The Lord's Prayer and Jewish Liturgy

Edited by

Jakob J. Petuchowski and Michael Brocke

A Crossroad Book
The Seabury Press · New York

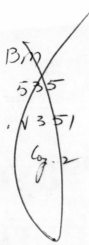
1978
The Seabury Press
815 Second Avenue
New York, N.Y. 10017

Originally published in part as *Das Vaterunser: Gemeinsames im Beten von Juden und Christen*. Copyright © 1974 Verlag Herder Freiburg im Breisgau, Federal Republic of Germany. English translation and new material copyright © 1978 Herder Publications Limited, London.

All contributions written originally in German and French were translated by Dr Elizabeth R. Petuchowski

Library of Congress Catalog Card Number: 77–014701
ISBN 0–8164–0381–3

Printed in Great Britain by Billing & Sons Limited, Guildford, London and Worcester

Contents

PART FOUR: PRACTICAL APPLICATIONS

Introduction

When the Oratio Dominica Foundation held its first international and inter-denominational conference in Freiburg im Breisgau, Germany, in November 1973, it chose the Lord's Prayer as the topic for discussion. The choice was significant. That prayer is *the* "Christian" prayer *par excellence*. Yet every phrase and sentence in it evokes in a Jew's heart echoes of his own liturgical heritage and of his own fundamental religious affirmations. Christianity and Judaism are different ways to the One God. Nothing is gained spiritually by attempts to ignore or disguise the differences. But Christianity and Judaism are nourished by common roots, and certain aspects of Christianity depend on post-biblical Judaism. It is well for both Christians and Jews to take note of that fact—not least in a world which increasingly challenges the basic assumptions of both Christianity and Judaism. It is well for Christians and Jews to realize that Synagogue and Church may not use one and the same version of what has become *the* Christian prayer, but that they are certainly at one in the affirmations underlying this prayer, and in the aspirations it voices.

The proceedings of the 1973 conference, edited by Michael Brocke, Jakob J. Petuchowski and Walter Strolz, were published in 1974 under the title *Das Vaterunser—Gemeinsames im Beten von Juden und Christen* by Verlag Herder of Freiburg. The present volume incorporates much, although not everything of the original German edition, and includes material not presented at the Freiburg conference; some of it was written especially for this volume. The articles originally in German and French were translated by Dr Elizabeth R. Petuchowski.

The present work is concerned with The Lord's Prayer in its setting. That "setting" presupposes the faith of biblical Israel and familiarity with its literary heritage. But it also implies a knowledge of the *religio laici*, as it were; of the kind of religion that is more characteristic of the synagogue than of the Temple of Jerusalem.

The institution of the synagogue, with its non-priestly service of prayer and of scriptural instruction, was one of the great contributions of Pharisaic-Rabbinic Judaism. It was from among the worshippers in the synagogues that Jesus and his original disciples came. This volume tries to introduce the reader to the synagogue and to the kind of worship offered within its walls. The attentive reader will, we hope, become aware of the features which the Lord's Prayer shares with the synagogal prayers, and of those elements of thought and formulation which may be unique to the Lord's Prayer.

Of course the *meaning* of some of the phrases in the Lord's Prayer has remained a matter for scholarly debate to this day. But "meaning" in religious texts is not only a question of what those texts originally meant. The situation in which the interpreter of those texts finds himself and the needs which he is trying to meet with his exegesis create another dimension of "meaning" which is of religious significance. Under the circumstances, the reader must be prepared to encounter in this volume a *variety* of different interpretations, and not only of phrases within the Lord's Prayer. No attempt has been made here to harmonize those differences. Every author, not the editors, is responsible for his contribution; and the reader will ultimately have to make up his or her own mind. Scholarly responsibility has been our sole concern.

We have also paid attention to the liturgical and the pastoral rôles of the Lord's Prayer in the past and present history of the Church. We have been aware of the challenges, particularly in relatively recent years, to its theological presuppositions. And we have not ignored the problems of teaching the Lord's Prayer today. Altogether, it is our hope that the Jewish reader will gain a deeper understanding of the Jewish heritage, the Christian reader of the Christian tradition, and each of the other's religious life and worship.

We warmly thank Dr Theophil Herder-Dorneich, whose enthusiasm inspired this work. We also gratefully acknowledge the co-operation of Dr Walter Strolz.

December 1976/Kislev 5737

JAKOB J. PETUCHOWSKI
Cincinnati, Ohio,
United States of America

MICHAEL BROCKE
Regensburg,
Federal Republic of Germany

Acknowledgments

Grateful acknowledgment is made to the following authors and publishers for permission to reprint from their publications:

Professor Gordon J. Bahr and the *Journal of Biblical Literature* for permission to reprint Gordon J. Bahr, "The Use of the Lord's Prayer in the Primitive Church", from *JBL*, Vol. LXXXIV (1965), pp. 153–9.

Professor Jean Carmignac and Éditions Letouzey & Ané, Paris, for permission to publish an English translation of Chapter 21 of Jean Carmignac, *Recherches sur le "Notre Père"* (Paris, 1969), pp. 387–95.

Ernest Benn, Ltd., Tonbridge, Kent, for permission to reprint a paragraph from Adolf Harnack, *What Is Christianity?*, translated by Thomas Bailey Saunders, Harper Torchbooks TB 17 (New York, 1957), pp. 64–5.

The Westminster Press, Philadelphia, for permission to reprint some paragraphs from their edition of Karl Barth, *Prayer According to the Catechism of the Reformation*, adapted by A. Ronlin, translated by Sara F. Terrien (Philadelphia, 1952), pp. 34–6.

PART ONE
THE HEBREW BIBLE

1

The Spirit of the Lord's Prayer in the Faith and Worship of the Old Testament

Alfons Deissler

The topic really presupposes a knowledge of the spirit of the Lord's Prayer. But what spirit animates and characterizes this pristine prayer of Christendom? New Testament exegetes are, as far as I can see, not fully agreed as to its interpretation. That is because the matter has many layers and many perspectives, and each layer and perspective is complex in itself. Still, we must try to disclose connexions between Israel's Bible (Holy Writ also for Jesus and the Primitive Church) and the New Testament, especially those which link the Lord's Prayer with the prayers of pre-Christian Israel transmitted to us by the Old Testament. We can make the attempt more readily because the question posed concerns the spirit of the Lord's Prayer, not simply its words and letters.

We may justifiably ask at the beginning if the Hebrew Bible of Israel is not rather far removed from the Lord's Prayer and its ambience. In fact it is constantly being shown that the closest point of contact between the Hebrew Bible and the Lord's Prayer lies in the interim period between the Testaments. Yet the Psalms of Israel occupied a central place in the worship of the later generations of God's people, even though in their fundamental strata many Psalms point back to pre-exilic times, and just as many to the early and middle post-exilic period. Rightly, the Book of Psalms is the OT book cited most frequently in the NT. It is the great bridge into all the Old Testament. But, as the response of God's people to the deed and word of the covenant Deity, psalmody is nurtured by texts of Old Testament revelation. It echoes them and gives them reality. That is also why the prayers of Ancient Israel have not been expressed here apart from the soil of belief which nurtured them, and why their widening perspectives have to be considered within the totality of the Old Testament.

1. *The Genre of the Lord's Prayer Against the Background of Old Testament Worship*

The Lord's Prayer is a biblical *tephillah*—a prayer in the narrowest sense of the word: that is, a petitionary prayer.[1] Throughout the OT, petitionary prayer is a part of the comprehensive genre *qinah* (the dirge) of which the structural elements usually comprise: invocation of God; lament; petition; expression of trust; promise of thanksgiving. Emphases can be variously placed in individual instances. That is how the sub-genre arose out of the wider genre "dirge": the Psalm of trust should be mentioned first here. But as far as I can see, there is no independent petitionary prayer in the OT, but only petitionary texts as smaller or larger units within the corresponding Psalms.

The situation verbalized in Israel's entreaties in the collective dirges (in the first person plural) is one of need and distress, and usually one of threat or oppression by enemies who, at the same time, appear as powers inimical to Yahweh. While admitting one's own guilt, one nevertheless earnestly implores the covenant Deity as a God of trustworthiness to turn his promise into mighty fulfilment by changing the dire condition and implementing his plan of salvation. The petitions aim at personal salvation but also at the realization of God's own cause.

The Lord's Prayer in the first person plural apparently also envisages a need: the enduring need of God's congregation which finds itself within an "exodus situation" within history and therefore looks forward both to the promised revelation of divine might and glory, and to the road thither; thus petitioning for earthly subsistence as well as the possibility of life within the sphere of salvation. Thus the twofold structure of the Lord's Prayer can be accounted for as: 1. the way and governance of God in history; 2. the way of man.

Petitionary prayer, however, remains petitionary prayer. It is not expressed in the lofty language appropriate to an address to God such as is exemplified in praises, such as a man may speak in his heart or even in public. Prayer in Israel responds to this very human limitation. Israel knows well, as is often expressed in the Book of Psalms, that praise is life. Israel knows joy before the Lord (thus it frequently designates the cult) and knows the ecstatic shout "Halleluyah!" (ie, "Praise ye the Lord!") which illumines the glory of God as he turns towards his people. Yet Israel has included all its songs of petition in the Book of Psalms (ie, tehillim) where they are in a majority. Genuine petition is also praise because it is grounded in faith and confidence and builds upon God's promise. And Israel always turns to the God who turns to it by means of an opening vocative which the "gospel" of the covenant of the charter takes up thus: "I am Yahweh your God who brought you out of Egypt, the house of slavery." Whenever the call goes up in Israel: "*Yahweh 'elohenu*" or "*Yahweh 'elohai*"—and this call goes up emphatically in the petitionary songs—the glory of the covenant Deity shines in the consciousness of the community and in the heart of each individual and lies like an aura round about all petitioning.

The Lord's Prayer has to be seen in this total setting; the prayers of Israel instruct us in this direction. Apart from that, the version in Matthew contains a doxology which takes up again at the end the full vocative of the beginning and develops it.

2. *The Basis of the Text of the Lord's Prayer in the Old Covenant and its Major Motifs*

(a) *The opening vocative*

The prayers in the Old Testament do not know of the opening '*abh* or *abhinu* (ie, "[Our] Father"). But Israel knows the title "father" as appellation for its covenantal God. All Israelitish names containing the theophoric element *abh*, beginning with the ancestor "Abraham", testify to that, and there are over forty. I will point to only one of them, the frequently occurring name for a man or a woman, "Abhiyah" or "Abhiyahu", which means nothing but "Yahweh is (my) father", and refers to an individual. There are sufficient proofs to show that Yahweh is called "father of the people" and "of the king". It is often pointed out that the authority aspect is primarily referred to here, because that grows out of the earthly father-experience. But since the time of Hosea at the latest (ie, around 750), Israel, at the mention of the word "father", is mindful of the unforgettable text:

When Israel was young, I loved him;
I called my son out of Egypt;
But the more I called them,
the further they went from me.

Yet it was I who taught Ephraim to walk,
I who had taken him in my arms.

5

But they did not know that I was their redeemer.
I drew them with human cords,
with strings of love.
I was to them like one who lifts a little child close against the chin.
I bent down and gave him to eat.   (11:1 ff.)

That the intensive power of this almost motherly father image has in no way diminished in illuminative intensity is shown by the verse concerning Ephraim in Jer. 31:20:

Is Ephraim my dear son,
a child in whom I delight?
As often as I threaten him,
I remember him:
my most inward parts are moved for him.
I must have mercy, I must have mercy upon him.

"The most powerful psalm of national lament in the Bible" (Westermann) is taken from this message which has also been handed down to us in the Trito-Isaic version: that is, from the post-exilic period:

Look down from heaven and behold
from this holy and glorious dwelling!
Where is your zeal and your strength,
the moving of your inmost parts and your mercy?
Stand not aloof!
For you are our father.
Abraham ignores us
and Israel does not acknowledge us.
You, Yahweh, are our father,
"Our redeemer" is your name from of old!   (Is. 63:15 ff.)

Before the eye of the believing congregation here stands "our Father in heaven" of whom the Lord's Prayer speaks in Matthew. This is not to deny that the *abba* of Jesus and the Primitive Church arose out of more central and yet more universal conditions. But we should not try, as has sometimes been done, to dim the il-luminative power of the OT tidings of the father by intensifying the splendour of its Christian counterpart. Finally, the father-son relationship alluded to in the Lord's Prayer, as it relates to the com-munity of the disciples, is an adoptive relationship analogous to that in Hosea 11:1.

(b) The first petition: Hallowed be your name!

This formulation is not characteristic of the New Testament, however possible it is to cast light upon it from new-covenantal texts. Its closest parallel can be found, apart from John 12:28 ("Father, glorify your name!"), in the Jewish *Kaddish* and the Prayer of the Eighteen Benedictions. These, in turn, point clearly to the OT.

The OT has developed a veritable theology of names for God. The revelation of the name in Ex. 3 constitutes its core. God steps out of his concealment and indefinability by means of his name and thus acquires personal traits which reveal a countenance which turns towards man. As God is holy (cp. Is. 6), so his name is holy.[2] Closely associated with this holiness is God's *kabhod*; ie, his glory and splendour. That is why "to hallow" and "to glorify" are interchangeable. In this perspective, "to hallow" means "to reveal the concealed glory". This is in the first instance an act on the part of God such as, for instance, Ezekiel quotes in a divine utterance in 36:23 f., and Ezekiel speaks of "hallowing" and of "to be hallowed" most often: "I will hallow my greatness which is profaned among the peoples, which you have profaned in their midst, so that the peoples will recognize that I am Yahweh, says Yahweh, the Lord, when I shall display my holiness through you before their eyes." (Ez. 36:23 f.).

As subsequent verses show, here it is a question of displaying divine power which works liberation and redemption for his people (cp. Ez. 20:41; 28:25; 36:23; 38:16; 39:7, 27). Surely our petition from the Lord's Prayer must first be interpreted in this perspective.

The manifestation of divine holiness in the OT calls for sanctification of his name by his people, as a correlative. According to Is. 29:23, the saved and redeemed people of Jacob will "hallow God's name", and this is expounded as "hallow[ing] the holy one of Jacob and stand[ing] in awe of the God of Israel". This, in the context of Isaiah's total message, can only mean faith, humility and justice towards one's fellow man;[3] that is: postures which show that the countenance of a God who reveals himself in the name Yahweh is becoming visible and perceptible. The open reflexive form in the first person plural petition under discussion here would indicate that a corresponding human deed is implied in addition to the divine act of the hallowing of the name.

In its official worship (ie, psalmody) Israel often, indeed over one hundred times, adjures Yahweh's name, mostly in such a manner that the term "name" points directly to the God who personally reveals himself. That is why the name is several times called holy (eg, 105:3; 106:47; 145:21). In view of the relevant Ezekiel texts (eg, 20:41; 28:25; 36:23 and others) the congregation prays:

Help us, o God of our salvation, for the glory of your name!
Deliver us and forgive us our sins for the sake of your
  name!   (Ps. 79:9)

In this manner Yahweh can and should, according to his promise through Ezekiel, "hallow his name". Therefore the congregation of Zion liberated from exile sings of Yahweh's redemptive act thus: "For the sake of your name you have magnified your word" (Ps. 138:2). In the above-mentioned prayer of Is. 63, Israel speaks in retrospect: "So did you guide your people, to win yourself a glorious name" (verse 14). In other instances where the name of God is mentioned in the Book of Psalms, it is in connexion with praise and glorification which the cultic community offers in celebration.

Our petition, then, in the Lord's Prayer, appears meaningful and with great brightness from the point of view of the OT. Here it is not so much a question of adjuring the *mysterium tremendum* of God but the *mysterium fascinosum* of his decisive turning towards man and, together with this, the thankful human response: namely, the praising word and the act of loyalty.

(c) The second petition: Your kingdom come!

Basileia is, in the NT, a word with several levels. Accordingly, there are differentiations and differences between it and its OT "premisses". The root *m-l-k*, applied in the OT to God in several ways (as verb or noun), not only designates God's rule but always signifies the pledging of his power in the service of justice. That is why the king is a soteriological figure in the ancient Orient. With the power given him by God he, in his domain, puts an end to the chaotic period when there is no king, and creates for man a place to live which is guaranteed by law, so that also the weak, widows and orphans also have human rights and can exist as human beings. As the title is transferred to the Godhead, this primary function remains fundamentally intact; that is shown, for example, by the Marduk myth where the powers of chaos are overcome and the cosmos is established. It remains a matter of contention precisely when this transference of the *m-l-k* terminology began to be applied to Yahweh in Israel. Whether, as Martin Buber asserts, it goes back to the time of the desert, is doubtful. Yet Buber reveals something decisive: the covenantal Deity assumes the leadership of his people as "ruler". This view of Yahweh's rule within the dimension of history dominates the other, also biblically-documented view which posits Yahweh's kingdom in the cosmos. We find both of them in Isaiah's vision of his call in which Yahweh is designated as "king" (*melek*) (6:5). This passage contains the first datable instance. No explanation is given. Only the prophets of the time of the exile point to Yahweh's kingly power as the source of a new future. Ezekiel proclaims: "With a strong hand and an outstretched arm ... will I be king over you and bring you out from the peoples ..." (Ez. 20:33 f.). Here the term "king" indicates promise and points to the end of days. Yahweh who had already proved himself king in the events of the exodus will surpass the earlier exodus and will put his power at the service of his covenantal striving before all the world and thus bring the chaotic history of his people to an end. Similarly, the kingship of Yahweh in Deutero-Isaiah means also God in his aspect as creator, but even more his aspect of redeemer at the end of time (eg, 52:7–10).

Yahweh's kingdom is a favourite theme in Israel's prayers.[4] Psalm 47, the first of the "King Yahweh" hymns, culminates in the proclamation:

King is Yahweh over the peoples,
Yahweh is seated on his holy throne.
The rulers of the peoples assemble
as the people of Abraham.
Because to Yahweh belong the shields of the earth.

Here is a clear reference to the final form of Yahweh's kingship in the *eschaton*.

A comparable eschatological perspective can be found in the related hymns Psalms 96, 97, 98. Here Psalms 96 and 97 end with hymnal praise for the coming God. Psalm 99:4 records what the kingdom of God brings about and desires to bring about: "The might of the king loves justice ... Justice and equity have you created in Jacob" (Cp. Ps. 145).

The kingdom of God understood in this way is echoed by Israel primarily in hymn form. Israel is mindful of Yahweh's kingship not only in the past and present but celebrates it already as a great future. From this position it is only a small step to the petition that God should manifest his kingdom in the glory of his might soon before all the world. This step is taken in our petition in the Lord's Prayer. As in the OT the community prays for the *basileia* of God, it expects that God will reveal himself and prevail at last against all the forces of this world. And with this expectation is combined the waiting for a kingdom where power, justice and love, so painfully divided in this aeon, will become one because at that time God (as "king") "may be all in all" (1 Cor. 15:28). Thus Psalm 85:11 is fulfilled: "Love and fidelity meet; righteousness and peace kiss each other."

(d) The third petition: Your will be done on earth as it is in heaven!

The exact interpretation of this petition is evidently still debated among NT exegetes, though there is a general consensus to understand it as follows: "In heaven God's will is done; on earth, may it be done!"[5] But what is this will? Is it the sum of the revealed teachings which, in this aeon, are to be fulfilled by men? Is it the plan which God has made with the world, with history and with the individual? Primarily with a view to the *eschaton*? But are such divisions really necessary? In principle, it is better, in Old Testament interpretation, to give preference in analogous cases to the typically Hebraic "both-and" over an "either-or", unless there is proof to the contrary. Perhaps this interpretative principle is applicable here, too, especially from the standpoint of the preceding petitions.

According to Job 38:4, God rules according to a comprehensive purpose for his actions (*'etzah*) which he executes according to his will. The emphasis is on Yahweh's cosmic providence. Israel has learned from Deutero-Isaiah that Yahweh's plan for creation and his sovereignty in history are to be seen in close connexion. Hence he admonishes in Is. 40:26:

Lift your eyes on high and look!
Who has created these?
He who led out their host by number
and called them all by names.
Before the greatness of his might and the strength of his power
not one dares fail.

In like manner he affects history. This is shown most clearly in the speech about Cyrus in Is. 44:24–45:3 where it says:

I am Yahweh who creates all things, (verse 24)
. . .
who says of Cyrus, "My shepherd,
and he will fulfil my whole purpose!"
who says of Jerusalem, "Let it be rebuilt!"
and of the Temple, "Let its foundation be laid!" (verse 28)

Similarly, Ps. 33:9 formulates more generally: "He speaks, and it happens, he commands, and there it stands." God's will permeates all history and even human aberrations will not deflect it. Joseph can teach his brothers: "You have purposed evil against me, but God re-planned it to good" (Gen. 50:20). God's will is profoundly a will for salvation (Ez. 18:23) and aims in the first instance at the future as the time for salvation:

I am God unrivalled
who from the beginning foretold the end . . .
I say: my purpose stands
and all my intentions I carry out.
. . .
I bring my victory near, it is not far;
and my salvation will not fail.   (Is. 46:9 ff.)

The culmination of such divine rule is prophesied by God's word to Is. 65:17: "Look, I create a new heaven and a new earth!"

As witnessed by the OT, man is God's earthly partner in the unfolding of the course of this history forwards and "upwards". He should walk God's ways with Him into the future. That is why Yahweh, revealing his will, has given him the saving guide (ie, *Torah!*). That is why Israel offers prayers not only for the fulfilment of Yahweh's historical will which has been revealed in the promises (cp. Ps. 9:20 ff.; 44:24–27; 60:13 f.; 68:29 ff.; 74:22 f.; 79:9 ff.; 80:18 ff.; 83:14 ff.; 85:5–8; 90:13–17; 94:1–7; 104:35; 115:1 f.; 126:4; Lam. 5:20 f.; Is. 63:15 ff.), but he prays for these: "teach me to do your will" (Ps. 143:10) or "teach me your statutes, explain to me how to walk according to your precepts" (Ps. 119:26 f.) or "To do your will is my desire, o my God, and your law is innermost to me" (Ps. 40:9). This last quotation points to Jer. 31:33 and thus to a "New Covenant": "I put my teaching in their inmost part, writing it in their hearts."

11

Thus the petition "Your will be done" describes a single large ark from the OT which encompasses cosmos, history and the final configuration of both, where the distinction between "heaven" and "earth" is de-emphasized.

Thus much, then, concerning the petitions of the Lord's Prayer which stress God's cause which thus becomes our cause. The following petitions emphasize the human partner of the covenant, the praying community and its members.

(e) The petition for bread

It is not my purpose to expatiate upon the well-known problem presented by the New Testament in connexion with this petition. From the point of view of the OT it can hardly be doubted that this petition has in mind man's daily major means of nourishment. But the very word "means" foreshortens the perspective. Of course, bread stills the hunger of the one who eats it, but in Israel bread is more than a dispenser of calories, and eating more than "tanking up". Normally, bread is eaten in the company of the family and is "welcomed", received and eaten as a basic gift bestowed by the beneficent convenant Deity upon his own. Ps. 104:14 formulates this concept in the form of praise:

It is you who makes grass grow for the cattle
and plants for man to till,
so that he brings bread from the soil
and wine to cheer man's heart,
that oil make the face shine
and bread strengthen man's heart.

Ps. 132:15 introduces God as the giver of bread even more directly in the divine oracle: "Its [Zion's] provisions will I bless, O bless, its poor I satisfy with bread."

Usually bread is prepared and freshly baked daily, not for lengthy storage. In Ex. 16:4, 16, 18, 21, it is expressly stated that the wandering Israelites should provide for only the respective day so that they will not forget the giver through a possible abundance and that they will hope on him alone. With the bread comes, as it were, a social mortgage. A fast pleasing to Yahweh consists, inter alia, in sharing one's bread with the hungry (Is. 58:7; cp. Ez. 18:7). Kindness means giving of one's bread to the poor, according to Prov. 22:9.[6]

No prayers preserved in the OT contain a petition for bread of such significance and in so central position as in the Lord's Prayer. But because famine is among the great disasters which befell Israel (cp. Gen. 12:10; 26:1; 41:54; Ruth 1:1; 1 Kings 18:2; 2 Kings 8:1 among others), many petitions for rescue out of distress imply supplications for food.[7] Lam. 1:11 is typical of this:

All her [ie, the city of Zion's] inhabitants groan,
search for bread;
their treasures they give for food
to support life.
Look, Yahweh, and see
how despised I am.

As the OT understands it—and the OT, too, is the word of God—petition for earthly bread and so for earthly existence is not astonishing. All consideration that such petitions are too earthy is, from the OT standpoint, decidedly impious and therefore probably not in character with Jesus. According to God's plan of creation, man is essentially a creature of flesh and should therefore hardly view the denigration of his corporeality as an ideal. Even where the OT speaks of "bread of angels" or "bread from heaven", the marvellous support of corporeal and earthly life is indicated (cp. Ex. 16:3–36; Neh. 11:4–9). This is not to deny that bread can at the same time be a transparent symbol for a higher gift, and all the more since God's personified wisdom, according to Prov. 9:1, in its own way sets the table for men and feeds them, according to Ecclesiasticus 15:3, "with the bread of insight".

(f) *The fifth petition: Forgive us our debt, as we forgive our debtors!*

Israel is acquainted with the first part of this petition. Already the tradition of Moses knows the pleading (by Moses for his people) for forgiveness (Ex. 32:32). Time and again, the prophets have confronted Israel with its guilt by measuring the breach of the covenant with the yardstick of the charter of the covenant contained in the decalogue, and by proclaiming as a consequence the "break-through" into calamity. In this way supplications for forgiveness are implicit in most of Israel's prayers for help and deliverance. Explicitly we find the collective confession of guilt and the corresponding plea for forgiveness and new pardon in Ps. 79:106 and Neh. 9. In the individual dirges which in the postexilic community were also collectively formulated in the first per-

13

son singular, the express supplication for forgiveness occurs relatively often, eg, Ps. 6:2; 25:18; 38:2; 51:3, 4, 10; 130:2 f.; in Micah 7:18, the pardoning of sin brings about the laudatory exclamation:

Who is a God like you, who takes away guilt
and forgives the sins of the remnant of his heritage,
who does not retain his anger forever
but delights in mercy.

The OT also knows of pre-conditions for divine forgiveness, as the second part of our petition contains it. Solomon's prayer at the dedication of the Temple enumerates return, confession of the name, prayer and supplication in 1 Kings 8:33 (cp. 8:35). Return from the wrong way and a turning toward Yahweh are not ever confined to the vertical thrust of the fundamental law but are applicable just as much horizontally to communal obligations. Micah 6:8 even formulates "existence before Yahweh" in this way: "to act justly, to love mercy, and to walk humbly with your God." Therefore, in the "liturgies of the gate", Psalms 15 and 24, entry into the Temple is made conditional upon deeds of communal loyalty. Ps. 34:15 identifies goodness with interpersonal *shalom* (cp. Is. 59:8). However, the creation of this fundamental relationship to one's fellow man is expressed in the protocanonical books not only by means of the word *salah* which is reserved for God. But the matter itself is brought home in Lev. 19:18 in this fashion: "Do not be vengeful and do not bear a grudge against the sons of your people, but love your neighbour as yourself." However Ben Sira, consistent with the given premises, formulated this admonition: "Forgive your neighbour his wrongdoing! Then, when you pray, your sins will be forgiven" (Ecclesiasticus 28:2). As the context shows (verse 4 below), God's forgiveness of sin is alluded to. Our petition in the Lord's Prayer can hardly have been formulated independently from this *locus classicus*.

(g) The sixth petition: Lead us not into temptation!

In continuation of the theme of "guilt", a petition that we should not fall again is made here. However, the manner of formulation harbours some difficulties for the interpreter. The question is often asked: how is this petition to be reconciled with the statement in James 1:13 "He [God] does not tempt any man?" The interpretation of *peirasmos* in Matthew can hardly be given without consideration of the concluding petition, the meaning of which is equally difficult to determine.

The famous text concerning Abraham in Gen. 22:1 (E) states: "God *nissah* Abraham." The Septuagint renders the Hebrew verb as *peirazein*. The point of the Hebrew expression aims indubitably at the meaning of "to test, to try". Such an action on the part of God vis-à-vis man is also mentioned in Ex. 16:4; 20:20; Deut. 8:2, 16; 13:4; 33:8; Judg. 2:22; 3:1, 4 and others. Many of the pious even seem to detect an opportunity in this. Thus the Psalmist of 26:2 prays, for instance: "Test me, Yahweh, and probe me!" It is true that the context would rather lead one to interpret this petition as functioning as a plea of innocence. Psalm 139:23 f. may be similar. However, in the collective song of thanksgiving, Psalm 66, Israel confesses:

God, you have tested us
and refined us as silver is refined.   (Verse 10)

This would seem to be an allusion to the exile which Yahweh has decreed. Job still says after the first test (loss of the sons):

Yahweh has given it, Yahweh has taken it.
The name of Yahweh be blessed.

In the face of the second test (boils), he already speaks in a more subdued way: "If we accept good from God, why not also evil?" (2:10). And in 3:1 ff. he indeed curses the day of his birth, and in the protestations of innocence the complainer turns into plaintiff against God.

From the OT perspective, the idea of God testing man appears, so to speak, as a matter of course; on the other hand, there is a manifest turning against an excess of tests. The collective dirges of Israel testify to this. It is in this sense that a worshipper from the old covenant would understand and receive that petition in the Lord's Prayer which has been under consideration here.

(h) The seventh petition: [But] deliver us from evil!

The verb here used has some ten corresponding expressions in Hebrew, the majority of which are used with reference to God. But the closest is *natzal*, used in the *Hiph'il* with the basic meaning "pluck out, tear away". Thus the hardpressed people plead in 1 Sam. 12:10: "Snatch us from the hand of our enemies!" Also the collective cry in Ps. 79:9 ("Snatch us") has this sense. Similarly almost all individual petitions for "snatching, tearing away" formulated with *hitz'il* envisages a personal enemy (Ps. 31:16; 51:16 among others). Ps. 39:9 provides an exception: "Snatch me from all my sins!" Possibly Ps. 79:9 is also to be interpreted in this manner. However, predicate clauses also express rescue from death: Ps. 33:19; 56:14; 86:13. If the petition here being considered were to be translated back into Hebrew, *hatzileni mera*, two interpretations would be possible: 1. deliverance from the "evil enemy", ie, the one who works injustice; 2. deliverance from calamity. However, from the point of view of Israel, both are many times closely connected, as especially the topic "enemies" in the Book of Psalms often indicates. If, as the direct connexion with the sixth petition leads one to suppose, the idea of keeping from evil-doing predominates, one would prefer to choose the verb *natzar* corresponding to the phrase: "to guard one's tongue from evil". To be sure, this connotation would not be altogether impossible in the first formulation above.

Coming from the OT, it is difficult in every case to want to settle the quarrel over the New Testament interpretation of this petition in the Lord's Prayer. Hebraic thinking is intent on synthesis and therefore on as many connotations as possible. In the formulation of prayers, such a tendency to aim, at the same time, at form and comprehensiveness offers special possibilities.

(i) The Doxology

These praises of God's *doxa* came into the Lord's Prayer at a later time but correspond excellently with the prayer of Israel, ie, its psalmody. The first and profoundest response of God's people to God's turning towards them is praise (cp. *tehillim* as title for the Book of Psalms). As if to recapitulate all OT doxologies, the Chronicler lets his hero David speak the "prayer" par excellence: "Praised be you, Yahweh, you God of our father-Israel, for ever and ever. Yours, Yahweh, is the greatness and the power and the glory and the splendour and the majesty ... Yours, Yahweh, is the sovereignty!" (1 Chron. 29:11 f.). The doxological ending of the Lord's Prayer is probably based on this text from Chronicles, at least according to the content.

I have only touched on the immense implications of this topic. All the same, a surprisingly large number of links have become apparent between the belief and prayer of Israel on the one hand and the Lord's Prayer on the other. Few direct literal derivations are among them. But again and again, wide comprehensive perspectives have opened up which make apparent or underscore the close homogeneousness of both Testaments. The individual petitions of the Lord's Prayer thereby gain an added radiance for many worshippers.

The whole, however, is always more than the sum of its parts or elements. This is also shown by an understanding of the Lord's Prayer in the light of the Old Testament. As a whole, and as such, it has no equivalent counterpart in the OT. In the Lord's Prayer many individual lines meet and are consolidated; in spite of all the analogies, its relative singularity is apparent. And yet a sketch like the above is justified not least because it shows, for the era of ecumenism, that a Jew can, in principle, join in the recitation of all its petitions and at the same time invest them with the content of an authentic revelation.

Notes

1. Cp. Ps. 17:1; 35:13; 72:20; 80:5; 86:1; 90:1; 102:1; 142:1; Hab. 3:1; Ps. 109:4 (*tephillah*, ie, petitionary prayer).
2. Cp. Ps. 111:9: "Holy and awe-inspiring is his name."
3. The "theologian" Isaiah especially puts decided emphasis on law and justice as "existential" before Yahweh (cp. 1:10; 1:21; 5:1–7). According to Amos 2:7, the "holy name" of Yahweh is "profaned" when a father and son sexually exploit a girl.
4. The much discussed question whether, in this, the Psalms are dependent upon the Prophets, or *vice versa*, will not be examined here.
5. Thus W. Grundmann in *Theologischer Handkommentar zum Neuen Testament*, I, p. 201.
6. In many places in the OT the word "bread" is used to represent "food" in general.
7. That is why starvation is, in effect, a stereotype in the prophets' predictions of punishment: Jer. 14:12; 15:2 and often; Ez. 5:12 and others.

PART TWO

THE PRAYERS OF THE SYNAGOGUE

2

Jewish Prayer Texts of the Rabbinic Period

(Selected and Translated)

Jakob J. Petuchowski

The "Hear, O Israel" and its Benedictions

1.
You are praised, O Lord our God,
Sovereign of the universe,
Fashioner of light and Creator of darkness,
Maker of peace and Creator of all.
In mercy You give light to the earth
and to those who dwell upon it.
In Your goodness You renew the work of creation
every day, perpetually.
How manifold are Your works, O Lord!
In wisdom You have made them all.
The earth is full of Your creations.

(Here follows a lengthy passage in which the heavenly luminaries
are identified with the angelic hosts who are continually praising
their Creator by singing such verses as the *trisagion* of Isaiah 6:3,
and Ezekiel 3:12. This passage does not seem to have been a part
of the original form of this benediction.)

As it is said: "(Give thanks) to Him who made the great lights, for
 His steadfast love endures forever!"
O cause a new light to shine upon Zion;
and may we all be worthy soon to enjoy its light.
You are praised, O Lord, Creator of the luminaries.

2.
With great love have You loved us, O Lord our God;
with great and exceeding pity have You pitied us.
Our Father, our King,
for the sake of our fathers
who have trusted You,
and whom You taught the statutes of life,

be gracious also unto us,
and teach us.
Our Father, merciful Father,
O Compassionate One,
have compassion upon us;
and set it in our heart
to understand and to comprehend,
to hearken, to study and to teach,
to observe, to do and to perform
all the teachings of Your Torah
in love.
Enlighten our eyes in Your Torah,
let our heart cling to Your commandments,
and unite our hearts
to love and to revere Your Name.
Then shall we never be put to shame.
For we trust in Your holy, great and awe-inspiring Name,
we jubilate and rejoice in Your salvation.
Bring us, then, in peace from the four corners of the earth,
and lead us upright to our land.
For You are a God who works salvation,
and You have chosen us from all peoples and language groups,
and You have brought us close to Your great Name in truth—
that we may give thanks to You
and proclaim Your unity
in love.
You are praised, O Lord, who has chosen His people Israel in love.

3.
Hear, O Israel: the Lord our God, the Lord is One.

(Deuteronomy 6:4)

Praised be His Name,
whose glorious kingdom is forever and ever.

Love the Lord your God with all your heart, with all your soul, and
with all your might. And take to heart these words which I command you this day. Teach them diligently to your children. Repeat
them at home and away, when you lie down and when you rise up.
Bind them as a sign upon your hand, let them be a symbol between
your eyes, and write them upon the doorposts of your house and
upon your gates.   (Deuteronomy 6:5–9)

If you will indeed listen to the commandments which I command you this day, to love the Lord your God and to serve Him with all your heart and all your soul, then I will give rain to your land in its proper season, the autumn rain and the spring rain; and you will gather in your grain, your wine and your oil. I will let grass grow in your fields for your cattle; and you will eat and be satisfied. Take care lest you be tempted to turn aside to serve other gods and to worship them. For then the wrath of the Lord your God will be kindled against you. He will close the heavens, and there will be no rain. The earth will not yield its produce; and you will soon disappear from the good land which the Lord is giving you. Therefore, impress these words of Mine upon your heart and upon your soul. Bind them as a sign upon your hand, and let them be a symbol between your eyes. Teach them to your children, speaking of them at home and away, when you lie down and when you rise up. Write them upon the doorposts of your house and upon your gates. Then your days and the days of your children will be long as the days of the heavens over the earth, on the land which the Lord swore to give to your fathers. (Deuteronomy 11:13–21)

The Lord said to Moses: Speak unto the Israelites and say to them that, in every generation, they shall attach fringes to the corners of their garments, and bind a thread of blue to the fringe of each corner. Such shall be your fringes. When you see them, you will remember and fulfil all the commandments of the Lord; and you shall not wander after your heart and your eyes after which you are wont to go astray. It is in order that you will remember and fulfil all My commandments and be holy unto your God. I am the Lord your God who brought you out of the land of Egypt to be your God. I, the Lord, am your God. (Numbers 15:37–41)

4.
True and certain,
established and enduring,
right and faithful,
beloved and precious,
desirable and pleasant,
awe-inspiring and mighty,
correct and acceptable,
good and beautiful
is this word for us,

forever and ever.
It is true
that the eternal God is our King,
the Rock of Jacob is the Shield of our salvation.
Throughout all generations
He endures and His Name endures,
His throne is established,
and His rule and His faithfulness endure forever.
His words are living and enduring;
they are faithful and precious
forever and unto all eternity—
for our fathers and for us,
for our children and for all our future generations,
yea, for all the generations of the seed of Israel, Your servants.

For the former as for the latter generations
it is a good and an enduring word,
forever and ever—
a truth and a faithfulness,
a law which will never pass away.
It is true
that You are the Lord our God and the God of our fathers,
our King and the King of our fathers,
our Redeemer and the Redeemer of our fathers,
our Maker, the Rock of our salvation,
our Deliverer and Rescuer.
Eternal is Your Name;
there is no God beside You.

You have been our fathers' help from of old,
a Shield and a Saviour to their children after them
in every single generation.
In the height of the universe is Your habitation;
Your judgments and Your righteousness reach the uttermost ends
    of the earth.
Happy is the man who obeys Your commandments,
who places Your Torah and Your word upon his heart.
It is true
that You are the Lord of Your people,
and a mighty King to champion their cause.
It is true
that You are the First and the Last,

and that beside You
we have no King, Redeemer or Saviour.

From Egypt You have redeemed us, O Lord our God,
and from the house of bondage You have delivered us.
All their firstborn You have slain,
but Your own firstborn You have redeemed.
The Sea of Reeds You have split,
the arrogant You have drowned,
but those You befriended You have brought across.
The waters covered their adversaries;
not one of them was left.
For this
the beloved people praised and extolled God.
Those You love offered hymns and songs,
praises, blessings and thanksgivings
to the King,
the living and enduring God.
Lofty is He and exalted,
great and awe-inspiring,
bringing low the proud
and raising up the lowly,
freeing the captives
and delivering the meek,
helping the poor
and answering His people
when they cry out unto Him.
Praises to God Supreme,
praised is He,
and ever to be praised!
Moses and the children of Israel
intoned a song unto You
in great joy,
as all of them said:
"Who is like You, O Lord, among the gods men worship?
Who is like You, majestic in holiness,
awe-inspiring in renown, doing wonders?"

(Exodus 15:11)

With a new song
the redeemed praised Your Name
at the shore of the sea.

All of them together
gave thanks
and proclaimed Your sovereignty,
and they said:
   "The Lord shall reign forever and ever."   (Exodus 15:18)

O Rock of Israel,
arise to the help of Israel.
Deliver, as You have promised, Judah and Israel.
Our Redeemer,
the Lord of hosts is His Name,
the Holy One of Israel.
You are praised, O Lord, who has redeemed Israel.

From the Evening Version of the "Hear, O Israel" and its Benedictions

5.
You are praised, O Lord our God,
who by His word brings on the evening twilight,
who in wisdom opens the heavenly gates,
who with understanding changes the times and varies the seasons,
and arranges the stars in their watches in the sky,
according to His will.
He is the Creator of day and night.
He rolls the light away from before the darkness,
and the darkness from before the light.
He makes the day to pass
and the night to approach,
dividing day from night.
The Lord of hosts is His Name,
the ever-living and enduring God.
May He reign over us forever and ever.
You are praised, O Lord, who brings on the evening twilight.

6.
Cause us, O Lord our God, to lie down in peace,
and let us rise again, O our King, to life.
Spread over us the tabernacle of Your peace,
direct us through Your own good counsel,
and save us for the sake of Your Name.
Protect us,

and remove from us
the enemy, pestilence and the sword,
famine and sorrow.
And remove the adversary
from before us and from behind us.
Shelter us beneath the shadow of Your wings,
for You, O God, are our Guardian and our Deliverer.
You, O God, are a gracious and merciful King.
Guard, then, our going out and our coming in
unto life and unto peace
from this time forth and forever.
You are praised, O Lord, the eternal Guardian of His people Israel.

7.
May our eyes see,
our hearts rejoice,
and our souls truly be glad
in Your salvation,
when Zion will be told:
"Your God is enthroned!"
The Lord rules;
the Lord has ruled;
the Lord shall rule forever and ever.
For Yours is the kingdom,
and unto all eternity You will reign in glory;
for beside You we have no King.
You are praised, O Lord, the King,
who, in His glory, will perpetually and eternally rule over us
and over all His works.

The Prayer of the Eighteen Benedictions. An Ancient Palestinian Version

8.
I
You are praised, O Lord our God and God of our fathers,
God of Abraham, God of Isaac, and God of Jacob,
the great, mighty and awe-inspiring God,
God Supreme, Creator of heaven and earth,
our Shield and Shield of our fathers,
our trust in every generation.
You are praised, O Lord, Shield of Abraham.

27

II

You are mighty, bringing low the proud;
powerful, judging the arrogant;
ever-living, raising up the dead;
causing the wind to blow and the dew to descend;
sustaining the living, quickening the dead.
O cause our salvation to sprout as in the twinkling of an eye.
You are praised, O Lord, who quickens the dead.

III

Holy are You,
and awe-inspiring is Your Name;
and beside You there is no God.
You are praised, O Lord, the holy God.

IV

Our Father, favour us with knowledge from You,
and with discernment and insight out of Your Torah.
You are praised, O Lord, gracious Giver of knowledge.

V

Turn us back to You, O Lord, and we shall return;
renew our days as of old.
You are praised, O Lord, who delights in repentance.

VI

Forgive us, our Father, for we have sinned against You.
Blot out and remove our transgressions from before Your sight,
for Your mercies are manifold.
You are praised, O Lord, who abundantly pardons.

VII

Look at our affliction, and champion our cause,
and redeem us for the sake of Your Name.
You are praised, O Lord, Redeemer of Israel.

VIII

Heal us, O Lord our God, of the pain of our hearts.
Remove from us grief and sighing,
and bring healing for our wounds.
You are praised, O Lord, who heals the sick of His people Israel.

IX

Bless, O Lord our God, this year for us,

and let it be good in all the varieties of its produce.
Hasten the year of our redemptive End.
Grant dew and rain upon the face of the earth,
and satiate the world out of the treasuries of Your goodness;
and grant a blessing to the work of our hands.
You are praised, O Lord, who blesses the years.

X
Sound the great horn for our freedom,
and lift up a banner to gather in our exiles.
You are praised, O Lord, who gathers in the outcasts of His people
Israel.

XI
Restore our judges as at first,
and our counsellors as at the beginning;
and reign over us—You alone.
You are praised, O Lord, who loves justice.

XII
For the apostates let there be no hope,
and uproot the kingdom of arrogance, speedily and in our days.
May the Nazarenes and the sectarians perish as in a moment.
Let them be blotted out of the book of life,
and not be written together with the righteous.
You are praised, O Lord, who subdues the arrogant.

XIII
May Your compassion be aroused towards the true proselytes;
and grant us a good reward together with those who do Your will.
You are praised, O Lord, the trust of the righteous.

XIV
Have compassion, O Lord, in Your abundant mercies,
upon Israel, Your people,
upon Jerusalem, Your city,
upon Zion, Your glorious dwelling-place,
upon Your temple and upon Your abode,
and upon the kingdom of the house of David, Your righteous
anointed.
You are praised, O Lord, God of David, Builder of Jerusalem.

XV
Hear, O Lord our God, our prayerful voice,

and have mercy upon us,
for You are a gracious and merciful God.
You are praised, O Lord, who hears prayer.

XVI

Be pleased, O Lord our God, to dwell in Zion;
and may Your servants worship You in Jerusalem.
You are praised, O Lord, whom we worship with reverence.

XVII

We acknowledge to You
that You are the Lord our God and the God of our fathers;
and we thank You
for all the goodness, the loving-kindness and the mercies
which You have bestowed upon us,
and which You have wrought for our fathers before us.
And were we to say: "Our foot is slipping,"
Your loving-kindness, O Lord, would sustain us.
You are praised, O Lord, to whom it is good to give thanks.

XVIII

Grant Your peace
upon Israel, Your people,
upon Your city,
and upon Your inheritance.
And bless us—all of us together.
You are praised, O Lord, the Maker of peace.

*The Prayer of the Eighteen (really, Nineteen) Benedictions. The
Current Ashkenazi Version, of Babylonian Provenance*

9.

O Lord, open my lips,
that my mouth may declare Your praise.

I

You are praised, O Lord our God and God of our fathers,
God of Abraham, God of Isaac, and God of Jacob,
the great, mighty and awe-inspiring God,
God Supreme,
who bestows loving-kindnesses and possesses all things,
who remembers the loving-kindnesses of the fathers,
and who, in love, will bring a redeemer to their children's children,

30

for the sake of His Name.
King, Helper, Saviour and Shield!
You are praised, O Lord, Shield of Abraham.

II

You are mighty forever, O Lord,
quickening the dead, You abundantly save.
(You cause the wind to blow and the rain to descend.)
You sustain the living with lovingkindness;
You quicken the dead with great mercy.
You support the falling and heal the sick,
loosen the bound and keep faith with them who sleep in the dust.
Who is like You, Master of might,
and who can be compared to You,
O King, Author of death and of life,
who causes salvation to sprout?
You are faithful to quicken the dead.
You are praised, O Lord, who quickens the dead.

III

Holy are You,
and holy is Your Name;
and holy ones praise You every day.
You are praised, O Lord, the holy God.

IV

You favour man with knowledge,
and You teach mortals understanding.
Favour us with knowledge, understanding and discernment from
    You.
You are praised, O Lord, gracious Giver of knowledge.

V

Let us return, our Father, unto Your Torah.
Bring us near, our King, unto Your service.
And bring us back in perfect repentance into Your presence.
You are praised, O Lord, who delights in repentance.

VI

Forgive us, our Father, for we have sinned.
Pardon us, our King, for we have transgressed;
for You are pardoning and forgiving.
You are praised, O Lord, the Gracious One who abundantly
    forgives.

VII

Look at our affliction, and champion our cause.
And redeem us speedily for the sake of Your Name;
for You are a mighty Redeemer.
You are praised, O Lord, Redeemer of Israel.

VIII

Heal us, O Lord, and we shall be healed.
Save us, and we shall be saved;
for You are our praise.
Bring a perfect healing to all our wounds;
for You, God and King, are a faithful and merciful healer.
You are praised, O Lord, who heals the sick of His people Israel.

IX

Bless this year for us, O Lord our God,
and all the varieties of its produce for good.
Grant blessing upon the face of the earth,
and satiate us out of Your goodness.
Bless our year like the good years.
You are praised, O Lord, who blesses the years.

X

Sound the great horn for our freedom;
lift up a banner to gather in our exiles;
and gather us together from the four corners of the earth.
You are praised, O Lord, who gathers in the outcasts of His people
    Israel.

XI

Restore our judges as at first,
and our counsellors as at the beginning.
Remove from us grief and sighing.
And rule over us, O Lord—You alone
in loving-kindness and in mercy;
and clear us in judgment.
You are praised, O Lord, the King who loves righteousness and
    justice.

XII

Let there be no hope for the slanderers;
and let all wickedness perish as in a moment.
May all Your enemies be cut off speedily;

and uproot, crush, cast down and humble
the kingdom of arrogance,
speedily, in our days.
You are praised, O Lord, who breaks the enemies and humbles the
    arrogant.

XIII

May Your compassion be aroused, O Lord our God,
towards the righteous and towards the pious,
towards the elders of Your people Israel,
towards the remnant of their scribes,
towards the true proselytes,
and towards us.
Grant a good reward to all who truly trust in Your Name,
and set our portion among them.
Then shall we never be ashamed,
for we trust in You.
You are praised, O Lord, Stay and Trust of the righteous.

XIV

Return in mercy to Jerusalem, Your city.
Dwell in it, as You have promised.
Rebuild it soon in our days as an everlasting building;
and speedily set up in it the throne of David.
You are praised, O Lord, Builder of Jerusalem.

XV

Cause the sprout of Your servant, David, to flourish speedily.
Exalt his horn through Your salvation;
for we hope in Your salvation all day long.
You are praised, O Lord, who causes the horn of salvation to
    sprout.

XVI

Hear our voice, O Lord our God;
have pity and mercy upon us.
And accept our prayer in mercy and favour;
for You are a God who hears prayers and supplications.
Turn us not away empty-handed from Your presence, O our King;
for You hear the prayer of Your people Israel in mercy.
You are praised, O Lord, who hears prayer.

XVII

Be pleased, O Lord our God,

with Your people Israel and with their prayer.
Restore the service to the sanctuary of Your temple;
and, in love and favour, accept Israel's sacrifices
and their prayer.
May the service of Your people Israel ever be pleasing to You.
And may our eyes see Your return to Zion in mercy.
You are praised, O Lord, who restores His divine Presence to Zion.

XVIII
We gratefully acknowledge to You
that You are the Lord our God and the God of our fathers
forever and ever.
You are the Rock of our lives,
the Shield of our salvation,
throughout all generations.
We thank You and declare Your praise
for our lives which are committed into Your hand,
for our souls which are entrusted to You,
for Your miracles which are daily with us,
and for Your wonders and Your benefits
which You bestow at all times,
evening, morning and noon.
You are the Good One,
for Your mercies never fail.
You are the Merciful One,
for Your kindnesses never cease.
Forever do we hope in You.
For all of these, O our King,
may Your Name be praised and exalted
continually and forever and ever.
And all who live shall ever thank You.
They shall praise Your Name in truth.
O God, You are ever our salvation and our help.
You are praised, O Lord. Your Name is the Good One; and unto
    You it is fitting to give thanks.

XIX
Grant peace, welfare and blessing,
grace, loving-kindness and mercy
unto us and unto all Your people Israel.
Bless us, our Father, all of us together,
with the light of Your countenance.

34

For, by the light of Your countenance,
You have given us, O Lord our God,
the Torah of life,
the love of kindness,
righteousness and blessing,
mercy, life and peace.
May it be good in Your sight
to bless Your people Israel
at all times and in every hour
with Your peace.
You are praised, O Lord, who blesses His people Israel with peace.

(At this point of the service, a slightly abridged version of the prayer of Mar, the son of Rabina, is said. See below, No. 23.)

May the words of my mouth
and the meditations of my heart
be acceptable to You,
O Lord, my Rock and my Redeemer.

May He who makes peace in His high heavens
make peace for us and for all Israel.
And say: Amen.

"The Substance of the Eighteen"
(According to some early Rabbinic authorities, quoted in *Mishnah Berakhoth* 4:3, it was either sufficient to recite the "substance" of the Eighteen Benedictions for one's daily prayer in any case, or, at least, he could avail himself of the shortened version whose familiarity with the complete version left something to be desired. Those rulings were, of course, given centuries before there were any written prayerbooks. The "Substance of the Eighteen" has been retained in the traditional liturgy for use when sickness or some other emergency prevents full devotional concentration on the full text of the Eighteen Benedictions. It is envisaged that the first three and the last three benedictions of the regular Eighteen Benedictions are recited in their normal form. But all the intermediate benedictions are contracted into one single benediction, of which the text is here given.)

10.
Give us understanding, O Lord our God,
that we may know Your ways.

Circumcise our heart
that we may revere You.
Forgive us
so that we may be redeemed.
Keep us far from sorrow,
and feed us well in the pastures of Your land.
Gather our scattered ones
from the four corners of the earth.
May the erring ones be judged according to Your will;
and wave Your hand over the wicked.
May the righteous rejoice in the rebuilding of Your city,
in the establishment of Your temple,
in the flourishing of the horn of Your servant, David,
and in the perpetual dynasty of the son of Jesse, Your anointed.
Before we call,
You answer us.
You are praised, O Lord, who hears prayer.

The Short Prayer
(If the emergency is such that even the "Substance of the Eighteen"
cannot be recited with full devotional concentration, the Rabbis
make provision for a "short prayer" to take the place of the
Eighteen Benedictions. Various texts of the "short prayer" were in
use.)

11.
Save, O Lord, Your people,
the remnant of Israel.
In every time of crisis
let their needs come before You.
You are praised, O Lord, who hears prayer.

(Rabbi Joshua. *Mishnah Berakhoth* 4:4.)

12.
Do Your will in heaven above,
and grant equanimity to those who revere You below;
and do that which is good in Your eyes.
You are praised, O Lord, who hears prayer.

(Rabbi Eliezer. B. *Berakhoth* 29b.)

13.
The needs of Your people Israel are many,
yet their understanding is limited.

May it be Your will, O Lord our God,
to give to each one his sustenance,
and to every single body what it lacks.
You are praised, O Lord, who hears prayer.

(B. *Berakhoth* 29b.)

Four Forms of the Kaddish Prayer
The "Half Kaddish"
14.
(*a*)
Exalted and hallowed be His great Name
in the world which He created
according to His will.
May He establish His kingdom
    (*Some rites add:* and cause His salvation to sprout,
                        and hasten the coming of His messiah,)
in your lifetime and in your days,
and in the lifetime of the whole household of Israel,
speedily and at a near time.
And say: Amen.

(*b*)
May His great Name be praised forever
and unto all eternity.

(*c*)
Blessed and praised,
glorified and exalted,
extolled and honoured,
magnified and lauded
be the Name of the Holy One, praised be He—
although He is beyond all blessings and hymns,
praises and consolations
which may be uttered in the world.
And say: Amen.

The "Complete Kaddish"
15.
(*a*), (*b*), and (*c*) as in the "Half Kaddish". Then:

(*d*)
May the prayers and supplications
of the whole household of Israel

be acceptable before their Father in heaven.
And say: Amen.

(e)
May there be abundant peace from heaven,
and life,
for us and for all Israel.
And say: Amen.

(f)
May He who makes peace in His high heavens
make peace for us and for all Israel.
And say: Amen.

The "Rabbis' Kaddish"
16.
(a), (b), and (c) as in the "Half Kaddish". Then:

(g)
For Israel and for our rabbis,
for their disciples,
and for all the disciples of their disciples,
and for all who engage in the study of the Torah,
here and everywhere,
for them and for you
may there be abundant peace,
grace and loving-kindness,
mercy and long life,
ample sustenance and salvation
from their Father who is in heaven.
And say: Amen.

(e) and (f) as in the "Complete Kaddish".

The "Burial Kaddish"
17.
(h)
Exalted and hallowed be His great Name
in the world which He will renew,
resurrecting the dead,
and raising them up to eternal life.
He will rebuild the city of Jerusalem,
and establish His temple in its midst.

He will uproot idolatry from the earth,
and restore the worship of God to its place.
The Holy One, praised be He, will reign
in His sovereignty and in His glory.
May this be in your lifetime and in your days,
and in the lifetime of the whole household of Israel,
speedily and at a near time.
And say: Amen.

(*b*) and (*c*) as in the "Half Kaddish".

(*e*) and (*f*) as in the "Complete Kaddish".

"Our Father, Our King"
The Earliest Recorded Version (*Second Century*)
18.
Our Father, our King, we have no King but You.
Our Father, our King, for Your sake have mercy upon us.

> (Rabbi Akiba. B. *Ta'anith* 25b.)

"Our Father, Our King"
A Later Version (*Ninth Century*)
19.
Our Father, our King, we have sinned before You.
Our Father, our King, we have no King but You.
Our Father, our King, deal with us for the sake of Your Name.
Our Father, our King, nullify evil decrees from us.
Our Father, our King, renew for us good decrees.
Our Father, our King, nullify from us the designs of those who hate
us.
Our Father, our King, confound the counsel of our enemies.
Our Father, our King, send perfect healing to the sick of
Your people.
Our Father, our King, prevent the plague from Your people.
Our Father, our King, of pestilence, sword, famine and destruction
rid the partners of Your covenant.
Our Father, our King, remember that we are but dust.
Our Father, our King, do it for Your sake, and not for ours.
Our Father, our King, rend from us the evil judgment decreed
against us.
Our Father, our King, erase the records of our guilt.
Our Father, our King, pardon and forgive our iniquities.

Our Father, our King, blot out our transgressions, and make them
     pass away from Your sight.

Our Father, our King, let us return in perfect repentance before
     You.

Our Father, our King, inscribe us in the book of life.

Our Father, our King, inscribe us in the book of remembrance.

Our Father, our King, inscribe us in the book of merits.

Our Father, our King, inscribe us in the book of maintenance and
     sustenance.

Our Father, our King, let salvation sprout for us soon.

Our Father, our King, hear our voice, pity us, and have mercy
     upon us.

Our Father, our King, accept our prayer in mercy and in favour.

Our Father, our King, do it for the sake of Your great Name.

Our Father, our King, do it for the sake of Your abundant mercies;
     and have compassion upon us.

Our Father, our King, be gracious unto us and answer us, for
     we have no good works to show. Deal
     charitably and kindly with us, and save us.

 (*Seder Rabh 'Amram Gaon*, ed. E. D. Goldschmidt, pp. 138 f.)

From the Private Prayers of the Masters
20.
May it be Your will, O Lord our God,
to let love and brotherhood,
peace and friendship
dwell in our lot.
May You increase our borders with disciples,
prosper our latter end with good prospect and hope,
and set our portion in the Garden of Eden.
Improve us through a good companion
and a good inclination in Your world.
May we rise early
and find our heart's desire in the reverence for Your Name.
And may You be pleased with our equanimity.
      (Rabbi Eleazar. B. *Berakhoth* 16b.)

21.
May it be Your will, O Lord our God,
that our Torah be our occupation,

that our heart be not sick
nor our eyes darkened.

(Rabbi Hiyya. B. *Berakhoth* 16b.)

22.
Master of the worlds,
it is well known to You
that it is our will
to do Your will.
What, then, prevents us?
The leaven in the dough (=the "evil inclination". Cf. I Cor. 5 : 6 ff.)
and the subjugation to foreign kingdoms.
May it be Your will
to deliver us from their hand,
so that we may return
to do the statutes of Your will
with a perfect heart.

(Rabbi Alexandri. B. *Berakhoth* 17a.)

23.
My God,
keep my tongue from evil,
and my lips from speaking guile.
To those who curse me let my soul be silent;
and may my soul be as dust to everyone.
Open my heart to Your Torah,
and may my soul pursue Your commandments.
Deliver me from misfortune,
from the evil inclination,
from an evil woman,
and from all evils
which threaten to come into the world.

As for all those who devise evil against me,
annul their counsel speedily,
and frustrate their designs.
May the words of my mouth
and the meditations of my heart
be acceptable to You,
O Lord, my Rock and my Redeemer.

(Mar, the son of Rabina. B. *Berakhoth* 17a.)

41

24.

May it be Your will, O Lord our God and God of our Fathers,
that no hatred against us
enter the heart of any man,
and that no hatred against any man
enter our heart.
May no jealousy of us
enter the heart of any man,
and no jealousy of any man
enter our heart.
May Your Torah be our occupation
all the days of our life;
and may our words be
as supplications before You.

> (Rabbi Eleazar, as reported by Rabbi Pedath.
> Pal. *Berakhoth* IV, 2, p. 7d.)

25.

May it be Your will, O Lord our God and God of our fathers,
that You break and make desist
the yoke of the evil inclination
from our hearts.
For thus You have created us:
that we do Your will;
and we are obligated to do Your will.
You want it,
and we want it.
What, then, prevents it?
The leaven in the dough! (=the "evil inclination", See 22,
    above.)
It is well known to You
that we do not have the strength
to resist it.
May it, therefore, be Your will,
O Lord our God and God of our fathers,
to make it desist from us,
and to subdue it.
Then shall we make Your will
like our will
with a perfect heart.

> (Rabbi Tanhum b. Eskolastikai. Pal. *Berakhoth* IV, 2, p. 7d.)

26.

(*a*)

Our Father in heaven,
may Your Name be held holy.
Your kingdom come.
Your will be done
on earth as in heaven.
Give us today our daily bread.
And forgive us our debts,
as we have forgiven those who are in debt to us.
And do not put us to the test,
but save us from the evil one.

> (Jesus of Nazareth. Matthew 6:9–13,
> The Jerusalem Bible.)

(*b*)

Father,
may Your Name be held holy.
Your kingdom come;
give us each day our daily bread,
and forgive us our sins,
for we ourselves forgive each one who is in debt to us.
And do not put us to the test.

> (Jesus of Nazareth. Luke 11:2–4,
> The Jerusalem Bible.)

Alenu

27.

It is for us to praise the Lord of all,
To ascribe greatness to the God of creation,
Who has not made us like the nations of other countries,
Nor placed us like the other families of the earth.
He did not appoint our portion like theirs,
Nor our destiny like that of their multitudes.
For they bow down before vanity and emptiness,
Praying to a god who cannot save.
But we bow down, worship and make acknowledgment
Before the supreme King of kings,
The Holy One, praised be He.
For it is He who stretched out the heavens
And established the earth.
His glorious abode is in the heavens above,

And the domain of His might is in the exalted heights.
He is our God; there is none else.
In truth, He is our King; there is none beside Him.
As it is written in His Torah:
    "Know, therefore, this day,
    and lay it to your heart
    that the Lord is God
    in the heavens above
    and on the earth below;
    there is none else."

We therefore hope in You, O Lord our God,
That we may soon behold the glory of Your might—
When idols will be removed from the earth,
And non-gods will be utterly destroyed,
When the world will be perfected under the rule of the Almighty,
When all mankind will invoke Your Name,
And when You will turn unto Yourself all the wicked of the earth.
May all who dwell on earth recognize and know
That unto You every knee must bend,
And every tongue swear loyalty.

Before You, O Lord our God,
Let them bow down and worship,
Giving honour unto Your glorious Name.
May they all accept the yoke of Your kingdom,
So that You will reign over them soon and forevermore.
For Yours is the kingdom,
And unto all eternity You will reign in glory.
As it is written in Your Torah:
    "The Lord shall reign forever and ever."
And it is said:
    "The Lord shall be King over the whole earth.
    On that day the Lord shall be One
    And His Name One."

3

The Liturgy of the Synagogue

Jakob J. Petuchowski

I

The sacrificial cult was the main expression of biblical Israel's worship, but it was accompanied from the earliest times by liturgical formulae and extempore private prayers. "Calling upon the name of the Lord," as the biblical Patriarchs did when they erected their altars,[1] probably involved a liturgical formula. When the Priestly Code stipulates that he who brings a sin-offering to the sanctuary "shall make confession",[2] it implies that the sacrificial act was not thought to be sufficient, even though the exact wording of that "confession" is not specified in the biblical text. Deuteronomy is more informative when it gives the text of the "declaration" which had to be recited by an Israelite farmer when he brought his first-fruits to the Temple.[3] In addition, many of the Psalms were obviously composed for musical recitation during the sacrificial rites.

Moreover, the Bible leaves us in no doubt that individuals prayed. The examples of Moses, Hannah, Solomon, Jeremiah and Daniel come readily to mind. There are others. Those biblical prayers of individuals were spontaneous and follow no definite pattern.

Deutero-Isaiah, after mentioning the acceptability of the sacrifices to be offered by proselytes in the Temple of the future, goes so far as to call that Temple God's "house of prayer for all peoples".[4] Throughout the biblical period, the official worship of Israel was the sacrificial cult of the Temple—with its daily "continual offerings",[5] and the "additional offerings" on special occasions, particularly on the three Pilgrim Festivals: Passover, Pentecost and Tabernacles. The cost of the cult and of the officiating priesthood was borne by the people as a whole through an intricate system of taxes and tithes in which, in the days of the Second Temple, even the Diaspora Jews participated. The Temple cult thus "represented" the whole people on whose behalf it was performed.

Whether such "representation" through taxation and tithes really met the religious needs of the whole people, is, of course, another question. The rise and development of the synagogue with its non-sacrificial liturgy while the Temple was still in existence would seem to indicate that the religious needs of the people were not entirely met by the Temple cult, that there was room for an additional or alternative form of worship: the non-priestly service of prayer and Scripture reading.

The origins of the synagogue are mysterious. It is generally assumed that the synagogue originated during the Babylonian Exile, when there were weekly gatherings of the exiled Jews to read Scripture and listen to the words of the exilic Prophets. But that is no more than an assumption. One theory would even link the rise of the synagogue with the destruction of the "high places" at the time of the Deuteronomic Reformation. The populace, deprived of its local cultic sanctuaries (so it has been argued)[6] still needed an outlet for its religious feelings nearer home than the central sanctuary provided for by the Deuteronomic Reformation. If sacrifice could no longer be offered on the local "high place", then the erstwhile local sanctuary could at least serve as a place for prayer.

Whether the theories just mentioned are valid or invalid, there is more secure evidence from the days of the Second Temple. Not only were priests and levites organized in various "divisions" (*mishmaroth*) to take turns in officiating at the sacrificial cult, but the laity was organized in such a way that representatives of different localities would "stand by" at various times while the sacrificial cult was performed. Moreover, to heighten the sense of participation, the population of a given locality would gather in their own town for Scripture reading and prayer at the identical times at which their representatives, sent to Jerusalem, were "standing by" to witness the sacrificial rites. That was the institution of the *ma'amadoth* (lit. "bystanders"); and it is not unreasonable to assume that those local gatherings, devoted to Scripture reading and prayer, had a considerable influence on the development of the synagogue.

At any rate, the existence of synagogues, both in Palestine and in the Diaspora, is attested to by the New Testament[7] for the first century of the Common Era, while the Jerusalem Temple was still in existence. The popularity of the prayer service was so great that even the officiating priests at the Jerusalem Temple interrupted their daily sacrificial cult at dawn by adjourning to the Chamber of Hewn Stones on the Temple Mount in order to recite portions of the synagogue liturgy.[8]

II

When the Jerusalem Temple was destroyed by the Romans in 70 CE, Judaism was able to survive—not least because the synagogue was already there to take the Temple's place, while prayer and study could be seen as a substitute for the sacrificial cult.

The synagogue required no hereditary priesthood or ordained clergy. It was essentially the seat of a lay religion. Whoever had the requisite knowledge and learning could lead the congregation in prayer, read the Scriptures and expound them. Nor was a separate building an absolute prerequisite. Congregational worship could be held wherever ten adult male Jews gathered for prayer, although specific occasions like Sabbath and festivals made the availability of scrolls of the Pentateuch and the Prophets essential. Even when established synagogues were already common, some of the later Rabbis preferred to recite their congregational prayers in the House of Study rather than in the synagogue.[9]

Until the tenth century CE, there was no such thing as a fixed prayerbook, although many of the prayers went back to the first century and beyond. But there was a reluctance to commit prayers to writing, no doubt in an effort to preserve the spontaneity of the spoken word. Therefore it was natural for different versions of one prayer to be in use at the same time. For a long period, no one version was *the* "authorized" one. In fact, it was not until the end of the first century CE, under the auspices of Gamaliel II in Yavneh, that an attempt was made to bring some order and uniformity into the services of the synagogue. Even then, however, it was not the actual wording of the prayers which was fixed, but the number of the individual components and their sequence.

Only the heads of the later Babylonian academies, the *geonim* from the sixth to the end of the eleventh century, strove for uniformity in the actual texts and wording of the prayers. But they were not altogether successful. The Palestinian liturgy continued to be more flexible and innovative than the liturgy of the Babylonian Jews, and the latter itself gave rise to a variety of different rites, some of which have been in use to the present day.

Yet, in spite of all the variety, the basic rubrics of the synagogue service have remained constant from at least the first century, if not before. The most fundamental among them are "The *Shema* and its Benedictions" and "The Prayer" *par excellence*, which, on weekdays, consisted of eighteen benedictions (now there are nineteen), on Sabbaths and festivals of seven, and of nine benedictions in the Additional Service of the New Year.

III

The *Shema* (see above, chapter 2, selection 3) is a concatenation of three Pentateuchal passages: Deuteronomy 6:4–Deuteronomy 11:13–21, and Numbers 15:37–41. It derives its name, *Shema* (="hear!"), from the opening word of Deuteronomy 6:4. The *Shema* is not a prayer, if we understand prayer as man's word addressed to God; it is God's word addressed to man. That is why the Rabbis, always careful in their choice of terminology, speak about the *qeri-ah* (="reading", "recitation", "proclamation") of the *Shema*, thereby distinguishing it from *tephillah*, their word for "prayer". Indeed, the *Shema*, as the proclamation of the Jew's monotheistic faith, was originally meant to be recited by the Jew upon retiring at night and upon rising in the morning: in fulfilment of Deuteronomy 6:7, "when you lie down and when you rise up", quite independently of any synagogal or private prayer. It took an effort on the part of the Rabbis to get the people to recite the "proclamation of the *Shema*" in juxtaposition to the daily prayer.[10]

"Acceptance of the Yoke of the Kingdom of Heaven" was the name which the Rabbis gave to the first paragraph of the *Shema*, while they called the second paragraph, "Acceptance of the Yoke of the Commandments". The third paragraph, though primarily dealing with the ritual fringes which had to be attached to the four corners of one's garment, included, in Numbers 15:41, a reference to God who brought the Israelites out of the land of Egypt. On account of that reference, the whole paragraph was called "Exodus from Egypt".[11]

As a part of the daily morning and evening liturgy, the three paragraphs of the *Shema* were never recited on their own, but in a framework of *berakhoth* (="eulogies", "benedictions"). A "benediction", in Jewish liturgy, is a prayer which begins and/or ends with the phrase, "You are praised, O Lord, . . .". The recitation of the *Shema* in the morning was to be preceded by two benedictions and followed by one, while two benedictions both preceded and followed the recitation of the *Shema* in the evening.[12] Thematically, the first benediction before the morning *Shema* (see above, chapter 2, selection 1) dealt with God's fashioning of light and with his daily renewal of the work of creation. The second benediction (see above, chapter 2, selection 2) dealt with God's love which was made manifest by Israel's possession of God's revelation, the *Torah*. The benediction after the morning *Shema* (see above, chapter 2, selection 4) had a twofold purpose. In the first place, it expressed the worshipper's acceptance of, and confidence in the truths proclaimed in the *Shema*; and it also developed the theme of the Exodus from Egypt, Judaism's *heilsgeschichtliche* or salvation-historical prototype of Redemption. The memory of that first redemption led to the hope for the redemption yet to come. The three benedictions which surround the recitation of the *Shema* in the morning thus supplement the *Shema*'s formulation of ethical monotheism with a hymnic affirmation of the three cardinal doctrines of biblical religion: Creation, Revelation, and Redemption.

The identical doctrines are affirmed in the framework of benedictions around the recitation of the *Shema* in the evening, with the necessary change of the first benediction from one which praises God for the light of dawn to one which praises Him for bringing on the evening twilight (see above, chapter 2, selection 5). The wording of the second benediction and of the third is different in the evening service from that in the morning service, but the respective ideational contents are the same.

The second benediction which follows the *Shema* in the evening (see above, chapter 2, selection 6), basically a prayer for divine protection, can best be appreciated when we bear in mind that the *Shema* of the evening was originally recited very close to the time of one's going to bed at night; and, indeed, that benediction figures to this day in the prayer which the traditionalist Jew says at bedtime. However, according to one Rabbi in the Talmud, the second benediction after the evening *Shema* is to be considered as merely an "elongation" or elaboration of the benediction dealing with Redemption, apparently because the daily protection granted us by God is to be understood as an aspect of God's continuing redemptive activity.[13]

There is no public recitation of a formulated "creed" in the synagogue service in the way in which there is a recital of various Creeds in the services of the Christian Church. But the recitation of "the *Shema* and its Benedictions" can be said to represent the "credal" element of Jewish worship.

IV

Mention has already been made in the previous section of the *berakhah* ("eulogy", "benediction"), a prayer which begins and/or ends with the formula, "You are praised, O Lord ...". It is a distinguishing mark of statutory or mandatory prayer (as distinct from voluntary prayer, for which no time limits or prescription of form are given) that it invariably takes the form of the *berakhah*. The Grace before Meals consists of the following *berakhah*: "You are praised, O Lord our God, Sovereign of the Universe, who brings forth bread from the earth." The Grace after Meals consists of a series of four (originally only three) *berakhoth*, praising God for food, for the land, for the building of Jerusalem, and for being good and doing good. It is in the nature of the *berakhah* form of prayer that not only praise and thanksgiving are voiced as "benedictions", but even petitionary prayer turns out to be "praise".[14]

Berakhoth were already a part of the liturgy recited by the High Priest on the Day of Atonement in the days of the Second Temple. We are informed by the *Mishnah*[15] that the High Priest recited eight *berakhoth* on that day; concerning the Torah, concerning the cult, concerning thanksgiving, concerning the forgiveness of sin, concerning the sanctuary, concerning Israel, concerning the priesthood, and concerning "the rest of the prayers". We are, unfortunately, not given the actual texts of those *berakhoth*, any more than we are given the texts of the *berakhoth* recited by the priests as part of the prayers with which they interrupted the daily morning sacrifice.[16] Although the Rabbis were still arguing until the third century CE about all the requisite components of a *berakhah* (eg, whether or not God must be described as "Sovereign of the Universe"), the basic form of the *berakhah* is certainly pre-Rabbinic. The substitution of "You are praised, O Lord" for the more customary "I give You thanks, O Lord" in one of the Thanksgiving Hymns found among the Dead Sea Scrolls[17] shows that this formula was even adopted by some of the sectarians.

Whenever synagogal prayers originated, the statutory prayer of the synagogue was couched in the *berakhah* form. And statutory prayer was meant to correspond to the statutory sacrifices in the Jerusalem Temple.[18] That meant that there was a daily morning and afternoon prayer, and, on Sabbaths, New Moons and festivals, an "additional" prayer service to correspond to the "additional sacrifices" (*musaphim*) in the Temple. Since no evening sacrifice was brought in the Temple, the question of whether or not there should be an evening *prayer* (as distinct from the mandatory evening "recitation" of the *Shema*) was long debated by the Rabbis, and no definite conclusion was ever reached about it. Maimonides, in the twelfth century, tells us that the evening prayer is "voluntary", but, since the custom of saying it has spread among Jews "in all of their habitations", this prayer ought to be regarded "as though it were an obligatory prayer".[19]

Until the end of the first century CE, there seems to have been no uniformity either among individuals or among synagogues in the contents of the various *berakhoth* making up the daily statutory prayer, or even in the number of *berakhoth* that were to be said. Such standardization came about only under Rabban Gamaliel II (end of the first century CE), who, after the destruction of Temple and State, sought to help Jews and Judaism survive by—among other measures—bringing some uniformity into Jewish liturgical life. It was under Gamaliel's auspices that Simeon Hapaqquli "arranged the eighteen *berakhoth* in sequence".[20] That is, for whatever reason (and Rabbinic literature merely provides us with a number of homiletical "explanations"), the number of *berakhoth* making up the standard daily prayer was fixed at eighteen. (The Sabbath and festival prayer, as has already been noted, consisted of only seven *berakhoth*.) The number, which hitherto had been fluctuating, was fixed, and so was the content and the sequence. What was not fixed was the actual wording of the individual *berakhoth*.

The fact that eighteen *berakhoth* were "arranged" under official auspices at the end of the first century CE does not, however, tell us anything about the date when the various individual *berakhoth* originated. Two of them, corresponding in sentiment though hardly in actual wording to the seventeenth and eighteenth benedictions of the Palestinian version of the "Prayer of the Eighteen Benedictions" (see above, chapter 2, selection 8), were already a part of the daily prayer service of the priests in the Jerusalem Temple.[21] Others have a striking similarity to the contents and phraseology of a hymn in the Hebrew version of Ecclesiasticus.[22] Still others may have been taken over for daily use from original fast-day and New Year liturgies. Apart from a common scepticism about the Talmudic report that "the men of the Great Assembly" already "ordained" the Eighteen Benedictions,[23] there is no unanimity among modern scholars about the precise provenance of the individual *berakhoth*.

Whereas some Rabbis encouraged the worshipper to make daily innovations in the language of the Prayer of the Eighteen Benedictions,[24] generally accepted forms of this prayer gradually crystallized. Selection 8 in chapter 2, above, represents one such form, an ancient Palestinian one. There were others, some of them more poetic. None of the ancient Palestinian versions is in liturgical use by Jews today. Selection 9 in chapter 2, above, is the version of the Prayer of the Eighteen Benedictions used to this day by Jews of German and Polish origin and, with some rather minor verbal variations, by all other Jews. Unlike the Palestinian version, this one, which ultimately derives from a Babylonian prototype, consists of nineteen rather than eighteen *berakhoth*.

A comparison of the two versions shows that the fourteenth *berakhah* of the Palestinian version deals with the rebuilding of Jerusalem and the Davidic dynasty. In the Babylonian version, on the other hand, while there is a reference to David's throne in the fourteenth *berakhah*, a separate benediction, in which the theme of the Davidic messiah is more fully developed, has been added as a fifteenth *berakhah*, thus bringing the number of *berakhoth* up to nineteen, in spite of the significance the early Rabbis had attached to the number eighteen. It has been surmised that the Babylonian Jews added this particular *berakhah* (which in and by itself may well be of Palestinian origin) out of deference to their secular leaders, the exilarchs, who based their authority on a claim to Davidic descent.

On Sabbath and festivals, the statutory prayer consisted of seven, and not of eighteen (or nineteen) *berakhoth*. The first three and the last three benedictions were the same as on weekdays. But there was only one intermediate benediction, dealing with "the sanctification of the day", and concluding with either "You are praised, O Lord, who sanctifies the Sabbath", or with "You are praised, O Lord, who sanctifies (the Sabbath and) Israel and the festivals".

What distinguished the Sabbath and festival prayer from the weekday prayer was, therefore, the absence of the various petitionary *berakhoth* which figured so prominently in the weekday prayer. The suggestion that this was due to a conscious avoidance, on Sabbath and festivals, of the cares and concerns which find expression in those petitionary *berakhoth* may be no more than a homiletical conceit. Those cares and concerns do find expression in other parts of the Sabbath and festival liturgy as well as in the Grace after Meals recited on those occasions; moreover, the scheme of a "Prayer of Seven Benedictions" may, even for weekdays, be more ancient than the later scheme of "Eighteen Benedictions". At any rate, it is suggestive that a contemporary of Gamaliel II, Rabbi Joshua, requires the daily recitation of only "The Substance of the Eighteen" (see above, chapter 2, selection 10), a prayer which, in fact, consists of only seven *berakhoth*, while Rabbi Akiba (second century CE) rules that he who has liturgical fluency should recite the full eighteen *berakhoth*, whereas he who is lacking that fluency fulfils his obligation by saying only the seven *berakhoth* of "The Substance of the Eighteen".[25]

It has already been noted that there was no agreement among the early Rabbis about the obligatory character of the Eighteen Benedictions for the evening service, since the evening service did not correspond to any Temple sacrifice. Before the eighteen *berakhoth* nevertheless became widespread for the evening service, some Jews concluded their recitation of the evening "*Shema* and its Benedictions" with a cento of Scriptural verses which together contained eighteen mentions of the Name of God. Those Scripture verses were followed by a messianic *berakhah*, the text of which will be found in chapter 2, above, selection 7. Though technically no longer necessary once the "Prayer of the Eighteen Benedictions" found universal acceptance in the Jewish evening service, the rite of the German and Polish Jews—but no other rite—continued to feature the Scripture verses with their eighteen mentions of the Name of God as well as the concluding messianic benediction.

A unique structure distinguished the prayer of the "additional service" on the New Year festival and, perhaps, originally the New Year prayer as such.[26] It does not have eighteen (or nineteen) *berakhoth* like the weekday prayer. Nor does it resemble the Sabbath and festival prayer of seven *berakhoth*. Instead, it has nine, for this prayer has special insertions dealing respectively with God's Kingship, God's Remembering (and Judging), and the Sound of the Ram's Horn. Each insertion consists of ten biblical passages, and, in the fully developed form of this prayer

53

(third–fourth centuries CE), each set of Scripture verses is preceded by an introduction and followed by a conclusion. The introduction to the section dealing with God's Kingship is given in chapter 2, above, selection 27.

Whereas this prayer in its present form may go back to the third-century Babylonian teacher, Abba Arikha (Rabh), who is credited with the liturgical framework of the New Year prayer, the first paragraph (which differs stylistically from the second, as is evident even in the English translation) may be considerably older, and may have been composed quite independently of the New Year liturgy. By joining the two paragraphs into one unit to introduce a section of the New Year liturgy, eloquent expression was given to the particularist and the universalist components of Judaism.

This prayer, called, from its Hebrew opening word, *Alenu* (="it is for us", "it is our duty"), was on the lips of the Jewish martyrs on the point of death at the time of the Crusades; and, from the beginning of the fourteenth century on, it has been used as the concluding prayer of every single Jewish service. The German and Polish rite uses both paragraphs, and the other rites only the first.

V

The early Rabbis never ceased to stress the aspect of inwardness and spontaneity (in Hebrew, *kawwanah*) as an absolute prerequisite of Jewish prayer. As we have noted before, under Gamaliel II, the Eighteen Benedictions were merely "arranged in sequence". Their actual wording was not fixed at that time. But when a more or less fixed wording began to crystallize, a dialectic came into play between the prerequisite of *kawwanah*, on the one hand, and the need for familiar liturgical landmarks to make community worship possible, on the other, which is operative to the present day.[27]

To make room for the spontaneous, the synagogue provided some moments of silent devotion called "Entreaties", "Falling with the Face to the Ground", or simply "Words", after the "Prayer of the Eighteen Benedictions" had been said. There was no prescribed liturgy for those moments of strictly private prayer. Yet various groups of disciples could not be prevented from asking their respective masters to teach them how to pray, and from inquiring about their masters' own prayers.[28] The Talmud[29] gives us a number of the private prayers of the Rabbis which they offered after the conclusion of the "official" eighteen *berakhoth*. Selections 20 to 25 (and, perhaps, selection 26?) in chapter 2, above, offer examples of those "private" prayers. One of them in particular, that of Mar, the son of Rabina (selection 23 in chapter 2, above), achieved such popularity that, in time, it was said by everybody after the conclusion of the Eighteen (or Seven or Nine) Benedictions in every service; this practice continues to the present day in all Jewish rites. This is a good illustration of one of the laws of Jewish liturgical development: one generation's spontaneity becomes another's fixed routine.

VI

The "Recitation of the *Shema* and its Benedictions" and the "Prayer of the Eighteen Benedictions" are, as it were, the very heart of the statutory synagogue service (and of the statutory prayers to be said by the individual even when he is not attending synagogue). They are also, historically speaking, the earliest liturgical components of the synagogue service. But that service (as well as the prayer of the individual) became the repository of many other components.

One aspect of the synagogue service, the reading and the expounding of Scripture, is probably as old as the synagogue itself. Pentateuchal pericopes were read as part of the morning service of every Sabbath, festival, New Moon, Monday and Thursday as well as on Purim, Hanukkah, and the Ninth of Ab. Pentateuchal pericopes were also read as part of the afternoon service of Sabbaths and fast days. The morning reading of the Pentateuch on Sabbaths, festivals and the Ninth of Ab was followed by a pericope from the books of the Prophets, while a Prophetic lection was likewise provided for the afternoon service of fast days.

The Book of Psalms and other hymnic portions of Scripture figure prominently in various rubrics of the synagogue liturgy, and the Five Scrolls (Song of Songs, Ruth, Lamentations, Ecclesiastes and Esther) are allocated to various occasions within the Jewish ecclesiastical year. In addition, many liturgical compositions—prayers, litanies, meditations, hymns and poems—from the period of the Rabbis through the Middle Ages and beyond, have been incorporated into the liturgy of the synagogue, as have whole sections of Rabbinic (and, later, mystical) literature.

Two of those compositions, the *Kaddish* (selections 14 to 17 in chapter 2, above) and "Our Father, Our King" (selections 18 and 19 in chapter 2, above), are dealt with more specifically in other chapters of this volume.

But for the early Rabbis it was the "Prayer of the Eighteen Benedictions", or its Sabbath and festival equivalents, which was *the* "Prayer" *par excellence*—while they saw the daily recitation, morning and night, of the "*Shema* and its Benedictions as the fulfilment of a specific biblical commandment. The rest of the liturgy, though far more copious than these two rubrics, was of secondary importance, and entered the liturgy of the synagogue only very gradually. For an understanding of that part of the liturgy of the synagogue, see chapter 14.

Notes

1. Cf. Gen. 12:18; 26:25 and elsewhere.
2. Leviticus 5:5.
3. Deut. 26:1–10.
4. Isa. 56:7.
5. Num. 28:1–8.
6. Cf. Julian Morgenstern, "The Origin of the Synagogue", in *Studi Orientalistici in onore di Giorgio Levi Della Vida* (Rome, 1956), vol. II, pp. 192–201. For a brief survey of recent theories about the origin of the synagogue, see Menahem Mansoor, "How the Synagogue Came To Be", in *Jewish Spectator* (New York), vol. 41, No. 4 (Winter 1976), pp. 35–7.
7. Cf. Matt. 4:23; 9:35; Luke 4:16, 31 ff., Acts 6:9, and elsewhere.
8. Cf. *Mishnah Tamid* 4:3–5:1; and see b. *Berakhoth* 11b.
9. Cf. b. *Berakhoth* 8a.
10. Cf. b. *Berakhoth* 4b.
11. *Mishnah Berakhoth* 2:2; 1:5.
12. *Mishnah Berakhoth* 1:4.
13. B. *Berakhoth* 9b.
14. Cf. Jakob J. Petuchowski, *Understanding Jewish Prayer* (New York, 1972), pp. 41f.
15. *Mishnah Yoma* 7:1; and cf. *Mishnah Sotah* 7:7–8.
16. *Mishnah Tamid* 4:3–5:1.
17. *Hodayoth*, IQH V, 20; and cf. A. Dupont-Sommer, *The Essene Writings from Qumran* (Cleveland & New York, 1969), p. 216, note 1.
18. B. *Berakhoth* 26b.
19. Maimonides, *Mishneh Torah, Hilkhoth Tephillah* 1:6.
20. B. *Berakhoth* 28b.
21. *Mishnah Tamid* 5:1.
22. Cf. R. H. Charles, ed., *The Apocrypha and Pseudepigrapha of the Old Testament* (Oxford, 1913), vol. I, pp. 514 f.; and see Israel Abrahams, *A Companion to the Authorised Daily Prayerbook* (2nd edition, New York, 1966), p. 57.
23. B. *Berakhoth* 33a.

24. B. *Berakhoth* 29b.
25. *Mishnah Berakhoth* 4:3.
26. Cf. Jakob J. Petuchowski, "The 'Malkhuyoth', 'Zikhronoth' and 'Shofaroth' Verses", in *Pointer* (London), vol. VIII, No. 1 (Autumn 1972), pp. 4–6.
27. Cf. Petuchowski, *Understanding Jewish Prayer*, pp. 3–16, and *idem, Prayerbook Reform in Europe* (New York, World Union for Progressive Judaism, 1968), pp. 22–30, 348–55.

4

The *Kaddish* Prayer

Baruch Graubard of Blessed Memory

Editors' Introduction

One of the most frequently repeated prayers in the traditional synagogue service is the *Kaddish* (= Aramaic for "holy"), of which an English translation is given in chapter 2, above, 14–17. That prayer is the doxology *par excellence* of the synagogue liturgy, and its various forms serve to separate one rubric from another, and to conclude the worship service as a whole. It also figures as the conclusion of the study of a passage from Rabbinic literature, and a special form of it, 17 in chapter 2, above, is recited both at a burial service and at the festivities marking the conclusion of the study of an entire tractate of the Talmud.

The focus of the whole prayer, and probably its earliest component, is the congregational response, "May His great Name be praised forever and unto all eternity"—itself a variation on such biblical verses as Psalm 113:2 ("Blessed be the Name of the Lord from this time forth and for evermore!") and Daniel 2:20 ("Blessed be the Name of God forever and ever!").

At that, the original function of the *Kaddish* does not seem to have been as much liturgical as it was homiletical, ie, the congregation responded with this doxology to the preacher's homiletical discourse. Thus the prayer, or, at any rate, its major response, is referred to in b. *Sotah* 49a as *yehé shemeh rabbah de-aggadetha*, the "'May his great Name' of the homiletical discourse." Like the language of the latter, so the language of the *Kaddish* itself is a somewhat Hebraized form of Aramaic, the language of the common people, rather than Hebrew, the language of the liturgy. There may, however, also have been a Hebrew form of the *Kaddish*, as seems to be indicated by the form in which the major response is quoted in b. *Berakhoth* 3a. That the sentence, "May his great Name be praised forever and unto all eternity," was itself recited responsively is attested to by Rabbi Yosé (middle of the second century CE) in *Sifré*, *Ha-azinu*, 306 (ed. Friedmann, p. 132b).

On stylistic grounds, Joseph Heinemann (see also his contribution, in chapter 6 below) has argued with great cogency that the *origin* of the *Kaddish* is to be found in the House of Study, rather than in the synagogue proper. It is from the House of Study that the synagogue took, and later adapted, the *Kaddish* for its own liturgical use.

The first references to the *liturgical* use of the *Kaddish* come to us from the post-talmudic tractate *Sopherim*, which was compiled around the year 600 CE, and which reflects the liturgical usage of the Palestinian synagogues. There, in XXI, 6 (ed. Müller, p. XLII), we read that the *Kaddish* is to be recited at the end of the Torah reading. The same source, XIX, 12 (ed. Müller, p. XXXVIII), tells us that, after the termination of the Additional Service on the Sabbath, the prayer leader would comfort the mourners at the gates of the synagogue, and then recite the *Kaddish*. That is the first reference we have to a connection between this prayer and the mourners, a connection which was to become much more firmly established many centuries later. Since *Sopherim* does not give us the text of the prayer itself, it is to be assumed that such a text (that is, more than just the major response) must have been in existence for some time before *Sopherim* was compiled.

The custom of having the mourners themselves recite the *Kaddish* at the end of the daily synagogue service for eleven months after the death of a near relative, and then on every anniversary of the death, seems to have originated in medieval Germany. *Mahzor Vitry* (eleventh century) does not yet know that custom. Isaac Or Zaru'a (twelfth–thirteenth centuries) reports that, in Bohemia and in the Rhineland, it was the custom for mourners to recite the *Kaddish* at the end of the service, but that the custom was not observed in France. Today the custom is universal among Jews, the mourners reciting a form of the *Kaddish* which is identical with the text we have given in 5, chapter 2, above—except that they do not recite the (*d*) paragraph, which is more appropriately said by the prayer leader when he recites the *Kaddish* at the point where, in an earlier recension of the ritual, a given synagogue service concluded.

The association of the *Kaddish* prayer with the mourners seems to have been related to the sentiment expressed in Job 1:21, "The Lord has given, and the Lord has taken away; blessed be the Name of the Lord." But, under the influence of a medieval legend (see *Seder Eliyahu Zutta*, ed. Friedmann, p. 23, note 52), and perhaps also under the influence of the Catholic Mass for the Dead, it more and more assumed the character of a Prayer for the Dead by which the survivors sought to affect the fate of the departed in the Hereafter. One of the consequences of this was an increase in the occasions, both during the service and at its conclusion, when the mourners were given an opportunity of reciting the *Kaddish*.

The following pages by Baruch Graubard mirror his associations with the *Kaddish* in the light of today's existential situation of the Jewish people.

For the scholarly background, the reader may wish to consult the following literature: David de Sola Pool, *The Old Jewish-Aramaic Prayer, the Kaddish* (Leipzig, Rudolf Haupt, 1909); Ismar Elbogen, *Der jüdische Gottesdienst in seiner geschichtlichen Entwicklung*.[4] (Hildesheim, Georg Olms, 1962), pp. 92–8; Joseph Heinemann & Jakob J. Petuchowski, *Literature of the Synagogue* (New York, Behrman House, 1975), pp. 81–4.

JJP/MB

1. *A Historical Memory*
It happened during the darkest time of the European tragedy, the effects of which are still felt. I was at that time an outlaw escaped abroad to Slovakia after many difficult experiences. I had surrendered and forgotten my identity. In 1944 I slid into an identity borrowed from a Franciscan monastery in Prescov. It hardly fitted me but fitted more than any other. Then I discovered a token of this identity in the Lord's Prayer. That was like a Jewish prayer, like an abbreviation of the Prayer of the Eighteen Benedictions. A calm prayer, only I missed the petition for peace. The Father was addressed only indirectly as King, and it seemed to me at that time that the Father, too, was in need of help just like me. Perhaps he was calmer, more certain of his goal and knew the future. The prayer opened an inner relationship to hope for me, and conquered fear.

In February 1945, a *minyan* of Jews (ten males) met together, from among the last surviving prisoners from Auschwitz. They wore concentration camp clothes and spoke the Jewish prayer. I could hardly understand how they linked up where the break had occurred in 1939. The continuity was incomprehensible to me. But when they said *Kaddish* I saw millions of dead before me and thought of those who left no trace anywhere, not even in someone's memory. Only in the *Kaddish* they still exist.

It has taken me a long time to discontinue seeing in the *Kaddish* nothing but a prayer for the dead. In order to do that I had to learn to understand Jewish history anew, scale it, plumb its depths and step far back until I discovered in the *Kaddish* a prayer of hope.

2. *Introductory Thoughts*

For an understanding of the relationship between the *Kaddish* and the Lord's Prayer, it is not essential to assume with Fiebig that the *Kaddish* is a model for the Lord's Prayer, although it would not be impossible.[1] Not only is a proof missing, but the habit, widely known to us from ancient times, of adapting and adjusting existing forms and formulae to different purposes, makes it unlikely that one prayer should be clearly dependent on another. However, this fact shows all the more that the essence of the *Kaddish*, its first sentence, and the Lord's Prayer, spring from the same source and are at home in one and the same world of belief.

3. *Kaddish Yatom*—the Orphans' *Kaddish*

Since the Middle Ages, in the popular mind, the *Kaddish* has been the prayer for the dead, those people near and dear to whom we were close. The Jew sees in the *Kaddish* a bridge to those who have gone on to another dimension. Of course the *Kaddish* did not originate and was not used as a prayer for the dead. E. Roth, in his essay about memorializing the dead, "*Haphtarah* and Orphans' *Kaddish*",[2] cites the legend of Rabbi Akiba from *Tanna debe Eliyahu*, a legend which probably was the impetus for the Orphans' *Kaddish* (cp. b. *Sanhedrin* 104a). In one version, Rabbi Akiba meets a deceased man who must atone for his sins with a severe punishment. Through the good deeds of his son he could have been relieved from this: the son was to read from the Torah, should say the blessing "Praise God who is to be praised" and induce the community to utter God's praise. Therefore Rabbi Akiba taught the orphan the *shema*, the Prayer of the Eighteen Benedictions and the Grace after Meals, placed the child in front of the congregation and the child said: "Praise God". The congregation responded with "Praised be . . ." and thus the punishment was lifted from the deceased. One can conclude from this that the significance of the prayer is to be sought in the call to the congregation to utter God's praises.

We read already in 2 Maccabees that after the end of the war, prayers and sacrifices were offered for the dead because the dead also had to achieve forgiveness, of course through the deeds of the living. The custom of saying *Kaddish* for the deceased for the course of a year arose only in the thirteenth century.[3]

4. *Origin of the Kaddish*

It is not so important for us here to set down exactly when the complete *Kaddish* texts were edited. Our question is directed towards the essential phrases of the *Kaddish*. The following remark is found in *Sepher Ha-Rokeah*:[4] "Why has the *Kaddish* been composed in Aramaic? Because the *Kaddish* originated in the Land of Israel, and when they left Babylonia, it was translated into Aramaic because also in the *Mishnah* there are Aramaic sentences, such as Hillel's sentence about the drowned man. Also in Jerusalem, Aramaic was spoken primarily ... The *Kaddish* was composed in Aramaic so that the people would understand it. Also one wanted to stress in this fashion that the *Kaddish* was instituted by the latter sages and not by the earlier ones."

During the time of the Saboraim, the *Kaddish* was a generally-known prayer also read after the Torah reading before the blessing of the *Maphtir*. There was also a version of the *Kaddish* for the installation of a new exilarch.[5]

5. *The Essence of the Kaddish*

As has been mentioned, the *Kaddish* evolved from the eulogy "May the great name be praised for ever and ever." We learn from *Mishnah Yoma* 6:2 that on the Day of Atonement in the Temple, when the High Priest pronounced the name of God, those assembled answered in response: "Praised be the name of the majesty of his kingdom for all eternity." That was the recognition of God's rule over the world. Together with this there is sounded the plea that God's rule may become known and manifest to the whole world. This eulogy is found as a prayer in I Chronicles 29:10 f.

"Wherefore David blessed the Lord before all the congregation: and David said, Blessed be thou, Lord God of Israel our father, for ever and ever. Thine, O Lord, is the greatness, and the power, and the glory, and the victory, and the majesty: for all that is in the heaven and in the earth is thine; thine is the kingdom ..."

Daniel 2:20 prays in Aramaic: "Blessed be the name of God for ever and ever: for wisdom and might are his."

As we trace the origin of the prayer we become aware how unsuitable it is to speak of a biblical and a talmudic Judaism. Whereas after the destruction of the Temple, views concerning obligations of the law, legislation, rites and liturgy underwent considerable broadening, there is hardly a dividing caesura which can be drawn between the piety of the biblical and that of the Talmudic period. The loss of the State narrowed and weakened the political arena of Judaism. All the energy of the people and their will to maintain themselves were concentrated into the world of faith. But the unity of Judaism was not interrupted. Only the non-Jewish world wanted to write off Judaism after the year 70 as a creative organism and deny its place in history.

After the destruction of the Temple, as Hadrian's policy of persecution began, a conspiratorial religious life developed. We know that from stories about the Ten Martyrs, about Rabbi Akiba, about Rabbi Simeon bar Yohai. The sages gathered the people together in secret and taught them to pray. This was something approaching a warlike attitude, a religio-political self-assertion. We know from b. *Ta'anith* 17 that the insertions in the New Year liturgy dealing with God's Kingship, his Remembering and the Sounds of the Ram's Horn were recited, and the doxology "Praised be the Lord, God of Israel, from eternity to eternity" as well as the response "Praised be the name of the majesty of his kingdom for ever and ever."

Rabbi Joshua ben Levi (ca 250) said: "Whoever says the response 'Amen, his great name be praised, . . .' can be certain that the punitive judgment against him will be annulled" (b. *Shabbath* 119b; cp. also b. *Berakhoth* 3a, b. *Sotah* 49). This view of the "power" of the response became popular and accounts for the fact that this response was regarded as the essential element of the doxology, and that the *Kaddish* concluded all individual parts of the service and the service itself.

6. *The Spirit of the Kaddish*

During the analysis of texts as they have been handed down to us in the oldest prayer books,[6] we find that the *Kaddish*, the prayer of the sanctification of the divine name, nowhere moves away decidedly into the realm of the other world.[7] The *Kaddish*, the prayer of sanctification, does not step beyond the framework of the Jewish feeling for the this-worldly task of man. Heaven and earth belong together: "The heavens are the heavens of the Lord, but the earth has he given to men" (Ps. 115:16). Also Jewish mysticism, as we clearly see from Hasidism, know no abrupt borderlines between heaven and earth. Mysticism sees it as its task to bring heaven closer to the earth and to make it understandable.

In the text of the *Kaddish* the desire is expressed that the worshippers may still live to see salvation, and that much good may come to those who occupy themselves with the law.

In principle, Jewish prayer does not focus on the problems of man but on the cause of God. The worshipping community is again and again called upon to hallow God's name, to show forth to all the kingdom of God because all wait for it. In the most ancient sources the *Kaddish* is not named as such but is referred to as "May his great name be praised". This ecstatic doxology has, in the course of time, developed into a complete doxology. In this way, the several variants of the *Kaddish* can be accounted for. The *Kaddish* is closely related to the *Kedushah* during the prayer leader's repetition of the Prayer of the Eighteen Benedictions. And the *Kaddish* resembles the text which is recited after the opening of the ark before the reading of the Torah: "Magnified and hallowed, praised and glorified, exalted and extolled above all be the name of the Supreme King of Kings, the holy One, blessed be he, in the worlds which he hath created . . . in accordance with his desire, and with the desire of them that fear him . . . . Now, therefore, thy name, O Lord our God, shall be hallowed amongst us in the sight of all living."

The special significance of the *Kaddish* is underlined in b. *Berakhoth* 21. If someone is occupied with the study of the law, he need not interrupt. However, for "May his great name" one does interrupt for prayer, even if the scholar be occupied with the esoteric speculations concerning God's throne. In b. *Sotah* 49, two doxologies are mentioned, the *Kedushah de Sidra* and *Yehé shemeh rabbah de-aggadetha*. From this one deduces that in Talmudic times a prayer of sanctification existed to which the congregation responded with "Amen. May his great name be . . .". This praise was said at the conclusion of the service or of a learned discourse.

People who immerse themselves in prayer, who concentrate their mind completely on the Creator of the world, can arrive at a state of emotion, of contemplation, of ecstasy. The doxology tries to formulate divine majesty with increasing intensity: from *kawwanah* via *hithlahabhuth* to *debhequth*.[8] By means of prayer, man pierces the curtain between his own limitation and divine omnipotence and prepares for the rule of the divine king. Man becomes the subject of the struggle for the dominion of God in the world of material objects. He storms the gate to the messianic kingdom so that God, the exalted one, can enter there: "And your name be praised and exalted above all, our king, for ever and ever."

Israel has to stand for and devote itself to the cause of God in this world. The great hope is not directed towards the other world. Life after death is understood as existence in the light of God. There can be no human activity and no human striving leading to the Beyond. The phantom realm of souls always remains in the shadow of nebulous sayings. Of course, every man is free to enter into God's kingdom, to absorb God's kingdom within himself if he accepts "the yoke of the kingdom of heaven". He fulfils the commandments, he lives under the law. But about him there is an unredeemed world from which he cannot withdraw. There were individuals and sects who practised flight from the world, but within Judaism they were marginal phenomena.

Israel lives in this world which is at the same time good and evil, which God created according to His will, and for which He drew up a future plan for happiness in peace and justice. That is the vision of the prophets. This future is the concern of God and of man. The kingdom of God, free from enmity between men and between nations, free from suffering, from misfortune and perhaps from death, will ripen in the course of time through human action and divine grace.

Two versions in the second sentence of the *Kaddish* point to two views of this expectation. The one: "May he establish his kingdom" and the other: "May he cause his salvation to sprout and hasten the coming of his Messiah." Both eventualities were considered but there was no doubt that the promised future will become reality at the end.

The sanctification of the divine name, man's subjection to the dominion of God hasten the redemption of mankind and of the world.

What would be worthy of aspiration—namely knowledge of the meaning of life, existence in truth and security—is bestowed only when divine rule itself holds sway. The Jewish people considered itself responsible for the way thither. A *mishnah* enumerates the principles of existence: "The world stands on three things: on Torah, on service and on good deeds" (*Abhoth* 1:2). These are the indicated paths. Service means prayer, service to God. The *Kaddish* is the clearest petition for the victory of God's cause in the world, unadulterated through any afterthoughts about the needs of the day.

7. *Sanctification and Sanctity*

First let us examine the individual sentences of the *Kaddish* prayer: "Exalted and hallowed be...", "May He establish His kingdom...". The concluding sentence "May there be abundant peace" is an adaptation of the Prayer of the Eighteen Benedictions which closes with a petition for peace. Perhaps we have here also a dismissal blessing after the comforting of mourners. The intermediary sentences supplement the second sentence with the petition for the realization of God's kingdom during the time of our earthly existence.

The first sentence contains the petition for sanctification, hope for it and confidence. The peculiarity of the future tense in the Hebrew language permits petition and confidence to be sounded at the same time. The sanctification of the name clears a space for sanctity in the secular area. The holy is a world differentiated from the profane, a totality in itself, existing by virtue of its own strength. Our world receives from it an emanation which endows the profane with vitality. Left by itself, the profane would be a world of fragments, of pieces of disintegrating matter. The holy is the source of being, cause and motive power of happening. The profane is never stripped completely of holiness. We human beings with our thoughts and deeds provide the bridge towards holiness. We can step out of the field of the profane and open ourselves to holiness. We can sanctify place and time. The Temple in Jerusalem was holy; the Day of Atonement is holy as is every place where people gather to learn and to pray, where "May His great name be praised" is spoken with devotion. The community of Israel in its totality is sanctified because a task has been entrusted to it. Jacob's ladder always exists and can always be raised up. Hence the mystics referred to the interchange between the absolute and the world of action.

"Be ye holy because I, your God, am holy" (Lev. 19:2). A bond of holiness exists between God and Israel. We cannot make statements concerning God's holiness, however we can concerning that of the people who were given the law and the commandment. Even when the people of Israel falls away from its obligations through disobedience, they remain within the circle of holiness which is not broken. This mystery is constantly stressed in the Pentateuch and in the Prophets. The election of Israel is the grace of God. Yet somehow the sanctification of the divine name through the people is essential so that the dominion of God should become manifest and recognized in our world.

"Thus will I magnify myself and sanctify myself; and I will be known in the eyes of many nations, and they shall know that I am the Lord" (Ezekiel 38:23, cf. the opening words of the *Kaddish*). "I will accept you with your sweet savour when I bring you out from the peoples and gather you out of the countries wherein ye have been scattered; and I will be sanctified in you before the eyes of the nations" (Ezekiel 2:41).

8. *Sanctification in History*

The name of God is sanctified through the works of God and his miracles, when he shelters his chosen people, liberates them and brings them back into his land as in the times of Moses. At the liberation from the last exile, God's miracles will be manifest to all the peoples of the earth. They will recognize that the God who has sanctified Israel, is the only God and that he will free the world from suffering.

Scripture expresses the hope that the community of nations will unite in the belief in the one God and submit to the just and beneficient rule of God. Thus one prays on the New Year: "That they may all form a single band to do your will with a perfect heart even as we know that yours is the dominion, strength is in your hand and might in your right hand and that your name is to be feared above all that you have created." The wonders of God are performed not only in the great work of redemption but also in natural events. When rain fell, the Amora Ezekiel (p. *Berakhoth* 14a) said: "Lifted up, sanctified and praised be your name, our king, for every single drop which you let fall for us."

One is admonished not to profane the name of God through disobedience. "And the Lord spoke to Moses and Aaron. Because ye believed me not, to sanctify me in the eyes of the children of Israel, therefore ye shall not bring this congregation into the land which I have given them" (Numbers 20:12).

"Neither shall ye profane my holy name; but I will be hallowed among the children of Israel: I am the Lord which hallow you" (Lev. 22:32).

During this historical phase when God's name was hallowed by miracles, man was not free from the duty of sanctification. It is sounded in the warnings not to serve idols: "Sanctify yourselves therefore, and be ye holy: for I am the Lord your God" (Lev. 20:7). The feeling for the method by which the sanctification was to be accomplished had to change with the changing historical situation. The will for sanctification remained unaltered in days of freedom and joy as in times of oppression and suffering.

In exile and oppression, the Jewish people so to speak took on responsibility for the sanctification of the name. Among strange peoples, it did not succumb to superior strength because it insisted on the fulfilment of God's commandments which are universally valid. If it lived among the peoples thus with its peculiarity, then such an existence demonstrated to the surrounding world the belief in God, and created the awareness that man has to bear much in order to trust faithfully in God's faithfulness. To be a Jew meant to bear a difficult lot, to suffer mockery and to fulfil God's will in subjugation. In the words of the Psalmist: "Thou hast given us like sheep to be eaten; And hast scattered us among the nations. Thou makest us a taunt to our neighbours ... Yet have we not forgotten thee, neither have we dealt falsely in thy covenant." (Psalms 44:12, 18.) They demonstrated hope through loyalty, through faith, through self-sacrifice as well as in religious custom and in external appearance. Moving scenes of steadfast faith are described in synagogal poetry, in the lamentations of many epochs, in the works of the historians of the expulsion from Spain and from other countries. This trait is to be found down to most recent times. The thoughts of the Jew move along an invisible yet strong path of sanctification throughout the long period of exile. Also in difficult situations, there existed in Judaism the hope, even if it was vague, that the Jewish way of life would contribute to the salvation of other peoples, that they would be stimulated through it to recognize the law and teachings of God: "When he, the stranger, seeth his children, the work of My hands, in the midst of them [the peoples], they shall sanctify My name; Yea, they shall sanctify the Holy One of Jacob and shall stand in awe of the God of Israel" (Isa. 29:23).

But the nations of the world did not accept the example of the Jews in the ghettos. In their eyes, their perseverance in their peculiarity was stubbornness, the work of Satan. Only seldom did some individuals recognize the religious essence of Jewish life which they saw shining through in spite of abuse and degradation.

In a third phase of Jewish life, the initiative and power of decision were transferred completely into the hands of the Jewish individual. Judaism took upon itself martyrdom. Already at the time of the Hasmoneans there were martyrs for the faith: "Nay, but for Thy sake are we killed all the day; We are counted as sheep for the slaughter" (Psalms 44:23). Martyrdom appears as often in Judaism as the fight for self-preservation among other peoples. Many generations regarded *Kiddush Ha-Shem*, sanctification of the name, ie, martyrdom, as a triumph of self-realization. Since the days of Rabbi Akiba's martyrdom, death for the sanctification of the divine name was a crowning of life, the fulfilment of the highest commandment to love God. According to a talmudic recommendation, man is obliged rather to suffer death than to be compelled to serve idols, to shed blood or to engage in sexual immorality. In time of religious persecution, however, he is obliged to face death even for less weighty sins so as to avoid any semblance of wrongdoing (b. *Sanhedrin* 74).

I do not wish to enter into the subject of the sacrifice of millions of European Jews who had to die simply because they were Jews. That was not only a crime but also a wild, mad absurdity for which we seek an explanation, yet find none.

9. *The Father*

"May the prayers and supplications of the whole household of Israel be acceptable before their father in heaven." The concept "father", often substituted for the name of God, originates from a period much older than the last redaction of the *Kaddish*. Here we cite some passages: "Is not He thy father that hath gotten thee?" (Deuteronomy 32:6). "Thou, O Lord, art our Father, Our Redeemer from everlasting to everlasting" (Isaiah 63:16). "But now, O Lord, Thou art our Father" (Isaiah 64:7). "And I said: 'Thou shalt call Me, My Father,'" (Jeremiah 3:19). "... for I am become a father to Israel" (Jeremiah 31:9).

The appellation "Father" is no longer easy to accept and to explain. Its reality no longer speaks to us. Perhaps in our day when religious language, as handed down to us, has become powerless, we have to go back to the beginning of the historical relationship between God and man to consider that passage which makes an original statement: "Thus saith the Lord. Israel is my son, even my firstborn. And I say unto thee: Let my son go, that he may serve me" (Exodus 4:22 f.). The eternal Father appears to lead his son into freedom, into the land of freedom. Perhaps this is an interpretation which can help us.

10. *Final observation*

In our connexion it is not important to formulate anew the problem of the origin of the *Kaddish*. A religious consideration should further the understanding and utilization of the prayer in our time. Probably the question of the relevance of this prayer is to be answered within the framework of Judaism in the same way as in other religions. A Jew who is not alienated from his heritage finds in the *Kaddish* the historical connexion of generations, a relationship between the present and the past. In the *Kaddish* there exists a tie with the deceased who were close to us, and with the martyrs of all times who surround our history with a special aura. There are few Jews who exempt themselves from saying *Kaddish* for the dead. Nay more: the *Kaddish* opens a more vigorous view on to the future because it is a prayer of hope. The worshipper is united with the dead, with the time of sanctification. Sanctification, however, exists not only in dying but also in daily life.

But the *Kaddish* as a prayer for the dead is rooted in the Jewish consciousness more strongly today than even fifty years ago. We have left too many dead in the recent past in foreign lands and in the land of Israel on cemeteries and in unknown graves somewhere where there is no marker for them. We cannot forget that; the thought of them we have enclosed within the *Kaddish* prayer.

If we seriously regard the hope which the *Kaddish* expresses, a new problem is forced upon us. Does the creation of the State of Israel perhaps indicate a point on the way to the messianic kingdom? If Jews take Judaism seriously and if Christians take Christianity seriously, they are bound to sense that a religious interpretation of the new statehood of Israel is no less, indeed: is more justified than merely a politico-pragmatic interpretation. Many sages derived the future not from a miraculous appearance of the Messiah but from a divine dispensation manifested to us in concrete facts. The messianic kingdom need not overpower us suddenly like a dream; it can also grow in time.

It is well known that the narrative of the exodus from Egypt—the Passover *Haggadah*—was edited by rabbinic sages of the second century of our common era. Strangely the role of Moses is not highlighted in this liberation from slavery. It is said in the *Haggadah*: "And he led us out of Egypt, he and not an angel; he and not a messenger. Only the Holy One, praised be he, he alone ..." For the Sages, only God can be considered as saviour in the greatest liberation epic. For the Sages, the past was always a

71

model for the future. An anointed one, a Messiah was not necessary, or not absolutely necessary, for salvation. They saw in God the king of the world, the king of the future kingdom. Rabbi Akiba said: "We have no king but you" (b. *Ta'anith* 25b). And Rabbi Yohanan said: "A benediction in which the kingship of God is not mentioned, is no benediction" (b. *Berakhoth* 40b).

Notes

1. P. Fiebig, *Das Vater Unser: Ursprung, Sinn und Bedeutung des christlichen Hauptgebets* (Gütersloh, 1927).
2. In *Talpiyoth* VII, 2–4 (New York, 1960), pp. 372–8.
3. He is known as Isaac Or Zaru'a (1220). Jacob ben Moses Mölln (*Maharil*, 1335–1427) knows the concept of "Jahrzeit". The *Halakhah* does not know of this custom.
4. Commentary to the prayer of Rabbi Eleazar ben Judah (thirteenth century), a disciple from the circle of Rabbi Judah Hehasid, the author of the *Book of the Pious*. The quotation is found in the Vienna MS 97b, on which Professor E. Roth is currently working.
5. Eliezer Levi, in *Yesodoth Hatephillah* (Tel-Aviv, 1959, p. 176), quotes the *Sepher Yuhasin* to the effect that "when an exilarch was appointed, he came to the synagogue on the Sabbath. The two heads of the academies of Sura and Pumbedita accompanied him. The head of the Sura academy gave a discourse on the scriptural pericope of the week. An interpreter stood in front of him, and transmitted his words to the people. After that, the prayer leader recited the *Kaddish*. At the point where that prayer reads, "in your lifetime and in your days", he inserted the words, "and in the lifetime of our prince, the exilarch". That was the enthronement of the new exilarch. Cf. also Ismar Elbogen, *Der jüdische Gottesdienst*[4] (Hildesheim, 1962, pp. 97 f.), who states that this custom not only lasted until the eleventh century, but that, a century later, it was reported that the Jews of Yemen expressed their reverence for Maimonides in a similar fashion.
6. Cf. *Seder Rabh 'Amram* (ca. 875 CE); the *Siddur* of Saadya Gaon (892–942 CE); *Mahzor Vitry*, which refers to Rashi (1040–1105 CE); and Maimonides (1135–1204 CE), *Mishneh Torah, Hilkhoth Tephillah*.
7. The sole exception, according to Tractate *Sopherim*, is the version of the *Kaddish* recited at the funeral of scholars: "*Be'alema di hu 'athid le-ithhadatha.*" He who occupies himself with the Torah deserves his portion in the World-to-Come.
8. These concepts of Jewish mysticism approximately mean: "concentration", "intention", "ecstasy", "*unio mystica*".

5

"*Abhinu Malkenu:* Our Father, Our King!"

Simon Lauer

The *Abhinu Malkenu* prayer is among the high points of the service on the High Holidays, and has deeply penetrated into the
people's consciousness. Ismar Elbogen writes: "The litany, the
verses all beginning with *Abhinu Malkenu,* goes back to a prayer of
Rabbi Akiba's which he once recited on the occasion of a fast
observed on account of a continuing drought. 'Rabbi Akiba
stepped (before the holy ark) and said: *Abhinu Malkenu,* we have
sinned before you! *Abhinu Malkenu,* if we have no deeds to our
credit, show us love[1] and help us!' These two sentences form beginning and end of the prayer still today."[2] There is a difference,
however, between our editions of the Talmud on the one hand and
the text as given in the prayer book and quoted by Elbogen:
"*Abhinu Malkenu,* we have no king but you! *Abhinu Malkenu,*
have pity on us for your sake!" The different versions of the prayer
will be discussed briefly below.

The Talmudic narrative which transmits Rabbi Akiba's prayer
deals with a fast which, according to rabbinic ordinance, is ordained for a time of drought. The report has it that before R. Akiba
spoke his prayer, R. Eliezer Hyrkanos had stepped before the holy
ark to recite the "twenty-four eulogies", but his request had not
been granted. What are these twenty-four eulogies? According to
the teaching of the *Mishnah,* they are the 18 eulogies of the Eighteen Benedictions, and in addition the *zikhronoth* and *shopharoth*
(Prayers of Remembrance and Prayers of Shofarblowing), as well
as Psalms 120, 121, 130 and 102, all of them inserted between the
seventh and eighth benedictions.[3] The first two of these added
prayers constitute part of the New Year liturgy, and on every fast
day a special eulogy (that is now the twentieth) is inserted at this
point: "Praised are you, O Lord, who answers in time of need."
The *zikhronoth* (section of the New Year liturgy dealing with
God's remembering) consist of Bible verses which tell of God's
promises that he will "remember", for instance the patriarchs; the

shopharoth (Prayers of Shopharblowing) consist of Bible verses mentioning the *shophar*; these are part of the fast day because the ram's horn (*shophar*) is being blown that day.

The connexion between the New Year Day (when the *abhinu malkenu* is recited) and the fast day will be dealt with below. First, however, another question arises which has not been posed in the Talmud: did R. Akiba recite his *Abhinu Malkenu* in addition to the twenty-four eulogies or instead of the six insertions? Is there a fundamental contradiction between R. Eliezer who offers a long, perhaps excessively long, prayer and R. Akiba? In the *Mishnah* quoted above, R. Yehudah who is, after all, the editor of our *Mishnah*, wants to substitute for each of the *zikhronoth* and *shopharoth* prayers, another coherent scripture passage referring to such an emergency.[4] That is to say: it is possible that R. Akiba departs from the formula which his colleagues have suggested. It should, however, be borne in mind that in ancient days the prayer leader prepared himself during the silent devotions of the congregation.[5] In that case, the *Abhinu Malkenu* would have fulfilled the function of the special prayer of the prayer leader which is customary today on the High Holidays. (Such a prayer is documented in published form since the sixteenth century, though not sooner; its author is unknown.)[6] The length of the prayer seems to have been of no significance to either R. Akiba or R. Eliezer. R. Akiba teaches explicitly that he who knows the Eighteen Benedictions should say them, and that anyone who does not know them should say the abbreviated form. R. Eliezer demands simply that one's prayer, whether full-length or abbreviated, should be regarded as entreaties, not as compulsory routine.[7] This is also indicated by a story according to which R. Eliezer defended a student who prayed very long and similarly one who prayed briefly: for Moses himself had prayed for forty days and forty nights (Deuteronomy 9:25) on one occasion and on another had pronounced only five words (Numbers 12:13).[8] A very short prayer by R. Eliezer has been handed down: "Your will be done in heaven above, grant contentment to those who fear you here below; do what is pleasing to you! Praised be you, O Lord, who hears prayer!"[9] Joseph Heinemann, referring to Strack-Billerbeck, has endeavoured to show that this prayer is something fundamentally different from the Lord's Prayer; I do not permit myself a final judgment in the matter.[10] Two points seem to me relevant in the present context: the prayer has a concluding eulogy—the same as the fifteenth (or the sixteenth respectively) of the Eighteen Benedictions—and it is to be said in an emergency: namely, when encountering hordes of wild animals or bands of robbers. Hence one might conclude that the Talmud in no way evades the problem when it lets a heavenly voice say that R. Akiba's prayer was accepted not because he was greater than R. Eliezer but because he could "forgo personal requests" whereas the other could not.[11] Neither the form of the prayer nor even its length are decisive but the character and bearing of the one who prays; Eliezer and Akiba agree on this.

What, then, is demanded? "Forgo personal requests" was my attempt to translate the Talmudic expression *he'ebhir 'al middothaw.* I find the *locus classicus* of this quotation in the tractate *Rosh Hashanah* where God's relationship to sin is discussed.[12] "A teacher from the school of R. Yishmael teaches as follows," so it says: "He omits the first (sin) from time to time, and that is his measure . . . . Rabha says: Whoever omits his measure, all his sins are forgiven; as it is said: 'He forgives sin and overlooks guilt.'[13] Whose sin does God forgive? The sin of one who overlooks guilt." *Middah,* "measure", means that which is his due, also the measure of punishment, and further the judicial procedure (God requites "measure for measure");[14] but it also means "attribute, characteristic": Rabbenu Hananel (first half of the eleventh century) interprets *middah* here as the sixth of the thirteen attributes (Exodus 34:6 f.), probably patience; the thirteen attributes are a permanent constituent of the penitential prayers.[15] The saying by Rabha quoted here is repeated in two instances which resemble each other and which occur in the tractate *Yoma,* namely in connexion with the requirement to ask forgiveness of a fellow man whom one has wronged, and the requirement not to withhold forgiveness if it has been asked.[16] The counterpart of the expression here under discussion can be found in yet another place: R. Akiba asks R. Nehunya the Great how he has managed to reach such advanced age, and receives, *inter alia,* this answer: "I have never insisted on my demands; for Rabha says: 'All sins are forgiven to him who overlooks his measure.'"[17]

One word more concerning the "twenty-four eulogies". According to a place in the Talmud, these eulogies correspond to twenty-four chants of praise which Solomon offered when he wanted to bring the Ark of the Covenant into the Holy of Holies.[18] (More precisely, the "praises, prayers and petitions" mentioned in

I Kings 8 : 22 ff. are meant here.)[19] Three reports agree that this was on a Day of Atonement.[20] On that occasion the gates of the Holy of Holies would not open, regardless of the twenty-four songs of praise. They only opened once Solomon prayed to God to remember the love of his servant David.[21] And that, in turn, was the sign that God had forgiven (namely David's famous sin and the festive banquet of the people on the Day of Atonement). Here, too, the twenty-four prayers were not heard; and here, too, the mention of the father brings about a decisive turning point.

So far, the *Abhinu Malkenu* has proved to be, as it were, a cypher for human qualities or bearings which correspond to divine attributes. Such attitudes assume existential significance in times of peril, and the days of divine judgment are surely of that kind. The *Abhinu Malkenu* prayer has no connexion with the remaining liturgy of the High Holidays. That the *Abhinu Malkenu* prayer should be said on the Day of Atonement is immediately clear if one considers that it is unmistakably part of the liturgy for fast days. But what about New Year's Day? As a matter of fact, many people evidently seem to have observed both New Year Days as fast days. For instance, the author of the *Shibbolé Haleqet,* R. Zedekiah Anav, who flourished in Italy in the thirteenth century, says that some people adhered to this custom whereas Yehudai Gaon (in the eighth century) forbids it.[22] Joseph Caro (died 1575) says tersely: "One does not fast on Rosh Hashanah." A hundred years later one of the most important commentators makes a decision in this spirit, but also quotes contrary opinions.[23] However, according to religious law fasting on New Year is likely to remain forbidden—indeed, eating would seem to be prescribed. According to custom, a tendency to fast remains apparent even today.[24] On the days between New Year and the Day of Atonement, individuals, but not communities, may fast.[25] In that period *Abhinu Malkenu* is said during the morning and afternoon prayer.[26] Hence the general character of those days is determined: they are the ten days of penitence.[27]

The Jewish calendar in general does not lack fast days; one can count up to roughly one to two dozen. But as far as I can see, *Abhinu Malkenu* is said only on the so-called "Minor Day of Atonement"; that is the day preceding the day of the New Moon, especially before the months of Nisan and Ellul. One does not say it on fasts which are commemorative days. Why *Abhinu Malkenu* should be omitted on other fast days I do not know.[28]

As was indicated at the beginning, there are differing versions of
the *Abhinu Malkenu*. Our editions of the Talmud attribute to
R. Akiba only two sentences: *"Abhinu Malkenu,* we have no king
but you" and *"Abhinu Malkenu,* have pity upon us for your sake!"
Rabbenu Hananel transmits this in a slightly altered form: *"Abhinu
Malkenu,* you are our father, and we have no king but you; *Abhinu
Malkenu,* have pity upon us!" His student, R. Isaac Al-Fasi (and
also R. Zedekiah Anav)[29] formulate it as follows: *"Abhinu
Malkenu,* we have sinned before you. *Abhinu Malkenu,* we have no
king but you. *Abhinu Malkenu,* deal with us for your name's
sake!"[30] Jacob ibn Habib (ca 1500) even has five formulae in his
'En Ya'akobh, a very popular compendium of the aggadic parts of
both Talmuds: *"Abhinu Malkenu,* you are our father. *Abhinu
Malkenu,* we have no king but you. *Abhinu Malkenu,* we have
sinned before you. *Abhinu Malkenu,* have pity on us! *Abhinu
Malkenu,* deal with us for your name's sake!" These two or five
formulae would seem to have been enlarged in early times into a
longer litany of nineteen, twenty-two and as many as fifty-three
verses. The *Tur*[31] attests twenty-two in the form of an alphabetical
litany according to Amram Gaon (ninth century), but that cannot
be correct.[32] Noteworthy is the number nineteen; it would correspond to the nineteen eulogies of the Eighteen Benedictions.[33]
Indeed, the *Abhinu Malkenu* has been related to this main prayer;
Baer sees in this also the reason for not reciting the *Abhinu
Malkenu* on the Sabbath. However, this reason is not convincing
because the Sepharadim who did not yet know the *Abhinu
Malkenu* prayer in the Middle Ages say it also on the Sabbath, and
also because the Prayer par excellence has only seven (or nine)
eulogies on the High Holidays. Nevertheless, attempts have been
made to find a clear parallel.[34]

The close connexion between the *Abhinu Malkenu* and the
Prayer remains striking; other abbreviated versions serve either as
substitute for the Prayer itself (*habhinenu,* perhaps also *barukh
adonai le'olam*)[35] or as a substitute for its repetition (for instance
on Friday night, perhaps also the just mentioned *barukh adonai
le'olam*);[36] neither is relevant here.

I refrain from a detailed interpretation not only because of the
variants in the individual versions but above all because very little
in this frame of reference strikes me as relevant: the historico-
theological framework of the origin of the prayer, the two to five

formulae handed down from antiquity, and especially the appellation "our Father, our King!"[37] I believe I have demonstrated that the brevity of the original prayer should not be interpreted too narrowly. Nor am I inclined to counterpose the suffix with the possessive pronoun to the *status emphaticus* of the Aramaic *abba*. A worshipper who has never in reality experienced a monarchy may find the royal title problematical. And lastly, that God is designated and addressed as simply (without connecting it with the title "King") "Father", happens also in other instances; for example in the litany which in the Roman rite concludes the daily petitionary prayer and at the end of which, in consonance with Psalm 20, *Abhinu Malkenu* occurs in four variations (without "we have sinned"). Another example can be found in the last *mishnah* of the tractate *Sotah* 9:15 which, however, is handed down in a rather remarkable way. "The men of good deeds have declined, men of violence and calumny have become powerful. No one enquires, no one is eager, no one asks. On whom can we rely? On our Father in heaven."[38]

Notes

1. For "love" as translation of *Zedakah*, cp. W. Gesenius, *Hebräisches und aramäisches Handwörterbuch*, 13th ed., s.v., 3b.—D. Michel's investigation (Habil. theol. Heidelberg, 1964) was unfortunately not accessible to me.
2. *Der jüdische Gottesdienst in seiner geschichtlichen Entwicklung*, 4th ed. (Hildesheim, 1962), pp. 147 f.—The source is b. *Ta'anith* 25b.
3. *Mishnah Ta'anith* II, 2 f.
4. *Ta'anith* II, 3.
5. B. *Rosh Hashanah* 34b.
6. *Mahzor layamim hanora-im*, ed. E. D. Goldschmidt, Leo Baeck Institute (New York & Jerusalem, 1970), I, 27 (Hebrew pagination).
7. *Mishnah Berakhoth* IV, 3 f. Cp. Albeck's comments in his edition of the *Mishnah*, p. 331.
8. B. *Berakhoth* 34a.
9. *Tosephta Berakhoth* III, 7; b. *Berakhoth* 29b.
10. Joseph Heinemann, *Prayer in the Period of the Tannaim and the Amoraim* (Hebrew) (Jerusalem, 1965), p. 116.
11. B. *Ta'anith* 25b.
12. B. *Rosh Hashanah* 17a.
13. Micah 7:18.
14. *Mishnah Sotah* I, 7; *Midrash Rabbah* Ex. 25:9; b. *Sanhedrin* 90a (beginning of Chapter 10). Note the explanation of the "celestial *talion*" in Isaak Heinemann, *Philons griechische und jüdische Bildung* (Darmstadt, 1962), pp. 369 ff.

15. The quoted passage (b. *Rosh Hashanah* 17a) is also alluded to in a stanza of the penitential prayer "Judge of all the Earth" which has survived in the Yemenite rite; see E. D. Goldschmidt, *op. cit.* (above, note 6), II, p. 272. The first part of the attributes (Ex. 34:6) is also contained in the *Alenu* Prayer attributed to R. Akiba. This prayer occupies an important place in the High Holiday ritual; cp. Gershom Scholem, *Jewish Gnosticism, Merkabah Mysticism, and Talmudic Tradition* (New York, 1960), p. 105.
16. B. *Yoma* 23a and 87b.
17. B. *Megillah* 28a.
18. B. *Berakhoth* 29a.
19. Rabbi Solomon ben Isaac (Rashi), *ad loc.*
20. B. *Shabbath* 30a; b. *Mo'ed katan* 9a; b. *Sanhedrin* 107b.
21. 2 Chronicles 6:42.
22. *Shibbolé Haleqet*, ed. Buber, para. 284.
23. *Turé Zahav* (David ben Samuel Halevi) to *Shulhan Arukh, Orah Hayyim*, para. 597.
24. *Mishnah Berurah*, para. 597 and *Sha'aré teshubhah* 584, 3.
25. *Tur* (Jacob ben Asher, fourteenth century), *Orah Hayyim*, para. 602.
26. *ibid.*
27. About an ancient fast day ritual extant in recent times cp. E. D. Goldschmidt in *Memorial Volume for Salomo S. Mayer* (Hebrew) (Jerusalem, 5716), pp. 77–89.
28. Monday–Thursday–Monday in the month after the Feast of Tabernacles and after the Feast of Passover, as well as on the fast days customary in Eastern Europe in winter (probably to guard against diseases of children).
29. Cp. Leopold Zunz, *Die Ritus des synagogalen Gottesdienstes* (Berlin, 1859), p. 118.
30. *loc. cit.* (above, note 22), para. 287.
31. *Orah Hayyim*, para. 602.
32. Zunz, *op. cit.* (above, note 29), p. 119.
33. Zunz, *op. cit.*; Seligmann Baer, *Seder 'Abhodath Yisrael* (Rödelheim, 5628) (ie, 1868), rpt. 5697 (ie, 1937), p. 109.
34. *Sha'are Teshuvah*, para. 584; in greater detail, Baer, *ibid.*
35. *Elbogen, op. cit.* (above, note 2), pp. 102–105.
36. Abudirham quoted by Baer, *op. cit.* (above, n. 33), p. 168.
37. Some sentences which refer to the martyrs, presumably to victims of the crusades, are contained in the Ashkenazi rite. Here I will point to two things. To the best of my knowledge no new martyrologies have found their way into the prayer book since that time; I know of only one *qinah* (dirge for the day commemorating the destruction of the Temple) which refers to the catastrophe of the twentieth century. Its author is Rabbi Breuer in New York, but it does not seem to have been included in the liturgy elsewhere. Professor Petuchowski draws my attention to the view of Rabbi Max Dienemann, in his time a leading Liberal rabbi. He refused to compile a *qinah* as long as he quarrelled with God (see Dienemann's letter of Jan. 12, 1939, in *Max Dienemann, Ein Gedenkbuch*, edited by his widow [privately printed, 1946], p. 58; see also p. 60). Dienemann never wrote a *qinah*. Secondly: Jacob Katz has shown the existence of different attitudes towards martyrdom at different times. "Sanctification of the name" has not meant

the same thing at all times and in all places, and has not always been accomplished in the same manner. See Jacob Katz, "From 1096 to 1648/49" (Hebrew) in *Y. F. Baer Jubilee Volume*, Historical Society of Israel (Jerusalem, 1960), pp. 318 ff. See also contributions by Baron, Dinur, Ettinger, Halpern.

38. In view of the contribution by Professor A. Deissler, a consideration of biblical passages has been omitted here.

6

The Background of Jesus' Prayer in the Jewish Liturgical Tradition

Joseph Heinemann of Blessed Memory

The form-critical approach to the study of the Jewish liturgy during the early Rabbinic period has proved fruitful and illuminating.[1] Prayers which differ from one another in their purpose and function exhibit quite distinct formal characteristics. Hence "form", in the widest possible sense, serves as a clear indication of the character of any particular prayer and helps us to answer questions like: to what category does a prayer belong? and what purpose did it serve in the liturgy? An attempt to assign the Prayer of Jesus its proper place must take account not only of Jewish prayer which may employ similar turns of phrase and share some motifs and ideas expressed in it but, first and foremost, of matters of style and liturgical function. To turn to a specific example: it has been claimed, with some justification, that there is "complete conformity of the *Paternoster* with Jewish norms of prayers", and that Matt. 6:9c–10a "have their exact equivalent in the *Kaddish*, except for the difference of person."[2] The *Kaddish* opens with the words: "Glorified and sanctified be His great name throughout the world which He has created according to His will. May He establish His kingdom in your lifetime and during your days ... speedily and soon; and say, Amen."[2a] But the *Kaddish,* in spite of the prominent place which it occupies in the prayers of the synagogue today, did not do so until the end of the Talmudic period in the fifth century CE; hence it can hardly be considered an example of "Jewish norms of prayers" in the first century. And "the difference of person" is hardly a negligible quantity when one prayer addresses God directly and unhesitatingly in the second person, and another speaks of Him indirectly and without even identifying Him by name or epithet—especially when, in place of the *Paternoster*'s direct address of God, we find the *Kaddish* turning to the congregation in the second person plural ("and say [ye], Amen").

For our purpose, three categories of Jewish prayer will be considered: the statutory liturgy of the regular synagogue service; private worship; and prayers associated with the public sermon (which was also frequently given in the synagogue, but did not constitute an integral part of the prescribed service). Only as far as set daily synagogue prayers are concerned—most of which can and must be recited also by individuals unable to attend the service—do we find strict rules and regulations regarding their contents, their structure and the precise formulae to be used in each of the constituent units. Hence, for example, in the "Eighteen Benedictions" which are to be recited daily on weekdays and which underwent their final editing at the end of the first century CE but, it is very likely, were customary in wide circles a considerable time before, not only the number, order and content of the benedictions are prescribed exactly, but each of its parts must be formulated as a "benediction" in the technical sense, using the concluding formula (and, at the beginning, also the opening formula): "Blessed art Thou, O Lord" (followed by a "specific praise" appropriate to each benediction, as eg, "Redeemer of Israel" or "Who hears prayer"). Moreover, the entire prayer is constructed according to the scheme: "praise—petitions—thanksgiving", and throughout (with the exception of some of the clauses immediately following upon the "benediction formulae", which cannot be discussed here) God is addressed in the second person, frequently in the imperative. The petitions themselves are of two kinds: the first group refers to general, human needs such as knowledge, forgiveness of sins, healing of the sick and sustenance; the second group is devoted almost entirely to the future redemption in its various aspects.

The other categories to be considered here have neither the broad sweep of synagogue prayers nor are they constructed in definite, intricate patterns fixed in all their details. Neither private devotion nor prayers connected with the sermon are, of course, statutory and regulated by rules. Nevertheless a number of favourite patterns are seen to emerge. Prayers following the sermon—of which the *Kaddish* (in its original function) is a prominent example—mostly strike the messianic note and contain fervent petitions for redemption and the establishment of the eschatological Kingdom of God; these arise organically out of the messianic promises with which the sermons themselves concluded most frequently. Stylistically, their most notable feature is the avoidance, in many instances, of both the direct address of God in the second person and the use of *adonai* ("The Lord"); instead, they prefer various epithets. Even petitions are formulated in the He-style, as in the *Kaddish*, quoted above. This style evolves naturally from that of the sermon itself, in which God is not addressed, but his actions and his mercies are recounted in the third person. In their discourses, the Rabbis avoided titles such as "Lord" or "God", and used other epithets in their place. Again, like the sermons themselves, the prayers following them would frequently be formulated in Aramaic.[3]

Private devotion, too, is limited in scope and does not normally consist of elaborate structures. Here, each prayer consists, at most, of two or three specific requests, and no lengthy, complex "series" are found. Again, Aramaic is often used. Nor are there any prescribed formulae which must be employed. Nevertheless, even in private prayers certain styles and patterns were eventually preferred, though they were never used to the exclusion of all others. The favourite one is undoubtedly the opening formula "May it be Thy will [literally: May it be the will from before Thee], O Lord, my God and the God of my fathers . . . ." In this pattern, *adonai* is used invariably, followed by the additional epithet, *elohai*, "my God" (with the first person pronominal suffix), and God is addressed in the second person. All of the foregoing points emphasize the intimate, personal relationship with God of which the worshipper is conscious.

This pattern is simple and extremely practical, for it allows the prayer to continue in almost any style, such as "May it be Thy will . . . that my wife give birth to a male (*Mishnah Berakhoth* 9:3), "that no mishap should occur through me" (*ibid.* 4:2) and the like. It would have been very difficult to phrase such petitions without an opening formula like this; for if a petitionary prayer were to open with another of the common forms, such as the one in which God is addressed by an epithet ("Our Father in heaven"; "Master of the universe", and so on), the continuation would have to use an imperative, and not every petition can be expressed in this style. In addition to its practicality, this formula also has the advantage of clearly indicating that the text which follows is a prayer. Hence a prayer becomes recognizable and identifiable as such by virtue of its own particular language, from the very first word.

But the primary reason for the widespread use of this formula is apparently its indirect and modest style; the worshipper does not address God forcefully in language which could be considered too direct and presumptuous, as if he were telling God what to do. A prayer which uses the stylistic device, "May it be Thy will...", expresses an appropriate amount of reverence and restraint, for the worshipper only asks that it be God's will to grant his request, and not that God do his bidding. Behind this formula, then, is the feeling that man should not approach God with his requests in too forceful a manner. Even though one attitude is reflected in sentences like "However much you bother Him, the Holy One, blessed be He, will receive you" (Palestinian Talmud *Berakhoth* IX, p. 13b), and "However much Israel presses Him ..., He is pleased" (*ibid.*), yet another attitude prevails: "The worshipper must humble himself" (*Numbers Rabbah* IV) and approach God with awe and reverence.

In public prayers, the Sages never disqualified the use of direct petitioning in the imperative form such as the petitions in the Eighteen Benedictions; but precisely in this respect the statutory public prayers, which are thought to be favoured by God, have a different standing. "What is the meaning of the verse, 'As for me, may my prayer be offered to Thee at an acceptable hour' (Psalms 69:14)? When is an acceptable hour? It is that hour when the congregation is praying." (B. *Berakhoth* 7a.) So, too, "David, because he was an individual, said, 'an acceptable hour', but the congregational prayer never goes unanswered." (*Deuteronomy Rabbah* II, 12.) Moses, when praying on his own behalf, also says, "I do not claim that anything is due to me from Thee; but grant my prayer gratuitously ...." (*Ibid.*, 1.) But "whoever petitions for the needs of the people approaches as it were with force." (*Numbers Rabbah* XXI, 14.) And Moses "stood up before God with scant respect to request Israel's needs ... since he was not demanding his own needs, but those of Israel." (*Deuteronomy Rabbah* XI, 2.)

It is clear, then, that the individual must avoid using too presumptuous and demanding a style. Though the imperative form was not altogether abandoned even in private prayer, yet in most cases the formula "May it be Thy will" was preferred, because it expresses stylistically the requisite humility of the worshipper who can only request a gratuitous gift.

Furthermore, even though the use of the imperative form in petitions was allowed in public prayer, such petitions were nonetheless not recited at the very beginning of the prayer, but followed upon some expression of praise. "Let a man always declare the praise of God and afterwards present his petition." (B.

Berakhoth 32a.) So, too, "when Moses began [his prayer], he did not begin petitioning for the needs of Israel until he had first declared the praise of God. In the same fashion, the Eighteen Benedictions, which were instituted by the early Sages, do not immediately begin with the needs of Israel ... [but with a preamble of praise]." (*Sifré to Deuteronomy*, 343.) We do not, however, find such a pattern, namely one in which an expression of praise to God precedes the petition, in the private prayer of the talmudic period. The reason for this would seem to be not only the Sages' reluctance to burden the individual with such a demand—for the individual would not always have the leisure to attend to various formal requirements, nor, perhaps, would he know how to "declare the praise of God" in an acceptable fashion—but also their objection in principle to a pattern in which the worshipper is trying to gain God's favour through praise and appeasement. The use of the latter pattern is extremely ancient and widespread. In pagan cults, it took the form of extravagant flattery directed at the deity in an attempt to influence his will;[4] and the heaping up of divine epithets and attributes did not lack magic elements. The Sages took a firm stand against anyone who "recounts the praise of God excessively" (b. *Megillah* 17b), and although this pattern was retained in the Eighteen Benedictions, it was nonetheless limited to those attributes of praise "which Moses has written in the *Torah*, and which the men of the Great Assembly have instituted [in prayer]. " (B. *Megillah* 25a; b. *Berakhoth* 33b.) For "the Prophets know ... that their God is truthful, and they do not flatter Him." (Palestinian Talmud, *Berakhoth* VII, p. 11c.)

Although the Sages employed expressions of praise before the petitions in the Eighteen Benedictions of the public worship, if only sparingly, they apparently did not encourage the use of this pattern in private prayer which was, obviously, harder to oversee. Since the petition thus comes at the very outset of a private prayer, without prefatory words of praise, it is not fitting for it to begin in the forceful style of an imperative, and for this reason the indirect style of the formula, "May it be Thy will ...", came to be preferred.

In Jesus' prayer, on the other hand, it would appear that the opening clauses, "Hallowed be Thy name. May Thy kingdom come, Thy will be done on earth as it is in heaven," do, in fact constitute an "expression of praise" preliminary to the petitions. Similarly, we find brief words of praise and adoration again in the doxology at the end: "For Thine is the kingdom and the power and the glory for ever." In this respect, then (but not in others), Jesus' prayer appears to have been modelled upon the pattern employed in the set synagogue prayers, especially the Eighteen Benedictions (although the actual wording of the preamble may have been inspired by the *Kaddish*).

There is reason to inquire whether the formula, "May it be Thy will", expressed the same kind of abject deference and surrender to the will of God which is found in the prayer of Jesus: "Not as I will, but as Thou wilt" (Matt. 26:39, 42; Mark 14:36), as well as in the verse: "Thy will be done on earth as it is in heaven" (Matt. 6:9 ff.). Heiler considers those verses to be "the highest moment in the history of prayer", and regards the passing over of the petitioner's prayer "into the complete surrender in which the wish is suppressed" as the great innovation of Jesus.[5]

Strack and Billerbeck[6] also hold that there is no Jewish prototype for such utter surrender by the worshipper (except the words of Judah, in I Maccabees 3:60, "As may be the will in heaven, so shall He do"—but this is not a prayer). They regard the short prayer of Rabbi Eliezer, "May Thy will be done in heaven above, and grant relief to those who revere Thee; and do that which is good in Thy sight" (*Tosephta Berakhoth* III, 7), as merely a faint echo of Jesus' prayer; while the other parallels from talmudic literature which are usually cited are not at all relevant according to their view. They do not mention the formula, "May it be Thy will", in this context.

It would appear that Strack and Billerbeck are right and that, notwithstanding the affinity of Rabbi Eliezer's prayer to that of Jesus, there is a fundamental novelty in the conception of the latter. When the Jewish petitioner surrenders his wish to the will of God, he nevertheless does not abandon it altogether. His request still stands, and, if it remains conditional upon God's will, this is only because he trusts that it shall, indeed, be God's will to grant the request. We do not have here the same categorical surrender in which the petitioner's request is completely given up. If Jesus' conception represents the "highest moment in the history of prayers", then it also seriously undermines the value of prayer. For if, from the very outset, the petitioner has already abandoned all hope of his request's being granted if it does not conform to the will of God, why is he praying at all? For Rabbinic Judaism, prayer only exists to be heard and answered. There is simply no point to a prayer which is not nourished by a sense of assurance that it is not being offered in vain. There is unquestionably an element of paradox in all prayer, and this element is certainly not lacking in the Jewish view of prayer. But the outlook which is expressed in the prayers of Jesus reduces the very possibility of prayer to absurdity, and it is not shared by Rabbinic Judaism.

Similarly, K. G. Kuhn[7] emphasizes the contrast between the NT passages quoted and the Jewish conception, in which men "perform Thy will". This conception is found, for example, in the Palestinian version of the Eighteen Benedictions. In Rabbinic Judaism, the role of mankind in general, and of the Jewish people in particular, is to perform the will of God, whereas in the passive form used by Jesus ("May Thy will be done"), no room is left for man as an active agent performing God's will.

According to the Talmudic Sages, there is no conflict between the will of God and the will of man, for, if man does God's bidding, he has reason to believe that God will also do his bidding. Rabbinic Judaism puts primary emphasis on the role of man and the demand that he "perform the will of his Father in heaven". The shift in emphasis in Jesus' prayer may perhaps be due to the fact that he no longer subscribes to the belief that man is autonomously capable of "performing the will of God".[8]

In addition to the pattern beginning with "May it be Thy will", private petitions may also open by addressing God with one of his epithets and proceed immediately to a request in the imperative form. Among such addresses we find frequently: "Master of the universe", or "My Master"; but also: "My God" and, especially in the so-called penitential prayers, "Our Father, our King", "Our Father who art in heaven", "O all-merciful One", and so on. The Jewish worshipper will sometimes view himself as a son standing before his father, but at other times "as a servant standing before his master" or "king". (B. *Berakhoth* 34a.) The two attitudes were not, apparently, felt to be incompatible. They were complementary; each of those metaphors was seen to express but one facet of the complex relationship between man and God. Hence the two styles appear interchangeably in both private and public prayer.

Rabbinic private prayer, then, though it lacks the standard forms and norms, still exhibits its own characteristic patterns and stylistic traits. It uses the second person in addressing God, and, in this respect, it is similar to the prayer of the synagogue. It will usually employ *adonai*, and frequently uses additional divine epithets with a first person possessive suffix, such as "my God", "our Father", and so on.

As a rule, this *genre* of prayer is characterized by stylistic simplicity and a lack of formal requirements. The formulae which it uses are also simple and practical. The prayers which belong to this category consist usually of only one or two sentences. There are no "series" or sequences of prayers of this kind, consisting of sections which are connected one to the other, and together constitute a larger unit, as is typical of the statutory liturgy.

There can be no doubt that the prayer of Jesus in Matt. 6 : 9 displays all of the characteristics of Jewish private prayer: it opens with an address employing one of the epithets used frequently in private petitions; it addresses God in the second person; its style is simple; it is quite brief, as are its component sentences; it lacks the form of the "liturgical benediction". It is true that the phrase, "hallowed be Thy name, Thy Kingdom come", is analogous to the opening of the *Kaddish*, which does not belong to the category of private prayers. But we should not forget that this style also occurs in private prayers: for instance, in the thanksgiving prayer for rainfall (Palestinian Talmud, *Ta'anith* I, p. 64b), where God is addressed in the second person (as in the prayer of Jesus), while the *Kaddish* refers to God in the third person. Moreover, the transfer of entire sentences from one prayer to another is a common liturgical phenomenon. No special importance should be attached to the fact that God is addressed as "Father" or as "our Father" at the opening of Jesus' prayer—instead of the address, "Master" or "God", often used in Jewish private prayer. For in the request "Thy Kingdom come", which follows immediately, the alternative concept, expressed in the metaphor of "the servant before his king", is clearly implied.

In his instructions preceding the actual prayer, Jesus unequivocally expresses his approval of the tradition of private prayer, which he considers preferable to the prayer of the synagogue: "And when you pray, you must not be like the hypocrites; for they love to stand and pray in the synagogues and at the street corners, that they may be seen by men . . . . But when you pray, go into your room and shut the door and pray to your Father who is in secret . . . ." (Matt. 6 : 5–6.) A prayer which is intimate and inward-directed in place of a public prayer; a brief prayer in place of a long series of benedictions; the simple popular style of private prayer in place of the more formal and elaborate style of the synagogue prayer; a prayer in the vernacular Aramaic tongue in place of the literary semi-Scriptural style, in which the common folk were not sufficiently fluent; and a prayer which every man can recite for himself, rather than one which he must hear recited by the Prayer Leader: that is the force of Jesus' instructions to his disciples and of his exemplary prayer. It is clear beyond all doubt that those words of Jesus are directed against the prayer of the synagogue, and against fixed, statutory public prayer in general. In its place, he prefers a simple prayer conforming to the tradition of popular private prayer.

Notes

1. Cf. J. Heinemann, *Prayer in the Period of the Tanna'im and the Amora'im: its Nature and its Patterns* (Hebrew) (Jerusalem, 1964). An English version is about to be published by Walter de Gruyter (Berlin & New York), under the title, *Prayer in the Talmud: Forms and Patterns.*
2. D. de Sola Pool, *The Kaddish*[2] (New York, 1964), p. 112.
2a. (*Editors' note:* For the different versions of the *Kaddish,* see chapter 2, above, selections 14 through 17; and chapter 4, above.)
3. Cf. J. Heinemann, "Prayers of Beth Midrash Origin", in *Journal of Semitic Studies,* vol. V (1960), pp. 264–80.
4. Friedrich Heiler, *Prayer* (New York, 1932), pp. 254 f.
5. Heiler, *op. cit.,* pp. 123, 266.
6. *Kommentar zum Neuen Testament aus Talmud und Midrasch,* vol. I (Munich, 1922), pp. 419 f.
7. *Achtzehngebet und Vaterunser und der Reim.* (Tübingen, 1950), pp. 21 f.
8. In complete contrast to the view of Jesus are the following instructions of Mohammed: "When you pray to God, do not say 'If it be Thy will . . .' but be importunate and demand great things, for nothing is difficult for God." Cf. Heiler, *op. cit.,* pp. 257 f.

PART THREE

THE NEW TESTAMENT

7

The Lord's Prayer: A Prayer for Jews and Christians?

Anton Vögtle

Luke 11:2c–4 and Matthew 6:9b–13 offer the earliest literary evidence for the Lord's Prayer.[1] They indicate what is true of the synoptic tradition in general: side by side with decided agreement there are considerable divergences in length and wording. But we must remember the special way in which the prayer has been handed down. The prayer instruction given by Jesus became a prayer formula. And it is almost universally agreed that both Evangelists present the Lord's Prayer in the manner in which it was recited in their respective time and congregations. The two differing versions of the Lord's Prayer point to the history of its transmission and the question of its original form.[2] We have to try to distinguish that original form from later formulations if we are to take due account of the historical point of view.

1. The Original Form of the Lord's Prayer

In addition to the problem posed by the quest for the historical Jesus and his *ipsissima verba*, there is a further complication in the consideration of our topic, first with a view to the original language. The exceptional *crux interpretum* connected with the word *epiousion* in the petition for bread is not the only instance where we wish to verify, or at least make probable, an attempted interpretation by re-translation into the language of Jesus. The most widely-held view that Jesus also spoke the Lord's Prayer in Aramaic has been refuted most recently by Jean Carmignac[3] and J. Starcky[4] who advocate the originally Hebrew form of the Lord's Prayer. Contrary to the well-documented *sentenia communis*, they posit a crucial intermediary document, a Hebrew original of the Gospel of Matthew[5] or at least an Aramaic *Ur*-Matthew, which would then underlie the "Hebrew" translation of the Gospel to the Hebrews as well as the Greek canonical gospel of Matthew.[6]

The supposition that Jesus also spoke the Lord's Prayer in Aramaic is certainly better reasoned and much more generally advocated, and *formal considerations* are regarded as factors determining the structure. K. G. Kuhn discovered end-rhymes in the Aramaic version of the Lord's Prayer which are also to be found in ancient Jewish prayers, especially in the main part of the Prayer of the Eighteen Benedictions.[7] According to Kuhn, the variants handed down in Matthew and Luke fit into the end-rhyme pattern observed in analogous cases in Jewish prayers, especially the Prayer of the Eighteen Benedictions.[8] Consequently Kuhn refrains from determining the original form of the Lord's Prayer solely on the basis of possible end-rhymes. In order to reconstruct these, he rightly looks for other criteria.[9] G. Schwarz, however, recently took another step in this direction. He, too, sometimes considers criteria of content.[10] However, he starts out from the conviction "that Jesus, in formulating his *logia*, must have consistently adhered to the metric rules governing Old Testament poetry"[11] and then finds he can reconstruct the exact length and wording of the Lord's Prayer with compelling evidence by basing himself on purely formal criteria. He would reconstruct the same structure for all petitions in the Lord's Prayer: two rhythmic stresses and end-rhyme; over and above that, he would introduce as a third formal criterion the *parallelismus membrorum*. This requires that a tripartite We-petition in Jesus' words corresponded to a tripartite Thou-petition.[12] The original Lord's Prayer then appears "as an artful product of a consciously poetic will for form".[13] This hypothesis forces K. G. Kuhn to undertake some doubtful and drastic textual emendations, especially in his reconstruction of the petition for bread and even more in his third We-petition.[14] To the extent that more recent discussion concerns itself at all with the significance of end-rhyme for the reconstruction of the original form of the Lord's Prayer, it is rightly more on Kuhn's than on Schwarz's side.

In general the following would hold true: "The decisive observation with regard to the original source is that the complete Luke version is contained in the Matthew version."[15] Examination and consideration of the individual versions,[16] which cannot be dealt with here, confirm, in my opinion, the generally held view: As far as the *length* is concerned, the Lukan version must be considered closer to the "original" (without the two additions in the address "Father", without the third Thou-petition of Matthew 6:10bc and without the fourth We-petition in Matthew 6:13b). Moreover, it is not only possible but even probable that the promise of one's own forgiveness which is common to both versions of the Lord's Prayer

94

(Matthew 6:12b; Luke 11:4a), was added in the Judaeo-Christian community only after Easter, probably at a relatively early date. If we consider what the two Gospels have in common and what is to be presupposed as the original dimension of the Lord's Prayer, then we have to conclude that the wording of Matthew's version has remained closer to that of the original.

I think we can thus presuppose the prayer instructions spoken by Jesus himself to have been these:

Father!
1. Hallowed be your name ⎱
2. your kingdom come ⎰ Thou-petitions

1. Our bread *ton epiousion* give us today ⎫
2. and forgive us our debts ⎬ We-petitions
3. and do not let us get into temptation ⎭

We could possibly consider as yet another original element, the second part of the second We-petition "as we forgive our debtors".

From a purely formal standpoint, the first two petitions are exclusively Thou-petitions, whereas the following three are both Us-petitions and We-petitions.[17] A certain caesura arises, as it were, between the Thou-petitions and the We-petitions, in that the second Thou-petition follows upon the first asyndetically, whereas the second and third We-petitions are each connected to the preceding one through "and".

2. *Parallels from the Indigenous World of Prayer*

A prayer formula was nothing new in the land and among the people of the Bible. Although it is possible to call to mind almost only those parallels which are often cited,[18] the requirements of this dialogue call, in the first instance, for prayers and prayer formulae which can be assumed with greater or lesser certainty to be contemporary with Jesus.

Until today, the oldest form of the *Kaddish* prayer which concluded the service of the synagogue is adduced as evidence.[19]

> Exalted and hallowed be His great Name
> in the world which He created
> according to His will.
>
> May He establish His kingdom

in your lifetime and in your days,
and in the lifetime of the whole household of Israel,
speedily and at a near time.
May His great Name be praised forever
and unto all eternity.

If this prayer was really "familiar [to Jesus] from his childhood",[20] then the two Thou-petitions of Jesus must be regarded as a powerful shortened version of it. The doxology of the "Holy"-prayer which is not to be expected in Jesus' prayer instruction, may be disregarded to start with. Further, as far as content is concerned, the model named only *one* need,[21] namely the eschatological revelation of God articulated in two motifes: the sanctification of God's name and the manifestation of his dominion. Jesus speaks exactly like that. And there can be no doubt that Jesus requests the revelation of God's kingdom "speedily and at a near time", that is to say: as soon as possible, even if his formulation lacks a specific point in time which would correspond to that which begins emphatically with "in your lifetime". As in the *Kaddish*, here too the two petitions are next to one another but unconnected; the verbs come first and a direct request to God is avoided. In the petition concerning the sanctification of God's name, the phrase "God alone and only He, not man" is probably the logical subject which is mentioned in a veiled manner precisely through the passive *hagiastäto*.[22] The pious Jew does not want to give the impression that he would presume to give God instructions in personal matters.

Jesus mentions in his prayer three other petitions apart from those of the *Kaddish*. The mention of further petitions was of course customary, as is shown by other ancient prayers, above all the important prayer of the Eighteen Benedictions which might have existed already in the first half of the first century AD, before the Great Assembly at Yavneh, at the end of that century, regulated the order of its petitions and their wording, not least that of the *birkath haminim*.[23] The 12 *berakhoth* of the middle and main part contain the petitions proper and, like the We-petitions of Jesus, regard the Jew both as an individual before his God and as a fellow man in a community. If Kuhn is correct, this main part takes the same view of the differentiation as is taken in Jesus' prayer formula. The petitions of the first part (benedictions 4–9) look at the present situation, especially with regard to the individual, whereas the petitions of the second part (benedictions 10–14) concern essential needs with regard to eschatological fulfilment.[24] Jesus found in the liturgical world of his forefathers, though in a different order, the distinction between and connexion of petitions for eschatological fulfilment with petitions for the present situation and behaviour of men. Why Jesus should have rearranged this sequence (which, incidentally, is perfectly compatible with the biblical beliefs of Israel) is not a question to be raised yet. Nor is the question why he made the petition for *bread* the first of the We-petitions, whereas in the prayer of the Eighteen Benedictions it comes last (benediction 9) and clearly represents, in content, a petition for the blessing of the fields for all the current year: that is, for annual bread. All the same, there is a certain correspondence which is also formulated as a We-petition: "Bless, O Lord our God, this year for us, . . . and satiate the world out of the treasuries of Your goodness."

The sixth *berakhath* "in its emphatic simplicity",[25] "Forgive us, our Father, for we have sinned against You; blot out and remove our transgressions from before Your sight, for Your mercies are manifold", corresponds to the second We-petition of Jesus. The next, the seventh petition for God's help in present trouble, struggle and distress offers at least a certain correspondence to the next, Jesus' third *We-petition*: "Look at our affliction and champion our cause, and redeem us for the sake of Your Name." The correspondence is especially noteworthy if the word for "redeem" is here used in a transferred sense and could mean "redemption from everything that would remove man too far from his creator and his God-relatedness".[26] The third We-petition of Jesus bears much closer resemblance to some lines of an ancient Jewish morning- and evening-prayer (b. *Berakhoth* 60b, twice) with which, according to Joachim Jeremias,[27] Jesus "is perhaps even making a direct reference":

> Lead me not into the power of sin,
> not into the power of transgression
> and not into the power of temptation
> and not into the power of shame!

Regarding the juxtaposition of the petition for forgiveness of sins with the petition for prevention from situations of temptation, two recently found prayer texts should be compared to which Jean Carmignac has drawn attention.[28] The relevant verses of the third apocryphal Psalm (11 QPs^a , Col. XXIV, 11–12) are in James A. Sanders' translation:[29]

> 11 Remember me and forget me not
> and lead me not[30] into situations too hard for me.
>
> 12 The sins of my youth cast far from me,
> and may my transgressions be not remembered against me.

A Psalm fragment (11 QPs^a , Col. XIX, 13–16) probably inspired by Psalm 119:133, which itself probably may not come from Qumran, contains the following verses:[31]

> 13–14 Forgive my sin, O Lord,
> and purify me from my iniquity.
>
> 14–15 Vouchsafe me a spirit of faith and knowledge,
> and let me not be dishonoured in ruin.
>
> 15 Let not Satan rule over me,
> nor an unclean spirit;
>
> 15–16 Neither let pain nor the evil inclination
> take possession of my bones.

3. *Old and New Over-interpretations of the We-Petitions*

Before summing up answers to the question how Jesus himself may have regarded his enumeration of the prayer requests, we must consider the interpretation of the controversial We-petitions. It may seem surprising at first that it is a question of *the petition for bread* and that its interpretation can go in several directions. The history of its interpretation has been comprehensively detailed in Jean Carmignac's imposing monograph and is, in my view, largely the history of an overinterpretation. The word *epiousios*, which has been etymologically derived in a variety of ways, has afforded opportunity for several interpretations. Since the days of the Church Fathers, *artos* has been understood as relating to concrete bread and/or the spiritual word (Matthew 4:4) as well as to the new manna and/or the bread of the eucharist.

The *expressly polysemous interpretation* of the petition for bread has of late found a famous defender in the person of Jean Carmignac.[32] He, too, thinks that the inner logic of the Lord's Prayer would be compromised if Jesus were to enjoin prayer for mere earthly bread.[33] Carmignac adduces the word *mahar* which

Jerome documents (as equivalent for *epiousios*) "tomorrow", and which, he says, suggests a connexion with Exodus 16.[34] Thus Carmignac has Jesus say with reference to the manna-tradition: "Give us day by day our bread (manna) for tomorrow" (*lemahar*), that is to say: "until tomorrow" (*ad mahar*): that is, bread which will suffice until the next day. Jesus' audience would have been able to understand that he meant "bread" to the extent of the biblical meaning, namely including the new and true manna. For modern listeners, therefore, one would really have to translate: "Give us every day our manna until tomorrow". The mention of "manna", for which there is no more room in today's religious thinking, would, according to Carmignac, enable Christians to understand Jesus' prayer instruction once more in its complete meaning, namely as petition for threefold nourishment: nourishment for the body, the word of God and the Christ of the Eucharist.[35] J. Starcky's[36] more recent hypothesis is to be distinguished from this, as well as the explanation by R. E. Brown[37] put forward in 1961: the latter was mainly concerned with a post-Easter understanding of the Lord's Prayer.

Joachim Jeremias, the most determined and most renowned protagonist of an *"eschatological" understanding of "bread" in the first We-petition*,[38] in contrast to Carmignac, renounces both the manna-motif and an Aramaic or Hebrew *Ur*-Matthew. With equal justification, he assumes *saemeron* = "today" as original. Although Jeremias, surely appropriately, sees in the Gospel according to the Hebrews only a later *targum*-like translation of the Greek Gospel of Matthew, we can support his view "and maintain for good reason that *mahar* is older than the Gospel of Matthew; because the translator who translated Matthew into Aramaic stopped translating, of course, the moment he came to the Lord's Prayer and instead wrote down what he prayed daily. In that case there can be no doubt that *mahar*, 'tomorrow',[39] is the Aramaic expression behind *epiousios*." Jesus said: "The bread for *tomorrow*—give us *today*!" and he meant this sentence "as petition for *bread at the time of salvation*, the bread of life", moreover the bread which he broke at the supper with the publicans was for Jesus "earthly bread and at the same time the bread of life".[40]

However much this "eschatological" interpretation may convince at first sight, especially in view of the immediately preceding petitions for eschatological fulfilment, one cannot help an impression of overinterpretation,[41] although a few degrees less than in the case of the polysemous interpretation of Carmignac. But a *mahar* does not have to stand behind *epiousios* because *epiousios* equally permits of other derivations: "Our bread for the approaching (=current) day give us today!" fits in better with the determination of time as "today" which is emphatically placed at the end: "our necessary (amount of) bread, the bread which we need, give us today!" This interpretation of *ton epiousion* seems to be gaining adherents,[42] though whether that is justifiable is something to be determined only through further examination of context: the immediate context of the Lord's Prayer, the indirect context of the message of Jesus, and the further context of Jewish belief and prayer (see below).

"And forgive us our debts". The final forgiveness of God, or its confirmation, is accomplished by the Judgment. Where the tradition of Jesus links God's forgiveness to our own forgiveness, it is emphasized quite rightly that this refers to the final forgiveness in the Judgment (6:14 f.; 5:23 f.; 18:23–34:35; Luke 6:37). But some authors who interpret the first ("bread") and third (*peirasmos*) We-petitions eschatologically and as referring to the future (that is, who in the second We-petition are interested in an implicit reference to the future Judgment), quite properly also detect here a petition for the remission of a debt of sins acquired here and now. This interpretation is valid although the self-reminder of one's own, inter-personal forgiveness, "which concerns daily events here",[43] was probably not added by Jesus. H. Schürmann seems to me to capture Jesus' meaning of the petition: "God's forgiving amnesty is being prayed for in the face of the approaching Judgment. But the worshipper wants to receive this divine act of forgiveness already here and now probably so as to obviate the need for his being judged at the time of Judgment."[44]

The same connexion of ideas may be present in *the third and last We-petition*. Finally, the purely eschatological, future-orientated interpretation[45] had decisive protagonists in Joachim Jeremias and S. Schulz; the latter, however, regards the Lord's Prayer as a whole as having been composed only by the primitive Church in Palestine. He sees it as the petition for preservation from defeat in the last great battle.[46]

If we examine more closely a different formulation of our petition as contrasted with the ancient morning and evening prayer cited above, and if we compare different ancient Jewish prayers and different Qumran texts, the right opinion seems to be that of the probable majority who would have Jesus think not of the dis-

tress at the end of time but of the threatening situations of temptation in the now.[47] In content the petition is probably to be rendered
as: "and let us not be led into temptation".[48]

If Jesus also has in mind (indeed, has primarily in mind) in-
ducements to sin into which the believers can be led here and now,
even before the coming of the so-called "pangs of the Messiah",
then this idea fits well not only with the Jewish style of prayer but
with the immediate context of the Lord's Prayer: "forgive us our
debts and"—so that we may not incur new debts of sin—"let us
not be led into temptation".

The original Christian supplementary petition does not make
this interpretation more dubious but, rather, tends to confirm it,
perhaps especially because this petition should, according to its
meaning, probably not be translated as "save us from, snatch us
out of evil" (which, at least correctly, presupposes an *ek*) but as
"snatch us away from evil", "save us from before (*apo*) evil".[49] At
any rate *tou ponaerou* can very likely describe a quantity preceding
eschatological distress, whether evil or the evil one. Because the
basis for proving a pre-Christian designation of the devil as "evil"
is very slim,[50] we can certainly indicate with justification numerous
passages in the OT and early Judaism where evil is neuter, so that
it could designate either "evil" or "the evil one".[51] Parallels in
Jewish prayer[52] like, for instance, a prayer from the *genizah* fragment, "Save me out of every evil thing", could bring in evil comprehensively, including temptation and sin.[53] From a linguistic
point of view, one could, however, object that if a plurality of
evils,[54] that is to say: preservation from every evil, was meant, at
least the article before *ponaerou* should be omitted so that the
phrase would have to be: "preserve us from every evil". This objection does not arise if evil in general is meant, namely becoming
guilty before God, sinning.

Because our final petition was added almost certainly after
Easter, arising probably from a Judaeo-Christian environment, it
could, in view of commonly employed Testamental use of
language, mean simply: evil, the devil. Not a few recent authors
venture to side with the Greek Church Fathers in favour of this
interpretation.[55]

Among newly discovered texts, the verses from the Psalm fragment 11 QPs[a], Col. XIX, 13–16, cited above, deserve attention.
Within the framework of the petition for the granting of a good
spirit and preservation from the evil spirit and from ruinous in-

clinations, the theme of "temptation" is, indeed, not specifically mentioned, which in Old Testament thinking, however, could be regarded as normal. But a thought sequence close to one of the last two We-petitions of the Matthew version nonetheless obtains here. The pious man pleads for forgiveness of his sins and for preservation from the dominion of Satan over him: "Let not Satan rule over me, nor an unclean spirit."

In the case of the first interpretation and also in terms of contentwise, the addition represents little more than a positive formulation of the third and last We-petition of Jesus: preservation from temptation implies at the same time preservation from the guilt of sin. In the case of the second interpretation, the addition specifically names a new factor: it refers to the devil as author of temptations—effective of course up to the End—and it could, one may add, reveal him as the real and main power of temptation.

4. How did Jesus Understand the Lord's Prayer?

As, above all, a comparison with the prayer of the Eighteen Benedictions shows, Jesus has placed the main concerns of the *Kaddish* prayer emphatically at the beginning of his instruction for prayer by means of his significantly formulated Thou-petitions. In view of the basic theme of his preaching of God and his Kingdom, his proclamation of the eschatological acts of God indicated by his speech and action leads us to expect nothing else; in other words, the final revelation of God, understood as the essence of salvation, is the primary concern of Jesus; and this concern determines, too, the remaining contents of the prayer as enumerated by him. One may, therefore, presume from the beginning that each of the following We-petitions must have an "eschatological" reference. The question is only wherein this eschatological reference is to lie.

A diacritical assessment of the discussion up to this point allows the following hypothesis: after Jesus has required worshippers to plead in the two Thou-petitions for the final revelation of the salvific action of God, he draws their attention to the situation of the Israelites who have been called to the attainment of salvation in the three We-petitions. He has in mind here three obstacles to the attainment of final salvation:

1. the complete preoccupation of men with one concern which makes it impossible for them to perceive the only necessary concern;

2. the sins through which they have become guilty before God;
3. the danger of new guilt through sin.

Only the first point now requires further proof. Those authors whose interpretations I have regarded as over-interpretations (see above) of the petition for bread, reveal nevertheless a fine sensitivity when, after all, they feel that, following upon a plea for the ultimate revelation of God's kingdom, a mere plea for physical nourishment would be a considerable anticlimax. And they feel it should strike one as strange that Jesus should mention, especially as the first of the We-petitions, a need which is in essence totally orientated towards the old aeon. This impression would, in my view, be largely justified if the petition in effect, asked "that one could go to sleep not, indeed, in superabundance and not secure against all time of need, but without worries because the needs of the coming day are taken care of."[56] This interpretation which, incidentally (at least without compelling philological grounds), interprets *ton epiousion* as (bread) "for the next day",[57] certainly misses the mark. Martin Dibelius comes closer to the real concern of Jesus when he has Jesus understand our request "in the spirit of that ideal freedom bestowed upon the goods of the world by eschatological faith: give us, for that yet short stretch of way, what we still need; and this is simply only the necessary food . . . because the relative frugality of the 'traveller', just like the situation of eschatological faith, no longer reckons with finite possessions."[58]

Indeed our petition for bread might be articulated out of that spirit of "ideal freedom" of which Dibelius speaks. "Jesus' request is always actively directed against that which prevents and hinders man from making a decision for the dominion of God."[59] Among factors which in the eyes of Jesus prevent and hinder man essentially is a wholly absorbing care for the finite possessions of this life. Hence his demand that we allow ourselves to be freed through the amazingly great goodness of the Creator God for the paradoxical state of not caring. From the total context of Jesus' summons to return, there can be no doubt towards what the really "necessary" care and activity of man should direct themselves. Even if Jesus had not spoken the well-known sentence: "But seek ye first the kingdom of God—and all these things shall be added unto you" (Matthew 6:33), namely from God, it would express exactly the only real aim of human cares, compared to which all the usual foreground cares and worries dwindle into insignificance.[60] Against

103

this background the eschatological reference and eschatological actuality of the petition for bread vis-à-vis the formulation cited by Martin Dibelius can be sharpened by one nuance of meaning. In accordance with its fundamental commitment to Jesus, the petition for bread is an interdiction of that forethought which prevents man from caring for the one truly necessary matter in the here and now: namely, to open up his thinking and doing towards the divine will for salvation and holiness. From this position, those whom Jesus addresses are to trust completely in the goodness of the heavenly Father and to ask literally only for the food necessary for "-today",[61] in order to be totally free for the call from Jesus and his appeal for the implementation of God's will.[62] What Eduard Schweizer says of the last We-petition, the petition for preservation from temptation,[63] already applies to the first We-petition: it, too, is spoken out of a very realistic estimation of the real man, his actual efforts and capabilities. The petition for bread, thus understood, incidentally allows at the same time an ideational association with the We-petition which follows. Completely submitting to the will of God means essentially: admitting to being a sinner before God and dependent on his forgiving mercy. The thesis that the petition for bread is, in Jesus' understanding, simultaneously and essentially a call to a situational activity on the part of the worshipper, cannot then, incidentally, be contrasted with the formulation of this first We-petition. One cannot expect anything other than that here, too, God appears solely as the one who acts and, more exactly, as the one who gives, and the worshipper solely as the one who receives. This formulation completely fits the immediate context of the Lord's Prayer: first, the two preceding Thou-petitions which look forward to the dominion of final salvation through the intervention of God himself and only from him; and no less the two subsequent We-petitions: only God can forgive committed sins and similarly prevent temptation leading to new guilt.[64]

5. *The Prayer Addressed to the One God and Father*

But what was the fate of Jesus' prayer instruction. By virtue of belief in the crucified Messiah Jesus and his ascension to God, the expectation of the final revelation of God, of the coming of God's dominion, has undergone not only a new intensification but a new direction, namely towards the "Messiah" Jesus. This is revealed most characteristically in the *maranatha*, the plea of the primitive church for the coming of *the Lord Jesus*. It cannot be gainsaid that this newly-won belief in the Messiah Jesus connects the final coming of the kingdom of God to the *parousia*, the manifestation of Jesus as Messiah. Has the prayer instruction of Jesus thus been rendered obsolete? One can say with a clear conscience: "Not at all!" The ancient biblical *telos* of the final revelation of God retains its complete validity, as an irreproachable witness to the new belief in the Messiah confirms, a belief which from the Jewish viewpoint is non-sense: "And when all things shall be subdued unto him [Jesus, the Messiah], then shall the Son also himself be subject unto him that puts all things under him, that God may be all in all" (I Corinthians 15:28). And not last: the pristine Christian fact of the transmission of the Lord's Prayer and its use as a prayer show that the continuing validity of Jesus' prayer instruction was not in the least diminished through the Easter faith.

Admittedly, we cannot at this point ignore the Jesus-like character of Jesus' prayer formula. Indeed, it is possible to adduce for every petition of the Lord's Prayer conspicuous, or at least partially suggested, lines which show connexions to the OT.[65] Moreover, ancient prayer texts and didactic sentences offer more or less direct parallels to the Lord's Prayer as a whole and to its individual petitions. All the same, the special accentuation and actuality of Jesus' proclamation of God and of God's kingdom are reflected in the requests of his prayer, and how he formulates and orders them, no less than in what he omits. But this, too, is part of the peculiar nature of the Lord's Prayer. Jesus the personage and his claim to a mission completely recede behind the action of God. Jesus has people pray for the coming of God's kingdom without pointing to the decisive turning point which has already been brought about with his coming; without indicating that, through him, God grants remission of sins. Nor does the Lord's Prayer even mention the coming of the Son of Man. Hence the Lord's Prayer forgoes what, with a view to the whole of Jesus' proclamation, is implicitly termed Christology. Nor can the address of God as *abba* claim to be that although it seems that *abba* as form of address to God in a prayer has as yet not been documented.[66] Moreover, David Flusser says that the fact that Joachim Jeremias has not found *abba* as address to God in Talmudic literature means "very little in view of the sparse rabbinic material about charismatic prayers."[67] And concerning the well known tradition about Hanan[68] he permits himself the rhetorical question: "Could it have been different but that such holy men [like Honi, Hanina bar

Dosa, Hanan] who stood to God as a son to his father, also spoke to God as 'Father' (*abba*)?"[69]

This much one apparently has to concede: even the intimate address of God as *abba*, preferred and recommended by Jesus and obviously fitting with his emphasis on the "near" God, does not in and by itself permit the conclusion that the eschatological Saviour is making claims. Precisely because it renounces "Christological" components, the Lord's Prayer is an "ecumenical" prayer in the widest sense of this word. From the first to the last petition, it speaks only about the one Father-God whom Jews and Christians acknowledge together.

6. *Christendom's Formulation of the Lord's Prayer*

Jesus' prayer instruction, in the extended version of the Judaeo-Christian community, has become the main prayer of all Christendom. Nor has its "ecumenical" character, which has just been explained, been impaired through partial expansions, beginning with the "who art in heaven" added by the pious Jewish worshipper, an addition which suggests the corresponding "on earth", and which was also added after Easter in the third Thou-petition of the Matthew version: "*Your will be done on earth as it is in heaven!*" The sanctification of God's name and the coming of his kingdom undoubtedly signify the final and unimpeded assertion of God's will in all creation. But the present formulation of the additional petition makes it possible to have simultaneously in mind the doing of God's will through man—a motif which truly fits, in the best way possible, with the language of prayer common to scriptures[70] and their pious readers.[71] The purpose of the additional, third Thou-petition was probably not merely to create a tautological explication of the two Thou-petitions but to alert the worshipper to a stance in keeping with the revelation of God's kingdom. At the same time a resounding conclusion[72] was created for the two fundamental Thou-petitions, as well as a certain thought-bridge from the strict *eskaton* of the two Thou-petitions to the We-petitions which look to the present situation of those who wait for salvation.

The supplement and *addition to the petition for forgiveness of the guilt of sin* made explicit, in paraenetic undertone, a demand on the worshipper which additionally fortified the petition for forgiveness, and which, in the spirit of Jesus, represents a self-evident implication of the petition for divine forgiveness of one's own sins because an indispensable presupposition for the petition for divine forgiveness is genuine preparedness for one's own interpersonal forgiveness. That, too, is an association of ideas already voiced unmistakably by the Scriptures themselves (Ecclesiasticus 28:2) and which is called to mind on the Day of Atonement by the quotation of the legal maxim "that God's forgiveness is valid only for him who previously reconciled himself with his fellow men."

The Lord's Prayer was brought to a sonorous conclusion by means of a positive formulation: "but deliver us from evil". The Old-Covenantal worshipper who accepts the language and mentality of Israel in the new epoch and, not least, its petitions and prayerful requests, could hardly be alienated by this Christian concluding petition whether it refers for the prevention of sin, a turning from God or preservation from the daemonic tempter.

Finally, no later than towards the end of the first century, *a fixed form of the eulogy* gradually[73] became indigenous. Without this, the first and last concern of biblical prayer is introduced, and it does this quite unmistakably in the prescribed language of Scripture and of its psalmody in particular. There can be no doubt that the final tripartite doxology which only late Matthew manuscripts document, is completely based on Scripture, more particularly on I Chronicles 29:11 ff.

Hence the enlarged version of the Lord's Prayer forgoes Christological implications and completely fulfils the requirement which Rabbi Yohanan made of a "benediction": "Every benediction without the mention of God and his kingdom is no benediction."[74] And just as particularly the Prayer of the Eighteen Benedictions can be said in the congregation as well as by the individual, so can the Lord's Prayer.

7. The "Ecumenical" Prayer for Today

Can a Jew recite the main prayer of Christendom? This question sounds as if it were the most obvious thing in the world that we Christians today still recite and can recite the Lord's Prayer. We should ask more appropriately: "Can we 'Moderns', Jews or Christians, recite the Lord's Prayer?"

We Christians have reason to rid ourselves of an at least subliminal assumption. The decisive *Thou-petitions* of the Lord's Prayer which do, indeed, determine the particular urgency of the subsequent We-petitions, are bound, if I may use the expression, to

107

embarrass Christians far more than Jews. Jews and Christians have used the same fundamental petitions for the speedy coming of God's kingdom for almost 2000 years and more—Jews above all in the *Kaddish*, Christians in the Lord's Prayer—and so far it has not been fulfilled. And truthfully we have to add: not for Christians either, although they confess belief in the Messiah Jesus who has long since been enthroned in heaven. In view of this major aspect of the Lord's Prayer the Christian worshipper faces a test of his belief no less significant than that which his Jewish brother faces.

Beyond that, the same onerous question arises for both: can we, in faith, still recite the petition for the redeeming intervention of our Father in heaven? Especially after the experiences of our century, the "father" concept has become highly problematical for all of us. We can understand only too well that Baruch Graubard, when as a refugee without rights, in a situation of extreme persecution, discovered in the Lord's Prayer "a symbol" for his identity: "That was like a Jewish prayer, like an abbreviation of the Eighteen Benedictions ... only the petition for peace seemed to me to be missing. The father was only indirectly addressed as king, and I thought at the time that the father was in need of help just like me."[75] How could "the father in heaven" permit what happened to Jews in Auschwitz, Treblinka and elsewhere? That was also the rousing question from Christian exegetes like the Marxist philosopher M. Machoveč: "To pray to God as father is today no longer possible for many people, and the actual pursuit of prayer, in this sense, has to undergo a most severe test. It has reached the fiery zone of doubt, of uselessness, of inapplicability."[76] I freely admit that "theodicy" with all its arts is no longer of avail here. But I would submit only one phenomenon which outstrips all attempts at rational justification. I am referring to the challenging and moving answer of experienced faith itself; that huge witness of a living faith in God which unites the old and the new People of God. Innumerable sons and daughters of Israel were not only murdered because they were Jews but died a martyr's death in conscious loyalty to a "Father in heaven" who was trying them severely. Graubard reminded us that it is the fate and the task of Israel, the people chosen by God, not to succumb to the pressure of exile but to bear witness to the faith in God's power, faithfulness and future in the face of the calumny and oppression of the surrounding world.[77] Can we, as Christians, close our eyes before the deepening crisis into which belief in divine redemption has fallen? In that case we have more reason than ever to recognize a prefiguration of our own future fate and task in Israel's fate and, together with our Jewish brothers, to implore God for the final glorification of his name and the coming of his kingdom.

Alert minds throughout the world bemoan the increasingly endangered *humanum*, or humane element and fear for its total loss—which would entail man's ruin. Who is more in duty bound and at the same time able to encounter this threat than Jews and Christians who are committed to the same God of the Bible who demands holiness and gives of himself paternally, the God to whom the *We-petitions of the Lord's Prayer* are addressed. Admittedly, it was beyond the viewpoint and thought-horizon of Jesus that millions of people should die of starvation. Nor, of course, is he, in his petition for bread, speaking on behalf of those who persuade others to labour and care for them. But his petition applies sharply to those who pursue the safeguarding of their continued satisfaction and repleteness as the real and only aim of their existence and therefore espouse a loveless egotism. The profound concern of the petition for bread is first of all care for the fulfilment of God's will: to do what God always desired and still desires today. This concern corresponds also to the purest faith and prayer of the OT. We would, in fact, thoroughly misunderstand the petition for bread were we to regard it, as it were, as a call to God's obligation to maintain and nurture us, instead of letting it obligate us. And because this petition, too, is a We-petition, it is part of this obligation to assume very concrete responsibility for one's fellow man: he, too, is to receive sufficient food so that he can open himself up to what is really essential.

Whether we acknowledge the Hebrew Bible or both Testaments, we always have reason to admit that we have incurred guilt and can exist before God only if we let forgiveness between man and man become a reality. The pious Jew prays three times a day: "Forgive us, our Father, for we have sinned", because he wants to become aware that God is a holy God before whom it is impossible to exist without sin. The Christian who recites the Lord's Prayer should be mindful of this. If we Christians think what injustice Christian nations and individuals even in the highest echelons of the Church have become guilty of, especially through their repugnant abuse and persecution of Jews, then we must not avoid the earnest obligation of interhuman forgiveness. We can have recourse to the same prayer of the Eighteen Benedictions, the twelfth petition of which calls for just punishment of the enemies' evil deeds, "all those who do evil". Towards the end of the first century AD, the Christian apocalyptist has the martyrs plead in even sharper language for the final intervention of the judge of wrath, in an hour of severest affliction in the presence of deadly earnest persecution of the Christian communities in Asia Minor: "And they cried with a loud voice: how long, Lord, holy and true, doest thou not judge and avenge our blood on them that dwell on the earth?" (Revelations 6:10). Beyond the understandable invocation of a God of wrath in an extreme situation of collective persecution, we must not overlook what the biblical tradition demands in regard to the relationship between man and man, and behaviour in face of the personal enemy. Claude G. Montefiore, arguing against Israel Abrahams' restrained evaluation of the assurance of one's personal forgiveness,[78] says: "What can be more closely parallel than Sirach XXVIII:2?" Should and must not the Lord's Prayer remind all of us, Jews as well as Christians, Christians as well as Jews, of the spirit of collective responsibility and conciliation? This spirit is breathed by the Scriptures we share and by Judaism's understanding of prayer inspired by those Scriptures.

It goes against the grain of our contemporary self-assured autonomy to see and admit "one's own evil potentialities" and to speak of temptation to sin, of becoming guilty before God, of the power of evil, let alone of the diabolical Tempter. This is in contrast to the ancient biblical tradition which demonstrated to us, through its teachings and especially its prayers, a deep understanding of the danger of situations and temptations which cause even the pious one to stumble. This can only mean that Jews as well as Christians are called upon to see the dangers of shortcomings, in the positive and productive sense, of the gift of human freedom, and thus the dangers to man and the human element in all its depths, and to call those dangers by their proper names. We should both, therefore, dare to pray: "and lead us not into temptation but deliver us from evil!" In this concluding supplication there is a yearning for that world where dualities disappear; dualities which weigh on the Old Testament and indeed its first pages. In this sense, the concluding petition turns our gaze back to the fundamental Thou-petitions for the final revelation of God.

This raises the kind of challenge that the Lord's Prayer has always represented. How can we today find it possible to believe in a Father-God and to hope for the coming of his kingdom? We are not shirking the issue if, at first, we turn to answer a preliminary

110

question, namely: through whom and through what is the coming of God's kingdom as the essence of salvation and life to be brought about? Through human *engagement* in history. (This is the average aim of new efforts which show individual variations, such as "God-is-dead-theology", "theology of revolution" and certain varieties of a self-styled "political theology".)[79] Through the gracious acts of God and the preparatory actions of the responding Covenant partner. This is the answer dominating the Old Testament and, above all, the answer as it lives on in early Jewish exegesis. Solely through God's intervening action. That is the response indicated in the late writings of the OT and typical in apocalyptic writings. Solely through God's actions and grace. Critical investigation also feels largely called upon to circumscribe Jesus' own answer in this manner. This, of course, does not mean that human *engagement* or commitment, the inevitable requirement of doing God's will by the earthly partner of the Covenant, was disregarded by Jesus. The difference concerns only the comparative significance of human action. If the critical view cited is correct, Jesus regarded the radical fulfilment of God's will as an inevitable condition and presupposition for entering into the salvation of God's kingdom, for the ultimate coming of which those he addressed could, and should, only pray. The demand for the fulfilment of God's will even to the point of loving one's personal enemy has in no way surrendered any of its compelling power. On the contrary. That demand undergoes an intensification and actualization which can hardly be surpassed because Jesus, in view of the anticipated coming of God's kingdom in the very near future, demanded an uncompromising surrender to God's holy and salvific will which brooked no delay. Consequently Jesus has four We-petitions follow upon the Thou-petitions. These We-requests look towards the situation of men called to be inheritors of salvation. That is why the later Judaeo-Christian community even added a third Thou-petition which was probably to implore not only the swift supremacy of God's will but also, and even primarily, the already present accomplishment of God's will by men.

The question posed above (namely, how salvation is to come) even gains in significance if we consider the hardly negligible fact that the expectation of Jesus and those who prayed the Lord's Prayer in the first Christian generation was no more fulfilled than that of the ancient reciters of the *Kaddish*. Not when as many people as possible, or when all men try to do God's will without hindrance, but through the God of Israel's Scriptures who intervenes in history and who is also the God of Jesus! What are we to make of this if Jesus really thought this, if he expected, in an "apocalyptic" understanding of the future hope—as undoubtedly based upon and anticipated in the OT—an absolute *eschaton* and salvation exclusively as action and gift of God? A realistic world-view can hardly cite another aim which allows us to dare recite the Lord's Prayer. In this sense I offer the closing thought: surely our experience, going back hundreds and thousands of years, should bring us together in deeper understanding of the primacy of God's actions? What better suasion to hope for a future of salvation is there than belief in a gracious, powerful intervention of God himself? Precisely this belief, surpassing the assumed illusion of a perfectibility of the world through purely human agency, is an uncontested common basis of both "Testaments"; nevertheless, a belief which we Jews and Christians can confess only in spite of all appearances.

Notes

1. The version in *Didache* 8:2 which is more recent and, except for unimportant deviations, corresponds to the Mt. version, would not contribute anything to the reconstruction of the original version.

2. One opinion encountered even today and, in my view, not convincing, is that both versions of the Lord's Prayer do not go back to a prayer formula recited by Jesus. S. Schulz attributes the original version to the oldest Judaeo-Christian "Q Community" which was completely governed by apocalyptic expectations, and which did, indeed, utilize old, in fact the oldest traditions: *Q Die Spruchquelle der Evangelisten* (Zürich, 1972), pp. 86–93. Continuing the hypothesis of M.D. Goulder (1963), S. van Tilborg, too, will have the Lord's Prayer originate in the Judaeo-Christian community, namely from a liturgical reflection of the Gethsemane story. He maintains that the reference to the "will of God" has brought about the influence of the *Kaddish*, and that the Jesus *logion* concerning *peirasmos* had brought about other prayer formulations of Jesus: "A Form-Criticism of the Lord's Prayer", *Novum Testamentum*, 14 (1971), pp. 94–105.

3. *Recherches sur le "Notre Père"* (Paris, 1969). According to Carmignac, the Hebrew original form "at least" is "rather probable" (pp. 32 f.).

4. "La Quatrième Demande du Pater", *Harvard Theological Review*, 64 (1971), pp. 401–9.

5. Jean Carmignac, *Recherches*, pp. 35–51.

6. J. Starcky, *op. cit.*, especially p. 409.

7. *Achtzehngebet und Vaterunser und der Reim*, Wissenschaftliche Unter-

suchungen zum NT (Tübingen, 1950); see especially p. 38: In the first stanza of both Matthew and Luke versions the rhyme is said to end in -āk = "your", and in the second stanza in -nā = "our", which is said to correspond exactly to the differences in content.

8. *Op. cit.*, p. 39.
9. *Op. cit.*, pp. 39 ff.
10. Above all, in order to be able to postulate as a structured third and last We-petition: "and save us from our temptation": Matthew 6:9–13/Luke 11:2–4: *New Testament Studies*, 15 (1969), 233–47. This passage on pp. 241 f.
11. Matthew VI, p. 234, Note 5.
12. *Op. cit.*, pp. 233–47.
13. *Op. cit.*, p. 246.
14. *Op. cit.*, pp. 237 f., 239–41.
15. Joachim Jeremias, *Neutestamentliche Theologie, I. Die Verkündigung Jesu* (Gütersloh, 1971), pp. 189 f.
16. The most comprehensive report of the discussion of the Lord's Prayer, beginning with the Church Fathers up to the end of the 60's is provided by Jean Carmignac's standard work cited above. Carmignac, as a Qumran expert, also includes an evaluation of the newly found texts. He cites almost 100 pages of relevant literature (pp. 469–553).
17. This differentiation between Thou- and We-petitions is surely preferable to that between "apocalyptic" and "this-worldly" petitions. Cf. S. Schulz, *Q.*, p. 90.
18. In addition to the work by K. G. Kuhn, already quoted, see especially Hermann L. Strack and Paul Billerbeck, *Kommentar zum Neuen Testament aus Talmud und Midrash*, I. (Munich, 1926), pp. 406–24; Paul Fiebig, *Das Vaterunser* (Gütersloh, 1927), pp. 28–58; Claude G. Montefiore, *Rabbinic Literature and Gospel Teachings* (London, 1930), pp. 125–35; possibly also Adalbert Hamman, *La prière I: Le Nouveau Testament* (Tournai, 1959), pp. 98 f.
19. According to Joachim Jeremias, *Theologie* I, p. 192 (with bibliography).
20. Jeremias, *op. cit.*, p. 192. About the period of the first two eulogies of the *Kaddish*, see above, chapter 4, "The *Kaddish* Prayer" by Baruch Graubard, and chapter 6, "The Background of Jesus' Prayer in the Jewish Liturgical Tradition" by Joseph Heinemann.
21. This is taken for granted by Jeremias, *op. cit.*, p. 192, as well as by Montefiore, *op. cit.*, p. 129.
22. O. Proksch, art. "hagiazo", in *Theologisches Wörterbuch zum Neuen Testament* (hereafter referred to as *ThWB*), I, 113, 15 ff.
23. See above, chapter 3, "The Liturgy of the Synagogue", by Jakob J. Petuchowski. About the *birkath haminim*, a malediction of heretics and evildoers which was a component of the Eighteen Benedictions even before a reference to the Judaeo-Christians was included at Yavneh, cf. Jakob J. Petuchowski, "Der Ketzersegen", in Michael Brocke, Jakob J. Petuchowski & Walter Strolz, eds., *Das Vaterunser* (Freiburg im Breisgan, 1974), pp. 90–101.
24. Cf. the Table of Contents in K. G. Kuhn, *Achtzehngebet*, pp. 25 f.
25. Kuhn, *op. cit.*, p. 44.

26. Johann Barta, "Das Achtzehngebet", in Brocke, Petuchowski and Strolz, *op. cit.*, p. 82. (*Editor's note*: The actual text of this prayer—see above, chapter 2, "Jewish Prayer Texts of the Rabbinic Period", selection 9, no. VII—does not preclude such an interpretation. But it does not compel its acceptance.)

27. Our citation of the prayer follows his *Theologie* I, pp. 195 f.

28. *Recherches*, pp. 287 f.

29. *The Psalms Scroll of Qumrân Cave 11* (Oxford, 1965), p. 71.

30. Carmignac, basing himself on roughly fifty other linguistic proof passages in Hebrew, emphasizes that 11b is to be translated as "Fais que je n'entre pas (and not: 'ne me fais pas entrer') dans des difficultés trop lourdes pour moi"—that is to say: in situations which would let me fall into new guilt; *Recherches*, p. 288.

31. Translation according to James A. Sanders, *op. cit.*, p. 78.

32. Carmignac's interpretation must be distinguished from that of H. Kruse, whose hypothesis, published slightly earlier, has Jesus speak the petition for bread with a view to the institution of the Eucharist, and he would thus almost go back to the exclusively "eucharistic" interpretation. "'Pater-noster' et Passio Christi", in *Verbum Domini*, 46 (1968), pp. 3–29; this interpretation on pp. 23–9. J. Swetnam, on the other hand, seems to want to claim the "eucharistic" interpretation of the petition for bread only for the post-Easter interpretation: "Hallowed Be Thy Name", in *Biblica*, 52 (1971), pp. 556–63.

33. *Recherches*, p. 190.

34. The next morning or day is alluded to nine times.

35. *Op. cit.*, pp. 118–221.

36. J. Starcky, too, presupposes a Hebrew formulation for the bread petition, however, with a different wording from that assumed by Carmignac. But this, according to Starcky, was understood by the original community in Jerusalem only after Easter—as against the original meaning of Jesus who uttered a petition for the speedy consumption of the new Passover sacrifice in the Kingdom of Heaven. This secondary understanding, which must be based on the Aramaic *Ur*-Matthew, Starcky sees proved by the *mahar* of the Gospel according to the Hebrews. Unlike this "tendentious" rendition, the translation of the canonical Gospels, especially Matthew, had rendered—or endeavoured to render—the meaning of the petition correctly. "La Quatrième Demande", especially pp. 403 f., 409.

37. Brown has the early Christians pray for "participation in the heavenly banquet", and at the same time think of the Eucharist, and he bases himself on OT and NT manna accounts. "The Pater Noster as an Eschatological Prayer", now in *New Testament Essays* (London & Dublin, 1965), pp. 217–53; this interpretation especially on pp. 238–43.

38. Considerable differentiations would have to be made with regard to the authors cited by Carmignac, *Recherches*, p. 337.

39. For the view that *mahar* can, in a transferred sense, also mean "God's morning", the future, ie, the end of time, see his proofs in *Theologie* I, p. 194, note 92.

40. *Op. cit.*, pp. 193 f.

41. For the reasons, see my contribution, "Der 'eschatologische' Bezug der Wir-

Bitten des Vaterunser", in *Jesus und Paulus: Festschrift für W. G. Kümmel*, eds. E. E. Ellis & E. Grässer (Göttingen, 1976), pp. 344–62.

42. Cf. W. Foerster, art. *"epiousios"*, in *ThWB*, II, 594, pp. 27 ff.; K. G. Kuhn, *Achtzehngebet*, pp. 35–7; W. Grundmann, *Das Evangelium nach Lukas* (Theol. Komm. zum NT, 3) 232, who, in his more recent Matthew commentary (1968), however, chose the translation: "Our bread *for tomorrow* give us today" (p. 197); S. Schulz, *Q.*, pp. 90 f., who can also cite Martin Dibelius, P. Stuhlmacher and E. Grässer; finally J. Starcky who, as translator, hazards the word formation "subsistential": "La Quatrième Demande", p. 409. This derivation has, of course, nothing to do with the resolving of *epiousios* into *epi* = "about" and *ousia* = "substance", to form a (*panis*) *supersubstantialis*—which today is being rightfully rejected by and large.

43. Eduard Schweizer, *Das Evangelium nach Matthäus* (NTD 2), (Göttingen, 1973), p. 97.

44. *Das Gebet des Herrn* (Freiburg i. Br., 1958), p. 83. For further proofs, cf. my contribution mentioned in note 41.

45. Older and more recent authorities cited by Schulz, *Q.*, p. 92.

46. Jeremias, *Theologie* I, pp. 195 f. and reference to pp. 130 f.

47. Thus according to Paul Fiebig, *Vaterunser*, pp. 49 f., 89 f. and *passim*; also H. Seesemann, art. *"peira ktl."*, in *ThWB* VI, 31, 6 ff.; Günther Bornkamm, *Jesus*, p. 126; E. Grässer, *Das Problem der Parusieverzögerung in den synoptischen Evangelien und in der Apostelgeschichte* (Berlin, 2nd ed., 1960), pp. 104 f.; Schweizer, *Mt.*, p. 98.

48. See my contribution cited in note 41.

49. For the philosophical aspect, cf. the thorough study by F. G. Chase, *The Lord's Prayer in the Early Church*. Texts and Studies I, 3 (Cambridge, 1891), pp. 71–167.

50. Cf. G. Harder, art. *"ponaeros"*, in *ThWB* IV, 560, pp. 39 ff.

51. Cf. Harder, *op. cit.*, 561, pp. 1 ff.

52. Cf. Harder, *op. cit.*, 552, 8 ff.; 561, pp. 12 ff.

53. Harder, *op. cit.*, 560, pp. 28 ff., Grässer, *Parusieverzögerung*, p. 105, are among those pleading for this comprehensive interpretation.

54. As they are enumerated in the parallel Jewish prayer texts.

55. In addition to Carmignac, *Recherches*, pp. 306–19, see his bibliography, pp. 311 f. H. Schürmann, *Das Gebet*, pp. 100–2, leads immediately from "evil" to "sin", from "the evil one" to Satan.

56. As thought, for instance, by Eduard Schweizer, *Mt.*, p. 97.

57. Schweizer, *Mt.*, pp. 85, 96, considers this translation "the most likely" because of the *mahar* of the Nazarene (Hebrews) Gospel.

58. *Evangelium und Welt* (1926), pp. 67 f. S. Schulz, *Q.*, p. 91, note 232, concurs.

59. H. D. Wendland, *Ethik des Neuen Testaments*, NTD Ergänzungsreihe 4 (Göttingen, 1970), p. 24.

60. Expounded in greater detail in my essay, " 'Theo-logie' und 'Eschato-logie' in der Verkündigung Jesu?", in *Neues Testament und Kirche, Festschrift für R. Schnackenberg*, ed. J. Gnilka (Freiburg, 1974), pp. 381–5.

61. In thought content this request is close to Rabbi Eleazar's *Mekilta* comment on Ex. 16:4, often quoted with justification: "He who has enough to eat for

today and says, 'What will I eat tomorrow?', behold he is of little faith."
(*Mekilta*, ed. Lauterbach, II, p. 103.)

62. Schürmann has Jesus ask his immediate disciples in particular to utter the request for bread necessary for the day; *Das Gebet*, pp. 68–70. This would seem to be too narrow a construction, which is contradicted by the subsequent We-petitions.

63. "One who recites the Lord's Prayer is not overly pious, no superstar of piety; he does not ask God for an opportunity to prove his faith but asks him, not to test him ... he asks for preservation from those specific opportunities in which a false move might almost certainly get the better over him, for preservation from a 'time of temptation'" (Luke 8:13). *Mt.*, p. 98.

64. Although it is correct—and understandable—that all petitions in the Lord's Prayer speak explicitly only of God's action, nonetheless Schwarz does not seem to me to aim at the logic of the Lord's Prayer, particularly the joining of the three We-petitions. Schwarz says in conclusion: "Jesus, at least in the Lord's Prayer, has, then, not considered human co-operation, no matter how constituted. (This is our conclusion, significant for the exegesis.) God was his only concern. His exclusive endeavour and aim in all six petitions of the Lord's Prayer was the action of God and nothing but that: in the first three petitions his ruling activity, in the last three his paternal activity." *Matthäus VI, op. cit.*, p. 247.

65. See above, chapter 1, "The Spirit of the Lord's Prayer in the Faith and Worship of the Old Testament" by Alfons Deissler.

66. M. Hengel and his colleagues (Institutum Judaicum, Tübingen) have kindly informed me in writing (August 22, 1974) concerning this point: The three passages cited by Kurt Schubert ("Geschichte und Heilsgeschichte", in *Kairos*, NS 15 [1973], p. 98) which deal with one and the same quotation, ie, one single citation, do not contradict Jeremias' finding. "The relevant proofs have probably been completely assembled by Jeremias, at least to the extent to which they yield something typical."

67. *Jesus in Selbstzeugnissen und Bilddokumenten* (Reinbek, 1968), p. 139, note 162.

68. "... Master of the world, do it for the sake of these (the school children) who do not distinguish between an *abba* who gives rain and an *abba* who cannot give rain." (B. *Ta'anith* 23b.)

69. *Op. cit.*, p. 91.

70. Cf. above, chapter 1 by Alfons Deissler.

71. Cf. the proofs cited by Billerbeck in Strack-Billerbeck, *op. cit.*, I, pp. 419 f.

72. Liturgical texts tend to end this way. Cf. Jeremias, *Theologie* I, p. 190.

73. First documented in two-part form by *Didache* 8:2.

74. B. *Berakhoth* 40b; see above, chapter 5, "The *Kaddish* Prayer" by Baruch Graubard.

75. Graubard, *loc. cit.*

76. See below, the chapter by Walter Strolz.

77. See Graubard, above.

78. C. G. Montefiore, *Rabbinic Literature and Gospel Teachings*.

79. Milan Machoveč, too, naturally interprets in this manner, in *Jesus für Atheisten*. Jesus had incited a new movement with his talk of the approaching kingdom of God, because he announces the future not as

something "which comes" independently of us, but leading men to the recognition that this future is their concern here and now, "the claim of the present ... challenge to the human capacity to utilize the moment as fully and as full of assumptions as possible" (Stuttgart, 1972), pp. 101 f. Incidentally, in contrast to some Christian representatives of the "new eschatology", Machoveč openly and emphatically admits that the beginning of the yearned-for change, in Jesus' sense, cannot be reduced to man's attitude, active or passive. "Without doubt, Jesus expected the arrival of the 'kingdom' also through the decisive active intervention of God himself or at least of some supernatural powers" (p. 108). Of course, allowance has to be made for this expectation which Machoveč sees as among "certain illusions" of Jesus and his followers (p. 111).

8

"Abba, Father!"
On the Humanity of Jesus

John M. Oesterreicher

Abba, Father, all things are possible to you. Take this cup away from me. Yet not what I will, but what you will.

(Mark 14:36)

Like every significant word of Scripture, Jesus' cry in the garden of Gethsemani is a "deed-word".[1] What other expression could offer a more passionate readiness for action than that absolute surrender: "Not what I will but what you will" (Mark 14:36)? To be sure, suffering has preceded this utterance. As he pays the toll for human existence, the man of Nazareth feels his heart near breaking. Fear and terror seize him (Mark 14:33) as in mind and body he anticipates his own passion.

Yet the hour on the Mount of Olives shatters the framework of a single life, the fate of one individual. The great preachers of the past held that Jesus let the world's suffering descend on him so that its weight hurled him to the ground. Servant of the Lord, thrown into the dust as he was by the terror of his own suffering still to come, indeed, by the terror of all suffering, he is not overpowered by those horrors. After ardent struggle, he offers them to his Father. The Father does not take the cup of bitterness from his Son, yet he does not leave him alone. He stays with him, suffers with him and with all those for whose sake he trembles. For the cause of Jesus is the cause of the all-merciful Father. To cite another Gospel account: "There appeared to him an angel from heaven, bringing him strength" (Luke 22:43).

1. At the Core of the Christ Event

The initial powerlessness of Jesus in the Garden of Olives, which levelled him with the earth, as it were; the trembling and flinching which rose from the very depths of human existence and ran counter to all notions of Greek heroism; the torment driven to such an extreme that one of the evangelists is moved to the point of seeing Jesus' sweat drip to the ground like drops of blood (Luke 22:44); the suffering with and for his brethren; the equally far-reaching surrender to the Father's plan for salvation and, finally, the union of the man Jesus with his heavenly Father, and of the Father with his Son in a suffering that is love—all this makes Gethsemani a focal point of the Christ-event, and thus of the whole Christian message.

What does "Christian" mean here? Is it synonymous with "un-Jewish" or even "anti-Jewish"? Not at all. In this context, I can give only a glimpse of the lasting kinship between Christianity and Judaism by pointing to the self-abasement of the Lord God vis-à-vis his creature. The rabbis' teachings about God, the Servant of his chosen people, about his devotion to men and his compassion with sinners do not, of course, form part of halakhic discussions but appear in haggadic disquisitions. Still, they cannot be dismissed as "homiletical exuberance".

Their profundity could be amply documented. Particularly moving is one example, an explanation of the Psalm verse: "Cast your burden upon the Lord, he will sustain you! He never suffers his righteous to be shaken" (55:22). In his interpretation, the Palestinian Amora R. Yohanan (d. 279 AD) ignores the last part of the verse and thus drops the limitation to the righteous. He then tells the following parable: A king's son had to carry a heavy beam. When his father saw how his son doubled up under the weight of the wood he said: "Put all your burden on me so that it becomes mine!" Just so does the Holy One, praised be he, say to the children of Israel: "Roll the burden of your sins off on to me; I will carry them!" (Midrash *Tehillim* XXII, 22).

In addition to this and other parables that depict God as the One who bears the burden of Israel's life, indeed the burden of its sins, there are other rabbinic sayings about the *Shekhinah*, God's grace-filled presence in the world. He suffers with Israel under Egyptian oppression, even goes with the people into all its exiles. To such an extent does God share Israel's distress, the thorns of its existence, that he manifests himself to Moses out of a thornbush. So profoundly does he feel with the people whom he has chosen that the destruction of the Temple, originally a punishment decreed by him, turns into his own pain and his loss. Almost disconsolate, he weeps and laments.[2]

In the light of these considerations, are Judaism and Christianity indistinguishable? No, they are distinct. When the rabbis concern themselves with the bond with which God has bound himself to the people Israel, they think undoubtedly of a genuine, real but mostly hidden bond. But the bond with which God has tied himself to mankind through Jesus is a visible one. In him God's compassion with sinners has become flesh.

2. Legend or History?

Before I examine the significance of Jesus' cry *Abba*! I should like to deal briefly with doubts cast on the authenticity of the Gethsemani scene as recorded by Mark. Mark, and Matthew with him, speaks of Jesus thrice walking "forward a little", away from his three companions in order to pray. But Luke mentions only one prayerful outcry. Some exegetes conclude from this that the triple structure of Mark's report is "artificial";[3] that it was possibly fashioned after the threefold denial of Peter (Mark 14:66–72), and the traditional threefold calls for help (see 2 Cor. 12:8; Daniel 6:11, 13). It is quite conceivable that "the second and third prayer walk ... are later stylistic embellishments".[4]

I cannot agree, however, with Bultmann's concept of the Gethsemani scene as a "faith- or cult-legend".[5] Is it to be supposed in all seriousness that a community believing in Jesus as the Christ and Lord, should have fabricated occurrences showing him in a condition of unimaginable weakness and fear, and a struggle which surpasses all their comprehension? Can we really imagine that the disciples invented a legend which proclaims their own wretchedness and failure? Some exegetes do not go so far in their criticism. While they let the pericope largely stand they reject the words of Jesus' prayer as unhistorical. They object that the disciples could not have slept and heard Jesus' words at one and the same time. Sometimes they go even further: the disciples could not have heard what Jesus said silently—"in private".[6] The counter-argument is simple and compelling. Mark's account tells first of Jesus' outcry (14:35), he does not mention the sleep of the disciples till afterward (14:37). Moreover, their response is never called a deep sleep.

Even if the New Testament contained no further statement on Jesus' anguished cry at the beginning of his passion, we would suppose that he, as a true son of Israel, would hardly whisper his soul's distress to himself but would rather shout it to heaven, with the silent world about him as witness.[7] There is such a statement in the Letter to the Hebrews. According to it, Jesus, "the priest for ever after the order of Melchizedek" (Ps. 110:4), when he still walked on earth, had 'offered up prayers and petitions, with loud cries and tears before him who could save him, and he was ... heard" (Hebr. 5:7). He was heard; he was given the opportunity to transmute the general subjection to death into a sacrifice for all, the senselessness of dying into the loftiest meaning.

The disciples must have heard his cry of despair even though they did not understand it. They must have seen how he suffered tortures as if the misery of all creation had been poured out over him, without fully understanding, however, what was happening. Later when they had comprehended the secret of Gethsemani, they testified. Thus we may interpret the meaning of the event with two contemporary and by no means uncritical exegetes.

Eduard Schweizer writes: "Here was real suffering ... It is quite striking how much complaining there is in the Old and New Testaments. This happens because there men keep their heart open to suffering, because they do not wish to protect or arm the heart against distress. This biblical posture is profoundly grounded in the fact that God himself assented to this road leading into suffering instead of skirting life; in other words, God himself assented to the real enduring, inwardly and outwardly, of the anguish of Gethsemani."[8]

In the first edition of the same commentary, Julius Schniewind observes: "As he speaks with his disciples, Jesus uses words like 'watch', 'stay awake', 'hour', 'temptation', words used of 'the end of days' (Mark 13:34 ff.; 1 Thess 5:6; Rev. 3:2 ff.; Mark 13:32; John 5:25; Rom. 13:11; Rev. 3:10). Here and now, the decisive struggle has begun."[9]

3. The Outcry of Jesus

The very wording of the prayer at Gethsemani testifies to its authenticity:

Abba, Father,
all things are possible for you!
Take this cup away from me.
Yet not what I will,
but what you will!

(Mark 14:36).

As elsewhere, when Jesus speaks either to proclaim or to pray, brevity and conciseness prevail. How could it be otherwise? The man Jesus who prays here has come "to cast fire upon the earth", and wishes "that it were already kindled" (Luke 12:49).

No less convincing is the invocation of God as *Abba*. Joachim Jeremias rightly sees in the Aramaic *abba* the *ipsissima vox Jesu*. As a category of biblical criticism *ipsissima vox Jesu*, "Jesus' very own utterance", means that he actually used the invocation *abba*; that it was not simply attributed to him. In our context moreoever, *ipsissima vox* signifies that the invocation *abba* carries the seal of Jesus' especial humanity, of his individuality.

No doubt, the vernacular *abba* began as lallation, but soon passed from infant speech into general usage. It may well have kept an aura of intimacy as, among other examples, an episode from the life of the miracle worker Hanan the Hidden proves.[10] From the lips of Jesus the address *abba* expresses a union that fills the depths of his being. When Jeremias maintains, however, that a pious Jew at the time of Jesus would have considered it "irreverent and therefore unthinkable to address God in this familiar way", this seems to me more than doubtful, unless the emphasis lies on the somewhat unfortunate expression "in this familiar way". Jeremias explains further: "It was something new, something unique and unheard of, that Jesus dared to take this step and to speak with God as a child with his father, simply, intimately, securely."[11]

The adverbs "simply, intimately, securely" hardly correspond to the stirring character of the event at Gethsemani. Jesus had just traversed the abyss of human suffering, just faced death eye-to-eye, just experienced the infinite distance between God's mandate and the beat of the human heart. It is unthinkable that after such an experience Jesus would turn to his Father saying: "Dad, take this cup from me. But not as I will but as you will!" Am I doing Jeremias an injustice if I push his interpretation to this extreme? The invocation *Abba!*, indeed the whole outcry of Jesus, visited as he is by fear, are not signs of "childlike confidence" but of an unlimited, indeed unique abandon.

By tying *Abba* to the childlike sound it once was, Jeremias—probably very much against his intention—robs Jesus' prayer of its gravity and turns his trust in the Father into a harmless attitude. This is not the only misunderstanding we must guard against. The occasional attempt to see Jesus' message about the Father in a false contrast to Israel's belief in the Father is no less misleading. Some theologians who examine the fatherhood of God in Scripture have found that in the Old Testament the idea of

God's fatherhood often appears together with his power of creation.

A few examples should suffice to show that we are confronted here with a wealth of theological insights unsuspected by many. For instance, in the song attributed to Moses, Israel is reminded of its election and dependency:

You foolish and unwise people!
Is it not your father
    who has created you?
Did he not make you and establish you?

                            (Deut. 32:6).

From a penitential liturgy of the sixth century BC, this confession comes down to us:

You, Lord, are our father.
"Our ransomer from of old" is your name. ...
You, Lord, are our father!
We are the clay
    and you the potter.
We are all the work of your hands.
Be not angry beyond measure, Lord,
    and do not remember our iniquities forever.

                        (Is. 63:16, 64:7).

The Lord is creator, not only because he calls into being, but also because he loves those he has called into being. His creative power has no limits. He forgives iniquities and renews the sinner.

Is Ephraim not my favoured son?
The child in whom I delight?
As often as I would threaten him,
    I still remember him with favour.
My heart stirs for him:
    I must have pity on him.
This is the word of the Lord.

                        (Jer. 31:20).

Joachim Jeremias offers the following comment: "This is the final word of the Old Testament with regard to divine fatherhood: the 'must' of God's incomprehensible mercy and forgiveness."[12] Is that not also the essence of the New Testament message? The words of Scripture I have just quoted testify to the all-encompassing character of the biblical concept of Creator. The almighty God is at the same time the all-merciful. This vision of the Torah and the Prophets becomes manifest precisely and most impressively in the prayer at Gethsemani. If we take "all things are possible to you" or "everything lies in your hand" not as separate sentences but as part of the address, then we could—indeed should—translate thus: "*Abba*, You all-powerful One!" This supreme power that rules all things is the power of love. Jesus' outcry is thus, not only supplication, but also a response, not only the Son's submission to his Father but the Father's to his Son: "No other title seems ... as well suited to express God's innermost being as the name 'Father'. It is the most human of all titles and describes God simply as the One who brings the sacrifice of his well-beloved Son ... If the name 'Father' is to be no empty word then it conveys that God suffers with his Son. ... The Father is with him, is in him. He makes the Son's sadness, fear, and loneliness his own and bears them with the Son.[13]

4. *Abba, The Key Word*

Jeremias sees in *Abba* the key to the secret of Jesus: "*Abba* was childish babble, an everyday word. No one would have dared address God in this way. But Jesus does so constantly in all prayers that have been transmitted to us with the sole exception of his cry on the cross: 'My God, my God, why have you forsaken me' (Mark 15:34; Matt. 27:46) ... Matt. 11:27 ["Everything is entrusted to me by my Father"] tells us that Jesus saw in the childlike address the expression of a unique knowledge and power of God bestowed upon him by his Father. *Abba* reveals the ultimate secret of his mission. The Father had bestowed on him perfect knowledge of God; thus he enjoyed the messianic prerogative of speaking to him in the intimate language of a child. *Abba*, then, contains in essence the claim to his mission and message."[14]

In his American lectures on "The Central Message of the New Testament", Jeremias muses once more on the significance the *abba* title has for Christology: "Thus, when Jesus spoke of God as 'my Father' he was referring not to a familiarity and intimacy with God available to anyone, but to a unique revelation which was bestowed upon him. He bases his authority on the fact that God has graciously endowed him with the full revelation, revealing himself to him as only a father can reveal himself to his son. *Abba*, then, is a word which conveys revelation. It represents the centre of

125

Jesus' awareness of his mission (*Sendungsbewusstsein*)."[15]

Because *abba* has its first home in a baby's paucity of words and its second in the people's treasure of speech, it denotes both worlds and, will, therefore, do the same on the lips of Jesus: his closeness to his Father as well as to the multitudes. His ministry was extraordinary, other than that of the great teachers of Israel; it was directed primarily to sinners, the outcasts, the lowliest in the land, those on the fringe of society. Thus he could say of his mission: "I have come to call the sinners, not the righteous" (Mark 2:17, Matt. 9:12; Luke 5:32). When a Canaanite woman loudly pleads that he heal her daughter, Jesus first answers with an apparent refusal: "I am sent to the lost sheep of the house of Israel, and to them alone" (Matt 15:24). The superficial hearer will assume that the issue here is the contrast between the covenant people and the pagans. But is it not more plausible to see in Jesus' stern avowal a deep concern for those that had been pushed to the periphery of the community, for those largely neglected by the shepherds of the people? How else could he fulfil his mission?

In order to do full justice to Jesus' stance in caring for those who had been driven from the very bosom of the community, even in making himself their companion, we have to try, without false pathos, to understand the position of the social outcasts at the time. The harsh measures by which, for instance, the lepers were separated from the rest of Israel's population were not essentially different from those decreed by modern authorities in cases of contagious diseases: "quarantine", "isolation ward" are only two labels to indicate measures, heartless as they may seem, issued for the sake of the common good and limited in their duration. The isolation of the lepers in Israel was essentially different from that of the "untouchables" of yesterday's or even today's India.

An inevitable fate was unknown in Israel. The tax collectors were shunned as public sinners, not because a merciless fate had condemned them but because they had, of their own free will entered into a contract with the occupying powers, in whose service they exploited their kinsmen. Again, however painful and embittered the antagonism between Jews and Samaritans may have been, its cause was not caprice or ill-will but a factual religious difference. In a certain sense women, too, were among these marginal figures because, at least in public, they played a secondary role. The scribes shunned them: they avoided looking at them or speaking with them—not because they thought little of them, but because they were conscious of their own weakness and the power of the *yetzer hara*[1], the "evil inclination".

How did Jesus meet those who ranked least among his people? As a guest in the house of a tax collector he never castigated the man's trade, nor did he preach to sinners as they stood before him about the terror of sin or even about God who waits for and forgives the sinner. Never did he seek to convince the lepers and other sick people that they were not punished by God but that, despite their sufferings, they were loved by him. Nor did he assure women that, regardless of their socially inferior position, they were equal to men before God. Such consolation was unnecessary. His presence alone inspired confidence and courage, brought blessing and salvation, convinced those near despair of the meaning and value of their lives. In his presence people sensed God's presence. For he was the divine habitation among his people, the *Shekhinah*.

At one point, Joachim Jeremias writes perceptively that *"Abba* contains in essence [Jesus'] claim to his mission and message."[16] At other times, however, the ground on which he stands is slippery: "[With *abba* as an address to God] we are confronted with something new and unheard of, which breaks through the limits of Judaism. Here we see who the historical Jesus was: the man who had the power to address God as *Abba* and who included the sinners and the publicans in the kingdom by authorizing them to repeat this one word: *'Abba*, dear Father!'"[17]

True, as saviour of the oppressed, Jesus was without equal. Yet even Luke, who came from a Greek milieu, could think of no more appropriate description of Jesus' unique mission than the words of the prophet:

The spirit of the Lord is upon me
    because He has annointed me.
He has sent me
    to announce good news to the poor,
    to proclaim release to the captives,
    and eyesight to the blind.
[He has sent me]
    to let the broken go free,
    and proclaim a year of the Lord's favour.

(Is. 61:1 ff.; Luke 4:18 f.).

According to this prophetic utterance, Jesus himself is a prophet. What, however, distinguishes him from the prophets before him is the direction of his concern. It cared, not only for the people as a whole, but also, indeed, primarily, for the man, woman, child who stood before him. He bestowed empathy and affection on each one. He taught as did other teachers; but his immediacy and power of conviction must have made him different (cf. Matt. 7:29; John 7:46). "A new kind of teaching! He speaks with authority", the people said of his message (Mark 1:27).[18]

Incontestible as the otherness and newness of Jesus are, they do not, as Jeremias thinks, "break through the limits of Judaism". In his otherness, too, Jesus remains a son of Israel: whatever he proclaims, does, or suffers is unthinkable apart from the root out of which he grew. With his appearance, no Greek philosopher or Indian guru arrived in the land of Israel but a Jew who characterized himself as a shepherd who goes after a single sheep that has ventured astray (Matt. 18:12; cf. Matt. 2:6). Like all heathens, Greeks and Hindus are seekers after God. But, seen in the light of the Bible, man is the one who is sought and questioned by God. There is hardly a biblical motif more Jewish than that of the God who goes after his people, who calls the sinner and draws the rejected to himself. If we keep in mind the profoundly Jewish character of this dominant theme, we must reject Jeremias' thesis that Jesus, by guiding the oppressed and despised to the Father, had left the path of Israel.

5. Theology of Prayer

Most exegetes agree with Jeremias that Jesus' form of address *abba* antedates the resurrection. As such, it significantly points to the historical Jesus. More than that, it permits a glimpse into his inner life, his soul. It is a *signum humanitatis suae*, a sign of his humanity and his "being for others". Although when speaking to his first disciples he never says "our Father" but always "my Father" or "your Father", he lets them and all future generations of disciples, participate in that great loving exchange, the love of the Father towards the Son and of the Son towards the Father.

In his volume on New Testament thought, Ethelbert Stauffer maintains that a whole theology of prayer is hidden in the one word "Father!" "The God of the New Testament is a God to whom one can say 'Thou'."[19] This dichotomy between Old and New Testaments is astonishing, not to say dismaying. Should the God with whom Abraham bargains for the fate of Sodom; to whom Moses confesses his dread about the mission given him; by whose call every prophet knows himself addressed; in whose presence the psalmists exult and lament, offer thanks and petitions—should that God not also be the "Thou" of man? Stauffer continues by describing prayer as a struggle with God's will, a struggle, to be sure, in which man does not seek to subjugate the will of the Lord to his own but in which, to the extent that the prayer is answered, God emerges as victor. The Father whom I address as "Thou" answers me with a "thou"—and in that moment my true self awakes to life. "Only when I pray am I wholly myself."[20]

Yet another commentary on faith in the Father needs to be considered. Karl H. Schelkle writes in his *Theologie des Neuen Testaments*: "In later Judaism at the time of the New Testament, God is removed so far away as to be confined to the beyond, and his personal intervention in the present is hardly known. In the recently discovered very profound prayers of the Qumran community, God is never called 'Father'. What is new in the Gospels and contrasts it with both Hellenism and Judaism, is that for Jesus God is very close and ever present. For him, God is Lord and Father who, though confining and challenging everyone, embraces him or her. For Jesus, God's innermost nature is his love in which man is secure."[21]

Apart from that unfortunate usage of calling the early stages of Judaism late Judaism, the fact that the Qumran psalms never address God as "Father" does not mean that for their poet God is utterly distanced and transcendent. Neither is the Lord in the New Testament canticles, the *Magnificat* and the *Benedictus* for instance, merely remote. The God of Israel is great and lofty yet intervenes in the life of his creatures: the mighty and the lowly, the rich and the poor, those oppressed by an enemy and those wrapped in darkness—all of them feel his saving or punishing arm. The Zealots wanted to wrest the land from the power of the idolatrous emperor and restore it to the rule of its only rightful Master, God. Their movement would have been a historical impossibility if these freedom fighters had regarded him as distant and unconcerned with the lot of his own.

Similarly the rabbis. Their care for the observance of the Torah could not be understood unless for them, too, God had been the near and ever-present one. "Be mindful of three things, and sin will not have power over you", is a saying in the *Ethics of the Fathers*. "Know what is above you: an all-seeing eye, an all-hearing ear and a book in which all your actions are recorded" (2:1). Another saying from the same book of Wisdom of the early rabbis disposes of the thesis that has God dwell no longer among men as he did in Israel's ancient days. "Where two sit together and occupy themselves with words of Torah, there God's presence, the *Shekhinah*, abides among them" (3 : 3).

Jewish awareness of God is never so narrow or one-sided as to forget his immanence while being alive to his transcendence. Infinitely far and infinitely near—such is the God of Israel. "Near is the Lord to all who call him, to all who call him in truth" (Ps. 144 : 18), says the daily morning prayer. Yet no word, no picture can contain the living God, nor the praise of a worshipper sufficiently extol him:

If our mouth were capable of song like the sea,
our tongue uplifted in rejoicing like the tumult of the waves,
and our lips full of praise like the spacious firmament;
if our eyes were shining like the beams of sun and moon,
our arms outstretched like the eagle in the sky
and our feet hastened [to your service] like a hind,
we would still be unable to offer you fitting thanks,
or your name fitting praise,
O Lord, our God and God of our fathers,
for even a thousandth part or a ten thousandth of the gifts
you have bestowed upon our fathers and on us.[22]

6. *"Father" in the Teaching and Worship of Judaism*

Awareness of our inadequacy in praising God, who is high above all praise, is part of Judaism. No less the confident supposition: whatever has been commanded to man he can also fulfil. Thus we read in the *Ethics of the Fathers:*

If you would do the will of your Father in heaven,
    be strong as a leopard,
    light as an eagle,
    swift as a hart,
    and mighty as a lion.

(5 : 23).

This advice of Judah ben Tema (second half of the second century AD) proves that the rabbis are familiar with the designation of God as "Father in heaven", even though they do not use it as frequently as, for instance, the phrase "the Holy One, praised be He". But the saying of ben Tema shows more than the mere fact

130

that "Father" was a familiar name for God among the early Jewish teachers. Its content shows that its counsel is not meant only for the community. Rather, every single member of the people is addressed. In Christian literature on Judaism we often find the assertion that for the pious Jew, God is indeed the father of Israel, the people, but not the father of the individual Israelite. For ben Tema, he is indubitably both.

The conviction that man is capable of fulfilling the Law must not be misconstrued. The self-assured man was not the rabbinic ideal. If a man, which means in our context a Jew, observes the Law and thus does the will of the Father in heaven, he resembles the angels; but if not, then he is altogether earthly. So R. Simai (beginning of the third century, in *Sifré, Deuteronomy*, par. 306, ed. Friedmann, p. 132a). But if one who observes the law is tempted to break a commandment, let us say, to eat pork or to commit adultery, then he should not deceive himself, advised R. Eleazar ben Azariah (second century). In no case is he to say: "I do not wish to eat pork, I have no desire to sleep with a woman who is not married to me." Rather should he say: "Yes, I crave all this. But what am I to do? My Father in heaven has forbidden it" (*Sifra, Qedoshim*, ch. 11, ed. Weiss, p. 93d). For the Jew devoted to the Torah God's will is the beginning, God's honour the end of his life. R. Levi (third century) teaches:

Whatever the bee collects
    it collects for its owner.
Whatever Israel accumulates in merits and good works
    it accumulates for its Father in heaven.

(*Deut. Rabbah* 1:6)

The fact that the rabbinic sayings cited here have their origin at a time following Christ's ministry in no way diminishes their significance. For I am not concerned here with finding parallels or determining the age of a given saying but to portray a spiritual atmosphere. That the invocation of God as "Father" has outlasted centuries of rivalry and alienation between Judaism and Christianity surely proves that it is part of the oldest and therefore truly inalienable Jewish heritage.

It seems significant that the compiling of a few rabbinic texts which speak of God as "Father" quite naturally yields the rabbinic picture of man as a being open to God. What is more important, the texts and all the prayers addressed to God as Father, reveal him as one whose heart is turned toward man. The God of Scripture and therefore the God of the rabbis and of the Jewish prayer book is fond of all humanity and every human being.

In the Jewish tradition the title "Father" is only one of several names that testify to God as the lover of men and women. A litany in the evening prayer of the Day of Atonement, for instance, contains the following petition: 'Anenu abhinu 'anenu, "Hear us, our Father, hear us". It is framed by other appeals. On the one side: "Hear us, O Lord, hear us!" and "Hear us, our God, hear us", on the other: "Hear us, our Creator, hear us!" This last entreaty is followed by others in which God is addressed as "Redeemer", "You pure and true One", "You who lives eternally". All these titles seem to be variations or, if you wish, concealments of the one, namely "the loving One".

In the petitions for forgiveness the worshippers, interestingly enough, always turn to God as Father and as King. So, for instance, it is said in the morning prayer of the Day of Atonement:

Forgive us, O our Father,
   because we have failed out of foolishness.
Pardon us, O our King,
   for numerous are our signs!

A form of address in the daily morning prayer is quite similar in its usage of the titles "Father" and "King". In the Eighteen Benedictions the congregations prays:

Lead us back, O our Father, to your teaching!
Take us, O our King, back into your service!
Through complete repentance bring us anew into your presence!
Praised be you, Lord, who delights in repentence.
Forgive us. Our Father, for we have sinned.
Pardon us, O our King, for we have failed!
For you are all forgiving and all pardoning.
Praised be you, Lord, the gracious one, who abundantly forgives.
                                                    (Benedictions 5 and 6).

God is addressed as "Father" not only in these prayers which ask for forgiveness; he is the giver of all good things. Thus the congregation exclaims every morning:

Give peace, welfare and blessing,
   mercy, favour and pity
   to us and all of your people Israel.

132

Bless us, O Father, all of us together
  as one in the light of your countenance . . .

7. The Uniqueness of Jesus

In my endeavour to grasp Jesus' outcry at the Mount of Olives in
its depth and thus to throw light on the prayer which he taught his
disciples, I have tried to avoid extreme standpoints—not because I
fear every extreme and consider the golden mean the ideal of life
and thus of thought. On the contrary, everything real is polar and
can be comprehended only by one who keeps this polarity in mind.
Applied to Jesus, this means that he is a Jew, wholly and totally,
and must be understood as such, but also that his humanity is not
exhausted by his Jewishness; that he is always himself; that as a
human being, as a man of prayer, as a teacher, he is unique and un-
repeatable. This an interpreter must never forget. Nor should he
ever fashion the Jewish humanity of Jesus—a statement of reality
and source of knowledge—into an instrument with which to rob
Jesus of his titles.

In order to dispel any doubts as to where I stand I wish to
declare emphatically that I consider Joachim Jeremias misleading
when he cites the dissimilarity between the gospels and Judaism as
a criterion for the identification of the authentic words of Jesus. As
much as I am convinced that Jesus' address to God as *Abba* is in
the spirit of Jewish prayer, that it does not burst open the
framework of Judaism properly understood; that Jesus' avowal to
do the will of his Father rests on the frequently used Jewish formula *yehi ratzon milephanekha*, "may it be your will", so I am
equally convinced that Jesus stamped his personal impress and
thus his particular meaning on both expressions.

Something similar is true about the *Oratio Dominica* which
should really be called *Oratio Discipulorum*, "Prayer of the Disciples". According to its form and meaning it is related to, indeed
analogous with, the prayer to be recited at times of crisis or
moments of danger which the rabbis teach in b. *Berákhoth* 29b. A
short *tephillath haderekh*, prayer for a journey, is also mentioned
there.[23] This is also true of the Lord's Prayer. It is one the Lord
gave his messengers to take along on their pilgrimages and
apostolic journeys as a vade mecum, a brief summing up of his
message.

Samuel Sandmel errs when he claims that "the Lord's Prayer
gets its Christian character from its association with Christianity".

133

Yet, he is right when he continues: "The words themselves are quite congruent phrases of prayer in habitual use in the Talmud."[24] This fact in no way prevents the same phrases from assuming a special sense when spoken by Jesus. Israel Abrahams is much more profound when he cites Wellhausen: "True prayer is a creation of the Jews, and the Paternoster follows Jewish models although it is not simply put together *ex formulis Hebraeorum*."[25] "To follow Jewish models" does not mean that the prayer which Jesus transmits to his disciples is a mere *cento*, a patchwork put together from synagogal prayers.[26] It is a gift which springs from the heart of the Master and one in which his heart continues to beat.

Notes

1. The Hebrew *dabhar* means both word or saying and thing, event or deed. *'Asereth Hadebharim* means "Ten Words", ie, the Ten Commandments (Ex. 34:28 and *passim*), while *dibhré hayamim* stands for the "events of days", ie, annals (1 Ki. 14:19 and *passim*).
2. Rabbinic sayings on God's offering of himself on behalf of his creatures and on his service to them have been collected by Peter Kuhn in *Gottes Selbsterniedrigung in der Theologie der Rabbinen* (Munich, 1968). The sources for the sayings quoted here about God's co-suffering with Israel are to be found on pp. 87–90.
3. Dennis E. Nineham, *The Gospel of St Mark* (London & Baltimore, 1963), p. 389.
4. Josef Schmid, *Evangelium nach Markus, Regensburger NT* (Regensburg, 1963), vol. II, p. 278.
5. Rudolf Bultmann, *The History of the Synoptic Tradition*, tr. John Marsh (New York & Evanston, 1963), p. 306.
6. Nineham, *op. cit.*
7. To cite biblical examples: David's lament at the death of Jonathan (2 Sam. 1: 19–27) and mourning for Absalom (2 Sam. 19: 1–2, 5); Judith's petition that God change the fate of his people (Judith 9); petition of the condolers at the house of Jairus (Mark 5:38); petition of pilgrims on the way to the grave of Lazarus (John 11:33); finally Jesus' cry on the cross (Matt. 27:46, 40).
8. *Das Evangelium nach Markus, NTD* (Göttingen, 1967), p. 169.
9. *Das Evangelium nach Markus, NTD* (Göttingen, 1949), p. 188.
10. During a drought school children were sent to the secret wonder-worker, to ask him to send rain. "*Abba, abba*, give us rain", called the children. Hanan turned to God: "Ruler of the world, do it for the sake of these here who cannot yet distinguish between an *abba* who has the power to send rain and an *abba* who has not (b. *Ta'anith* 23b). David Flusser, in his *Jesus* (tr. Ronald Walls; London & New York, 1969, pp. 94 ff., 144 ff.) offers some valuable points with regard to these and other Talmudic stories on charismatic wonder-workers: eg, Honi the "drawer of circles" (b. *Ta'anith* 23a).

Jeremias knows the corresponding pericopes but considers them of small importance in our connexion because they only use *abba* as a dative, never as vocative. In one case he is even a little perplexed by a jocular usage of the title *abba*, although this underscores precisely that intimacy which he otherwise cherishes. (See *The Central Message of the New Testament* [New York, 1965], pp. 19 f.)

11. *Central Message*, p. 21; also *Das Vater-Unser* (Stuttgart, 1965), p. 19. The view held by Jeremias is mirrored in most of modern literature about Jesus. Wilhelm Kasper writes in an essay "Jesus im Streit der Meinungen": "From a historical point of view it can hardly be doubted that Jesus polemicized against Jewish legalism, broke the Sabbath law, violated the regulations concerning purity, and addressed God as *abba*, 'Father', though [to Jewish ears] such an intimate address must have sounded alien, indeed scandalous." (*Theologie der Gegenwart*, 4 [1973], p. 235.) Every part of this statement is historically inexact. In fact, the whole sentence reflects gross misunderstanding of a situation hard to grasp for all not fully conversant with Judaism at the time of Jesus.

12. *Central Message*, p. 14.

13. Witold Marchel, *Abber, Vater, Die Vaterbotschaft des Neuen Testaments* (Düsseldorf, 1963), pp. 43 f. The following summation follows closely upon the last sentence cited in the body of this essay: "There is one who purchased the name 'Father' with the heart's blood of his own Son. Since then we, too, have a Father" (p. 44). Who is meant by "we"? The Gentile Christians who previously did not know the God of Israel? What goes on inside a theologian who first discusses the revelation of the fatherhood of God in Israel, but then ignores it as soon as he contemplates the proclamation of Jesus' message? Would it not be closer to the truth to phrase the sentence along the following lines: "Since Gethsemani the nations of the world who became Christians can also participate fully, indeed abundantly, in that paternal love of God with which he first drew, *and still draws*, Israel to himself."

14. *Das Vater-Unser*, p. 19.

15. *Central Message*, pp. 26 f.

16. *Das Vater-Unser*, p. 19.

17. *Central Message*, p. 30.

18. One has to agree with Jeremias when he states again and again that Jesus was the only teacher at the time of early Judaism who dared to address God, not only in the holy tongue of Scripture and worship, but also in the vernacular. This agreement, however, demands a qualification: The number of charismatic prayers by the rabbis that have been handed down to us is scarce (see Flusser, *op. cit.*, p. 145, n. 62). Jeremias is aware that later, at the time of the hasidic movement in the eighteenth and nineteenth centuries (and probably also today), God is addressed in a most intimate manner. But Jeremias fails to inform us whether he is acquainted only with that fact or also with the contents of such prayers.

19. *Die Theologie des Neuen Testaments* (Stuttgart, 41948), p. 156.

20. *Ibid.*

21. *Theologie des Neuen Testaments* (Düsseldorf, 1968), vol. I, pp. 112 f.

22. From the morning prayer said on the Sabbath, *Nishmath kol hai* ... ("The

breath of all living . . ."), cf. b. *Berakhoth* 59b.

23. I am indebted to my friend Professor Asher Finkel for the idea that the Lord's Prayer is the same as, or similar to, the prayer for a journey cited in the Talmud. As a prayer of pilgrimage, it permits the worshipper to express the fundamental distress that presses on him and on every human being, and to respond to the call to turn to God, which is addressed to him and again to everyone.

24. *A Jewish Understanding of the New Testament* (Cincinnati, 1956), p. 150.

25. *Studies in Pharisaism and the Gospels* (Cambridge, 1924), II, p. 94.

26. *Ibid.*

9

The Spiritual Wealth of the
Lord's Prayer

Jean Carmignac

The high reputation of the Lord's Prayer has prompted many authors to use it to support and propagate quite different theories. M. Hussey, who has collected several of these strange adaptations, has called the Lord's Prayer "a portmanteau of doctrine".

Similarly, various exegetical allegories have tried to link the Lord's Prayer with the seven gifts of the Holy Spirit, with the seven Beatitudes,[1] with the seven virtues (theological and cardinal), with the seven deadly sins,[2] with the seven sacraments, with the seven days of the week,[3] with the eight Hours of the breviary (by including the introductory invocation in the count),[4] with the successive stages of the spiritual life,[5] and so on.

But even without recourse to these more or less legitimate methods,[6] the Lord's Prayer is so rich it is enough to extract the objective theological content.

To someone who believes that Jesus was more than a prophet of genius and that he was indeed the Word of God become flesh (John 1:14), the Lord's Prayer is one of the essential purposes of his coming among us. Praying means speaking to God. How could man speak to God? After St Paul had discovered that inability, he answered that "the spirit itself maketh intercession for us with groanings which cannot be uttered" (Rom. 8:26). Now Jesus reveals to us, as it were, these "groanings which cannot be uttered" and teaches us to join our voice to that of the Spirit.

"Prayer is a grace, an offer of God".[7] By providing us with a model for prayer, Jesus offered us a priceless grace from God. For now we know what homage God wants to receive from us and what benefits he wants to bestow upon us.

"Now furthermore," says Calvin, "we must learn not only the manner of praying but the very style and formula which our Heavenly Father has given us through his beloved son, our Lord Jesus Christ. In which we may acknowledge his almighty goodness and clemency. For moreover he admonishes and urges us to seek him in all our wants (just as children have recourse to their father every time a need besets them). In the awareness that we do not even understand just how great our poverty and our distress are, what is good for us to request of him, what is useful and what is profitable, he wanted to provide for our ignorance and to give of himself to make up the lack in our spirit. And he has given us a formula for prayer according to which, as in a table, he has set forth all that we are allowed to wish for and desire of him; all that can benefit and profit us; all that is needed and necessary for us to ask of him. We can take uncommon consolation from this kindness and gentleness."[8]

Although the Lord's Prayer is the prayer suggested to the disciples and not the personal prayer of Christ, these two prayers cannot be separated, and the one undoubtedly throws light on the other: "Who would, without trembling and without invoking grace from above, dare lift his eyes towards what can be moments of unimaginable inwardness when the incarnate word silenced all within him so that his soul should be taken up with nothing but suffering in love, both in the light of the vision, the glory of his Father, and also in his own divinity and that of the Holy Spirit? ... The great wishes contained in the first three petitions: with what tenderness and what longing he must have pronounced them! These were his own wishes which he offered his Father, for the sake of the Name of his Father, for the Kingdom of his Father, for the Will of his Father; these were his own wishes before they became those which he, as chief among men, offered in the name of his brothers."[9] To have a view of Christ at prayer, to hear an echo of his voice, and to be able to repeat this echo, is surely a superior grace.

The essential revelation of this prayer is the fatherhood of God, a fatherhood brought to a point where it incorporates every other presentation of God and where God is only Father. John will say that "God is love" (I John 4:8, 16). Jesus shows that God is Father. The two concepts merge one more time. And, in the mouth of Jesus, this fatherhood is not only that of the creator towards his creatures, it is, above all, that of the Eternal Father towards his only-begotten Son (John 1:18), in which all the sons through adoption participate (Rom. 8:15–17): "*Our Father*, thou who hast begotten us, procreated us by thy Word, by thy Spirit; thou who art our Father because thou art our Creator, the Lord of the covenant which thou hast been pleased to make with men. Thou who hast begun in and with our creation and who art the end of our existence.

"Our Father, thou who hast made thyself responsible for our whole existence, temporal and eternal; God the Father, thou whose glory is our heritage and to whom we have free access as children to their father.

"Our Father, thou who by nature art ready simply to listen to us, answer us ... But we forget it always ... We may deny God, but he cannot forget us, nor can he deny us. Being Father, he is faithful by nature. His superiority and his good will toward us are unchangeable.

"This is what God is for us. But we must admit that we have no right to call him Father, to be his children, to address him in this manner. He is our Father, and we are his children by virtue of the natural relationship existing between him and Jesus Christ, by virtue of this Fatherland and this Sonship which were made real in the person of Jesus Christ; and for us they are made real in him. We are his children, he is our Father, by virtue of this new birth realized at Christmas, on Good Friday, at Easter, and fulfilled at the moment of our baptism. It is a new birth, that is to say, a new existence, really new, a life quite different from the one that can be born of our human possibilities, of our own merits ...

"Jesus Christ is the donor and the warrant of the divine Fatherhood and of our filiality. It is the reason for which this Fatherhood and this filiality are incomparably superior to any other, to any relationship suggested to us by the words 'father', 'son', 'children'. These human bonds are not the original, of which the other would be the image or symbol. The original, the true fatherhood, the true filiality are in these ties which God has created between himself and us. Everything which exists among us is merely the image of this original filiality. When we call God our Father, we do not fall into symbolism; on the contrary, we are in the full reality of these two words: 'father' and 'son'."[10]

Before this Father of Jesus who has become our Father, we must not primarily think of ourselves as we lay bare our requests, but primarily and above all of him as we offer our homage. The prayer is essentially "praise to the glory of God" (Eph. 1:6, 12). The Old Testament has already trained minds well in this direction, and the glory of God was the prime concern of the men of Qumran. Jesus enters into a current of thought which he brought to perfection. The highest degree of adoration is to desire and to want what God desires and wants: that is, that he brings towards his name, his persona, all the glory that creation is capable of offering him; that he governs the hearts of all men without impediment; and that in this manner his kingdom may be established on earth; that he takes up man's free will which could otherwise stray from him but which, through love, is allowed to merge with his supreme will; that he transforms the earth into an extension of heaven where even carnal beings will join in that praise which celestial spirits sing to him.

The Lord's Prayer aligns us immediately with the purest and most absolute theocentrism.

The first consequence of this theocentrism is the discovery of true human brotherhood. The church Fathers and preachers have expounded this theme so often that it runs the danger of appearing trite. Nonetheless Jesus has specified it for us: "All ye are brethren ... for one is your Father which is in heaven" (Mt. 23:8, 9). Because God has adopted us as sons, we can and we must adopt each other as brothers. A brotherhood based upon a common participation in the filial relationship of Christ towards his Father goes deeper than simply belonging to the same people, the same community, or the same family. The "we" used in the Lord's Prayer from beginning to end assumes that this fraternal inclusiveness is taken for granted through the fatherhood of God; that egotism has been renounced through true admission of other, rival personalities.

Hallowed be the name of God, that is to say "glorified". God be recognized as absolute being, as possessor of all sanctity, as centre of all glory.

His kingdom come! That his sovereignty over nature be implemented in an actual kingdom, that he should possess every human freedom to the point of governing it unhindered, until he become "all in all" (I Cor. 15:28).

His will be done! It should so transform obstinate human wills that they join themselves to the will of God, that is to say: to everything that is "good, acceptable and perfect" in his eyes (Rom. 12:2).

Because God is creator, it would be a kind of limitation of the glory of his name if we were to meditate only on him while forgetting his creation. Through care for his glory, we must think of his work. Theocentrism would be infringed if it did not include love and care for man.

Furthermore, by imploring our Father for the basic necessities of our brethren and for ourselves, we do not stop being aware of his power and his goodness, hence adoring him. H. Bremond isolates the essence of adoration implicit in the last petitions of the Lord's Prayer: "Elementary logic compels us to add that even the prayer of request is truly prayer only to the extent that it is also adoration. The simple beggar, one who is only beggar and all of whose activities unite under the one desire, namely to appease his hunger—this simple beggar does not pray in the religious sense of this word. He will pray only once he accepts and voluntarily, heartily, humbly and religiously recognizes all that his begging posture reveals, often without his knowledge and in spite of himself: namely both his own misery and the goodness of God. For his posture to have the value of prayer, it has to be shot through with an adoration which uplifts and transforms it. Raising one's eyes to heaven and stretching out one's hand are not two inimical gestures; on the contrary, one usually calls forth the other but is very different from it. By itself, the first is a gesture of prayer; the second becomes a gesture of prayer only once it is controlled by the first . . .

"If we can say that adoration is, in some way, the prayerful essence of all prayer, with how much more reason must this hold true for Christian prayer. The *Pater* starts off with a disinterested adoration; *nomen* TUUM; *regnum* TUUM; *voluntas* TUA; after which it permits, and it directs, the beggars that we are to think of ourselves: to stretch out the hand—*panem* NOSTRUM; *dimitte* NOBIS; *ne* NOS *inducas* . . . What could one imagine that is clearer and more decisive than this divine analysis? It demonstrates in all clarity the normal course of prayer: *ascensus*, elevation, adoration; and at the same time it teaches that this course need not flinch or go back on itself, that this thrust need not, does not buckle when we come to unfold our own need, and play our part as beggars. Asking for daily bread still and always means 'to pray', certainly; but it will cease meaning that if concern for our own interests, very legitimate in itself, were suddenly to change the initial, fundamental orientation of the *Pater*. If the thread of adoration would not connect the two series of petitions with one another—the *tuum* of the first series with the *nostrum* of the second—these would not only not continue but would even retract the others. The *fiat voluntas mea* would set itself over against the *fiat voluntas tua*, as one could justifiably maintain. If the adoration has vanished, then we are left with nothing but the beggar, and he does not pray."[11]

We do not, then, belittle our homage of filial adoration when we present to God the needs of our brothers and our own needs, provided that our requests, too, lead in the end to the glory of the Creator and of the Father.

When we ask him to nourish our life by reproducing for us daily the miracle of the manna, we proclaim that he is always just as powerful and just as attentive as the God of the exodus. And it is the spiritual life of our souls rather than the material life of our bodies which we are asking him to sustain with the manna of the word or of the body, and of the blood of his Son.

When we supplicate him to forgive our sins, we recognize in him the tenderness of the father towards the prodigal son, and we cherish his untiring pity while we know all the time that our ingratitude or our infidelities could never shake it. So that our prayer would not be hypocritical, we had, to begin with, to forgive the sins of our brothers, and in this way we have worked towards the coming of his reign and towards the fulfilment of his will.

When we implore his help against temptations, so that he might prevent our frail will from yielding to the lures of evil and from acquiescing to its seductions, we fall back on the power of his intervention which, without violating the autonomy of our freedom, can hold it fast to his precepts and his rules.[12]

When we beseech him to protect us against attacks of the enemy and to remove us as far as possible from his depraved influence, then we testify that he is always capable of overcoming the infernal spirits and that the course of events never escapes out of his all-powerful hand.

The voice of adoration dominates each petition. To serve him better, we ask him to aid us. The adoration of the three initial petitions sings the greatness of God our Father. Because it is mindful of that greatness, the adoration of the last four petitions pleads for the weakness of his earthly children.

Because with God word and action know no separation, the prayer of Christ has established itself not only on the level of words, but on that of actions. So far from being worthless verbiage, it already constitutes an act on the part of our soul which attempts to adore God, but especially an act on the part of God who instils within us his adoration. As Soloviev has put it: "Each one of the petitions (of the Lord's Prayer), pronounced with faith, contains at the same time the beginning of its realization. When we say with faith: 'Hallowed be Thy name', the name of God is already sanctified within us; when we wish for the kingdom of God, we recognize that we are part of this kingdom and it already spreads out over us; as we say 'Thy will be done', in other words, as we surrender our will to God, by that very act we accomplish his will in us; finally, to the extent that we reduce our material needs to a minimum (in the petition for daily bread for the one present day), we make their satisfaction possible; also, by pardoning our debtors we similarly justify ourselves before God; and finally, as we pray for divine help in the struggle against the temptations and suggestions of evil powers, we even thereby obtain most efficacious help against 'this foul spirit which could not be cast out but by fasting and prayer' (Mt. 17:20 and Mk. 9:28–29)."[13]

If we apply to prayer the classical distinction between "acts" and "states of being" that the masters of the "French school of spirituality" have formulated and such commentators as Bremond (*Histoire littéraire du sentiment religieux*, III, pp. 64–74) has presented, one can say that the Lord's Prayer generally tends to go beyond acts and reaches into that of states of being. It not only expresses *one* prayer, but contains in a pure state of being the very essence of all prayer. Usually, the Lord's Prayer puts us into a "state" of prayer because through it we achieve the abiding prayer of Christ to his Father. Raïssa Maritain says: "We have no other guide towards life eternal, life divine, towards bliss, but the life of Christ, the teaching of Christ, the passion of Christ, the prayer of Christ. The imitation of Christ is the act of love and of saintliness. Hence the *Pater*, taught us by Christ, is the truest of prayers, the most completely and perfectly true, fitting and acceptable to God, the flame of which must ever burn within us ... The prayer without words is itself based on the Word which is the Christ. It is based on the prayer of Jesus. The soul formed by the *Pater* prays—with or without words, in the murmur of words as in the bosom of the silence of pure contemplation—in the spiritual rectitude of the *Pater*, in imitation of Jesus ... Similarly we could say that it is in the impetus and quality of the *Pater* that desires and requests are uttered, no matter how unformulated; they are inherent in wordless contemplation where they have no voice other than the breath of love. The seven petitions are always there, at the bottom of the soul, but it is no longer necessary to articulate them in words, it is their spirit which the Spirit raises up towards God. If it were possible to come down again, without interruption, from the pinnacle of mystical experience, it would be the words of the Lord's Prayer which one would find at the base, because it is, indeed, starting out from them and because they are imprinted in the soul, that the soul has been lifted up towards a wordless union ... It is as if the petitions of the *Pater*—or the one or the other among them, or sometimes even the outline of some fulfilment, had dropped all the weight of human formulations so as to be nothing but a breath of love. One sees here that whether it be the busy man who can only recite his *paters*, or the contemplative man who, with sealed lips is carried towards a union with a known or unknown God and who, in these moments has only a sigh of the heart to offer as petitions taught by his Teacher: it is from one and the same road that all, whoever they are and no matter from what corner of the world, come towards God, to listen to the summons of his love and, to the best of their ability, imitate Jesus."[14]

Also Adolf von Harnack, beyond his arid technical research, is able to live in communion with the Lord's Prayer: "It was communicated by Jesus to his disciples at a particularly solemn moment. They had asked him to teach them how to pray, as John the Baptist had taught his disciples. Thereupon he uttered the Lord's Prayer. It is by their prayers that the character of the higher religions is determined. But this prayer was spoken—as every one must feel who has ever given it a thought in his soul—by one who has overcome all inner unrest, or overcomes it the moment that he goes before God. The very apostrophe of the prayer, 'Our Father', exhibits the steady faith of the man who knows that he is safe in God, and it tells us that he is certain of being heard. Not to hurl violent desires at heaven or to obtain this or that earthly blessing does he pray, but to preserve the power which he already possesses and strengthen the union with God in which he lives. No one, then, can utter this prayer unless his heart is in profound peace and his mind wholly concentrated on the inner relation of the soul with God. All other prayers are of a lower order, for they contain particularistic elements, or are so framed that in some way or other they stir the imagination in regard to the things of sense as well; whilst this prayer leads us away from everything to the height where the soul is alone with its God. And yet the earthly element is not absent. The whole of the second half of the prayer deals with earthly relations, but they are placed in the light of the Eternal. In vain will you look for any request for particular gifts of grace, or special blessings, even of a spiritual kind. 'All else shall be added unto you'. The name of God, his will, and his kingdom—these elements of rest and permanence are poured out over the earthly

144

relations as well. Everything that is small and selfish melts away, and only four things are left with regard to which it is worth while to pray—the daily bread, the daily trespass, the daily temptations, and the evil in life. There is nothing in the gospels that tells us more certainly what the gospel is, and what sort of disposition and temper it produces, than the Lord's Prayer. With this prayer we ought also to confront all those who disparage the gospel by representing it as an ascetic or ecstatic or sociological pronouncement. It shows the gospel to be the fatherhood of God applied to the whole of life; to be an inner union with God's will and God's kingdom, and a joyous certainty of the possession of eternal blessings and protection from evil."[15]

To sum up the findings of this also rather dry study, the most authoritative voice is that of the earliest exegete of the Lord's Prayer, Tertullian: "The Lord's Prayer is truly the epitome of the Gospel ... In a few words, how many utterances of the Prophets, the Gospels, the Apostles are touched on! How many discourses of the Lord, how many parables, lessons, precepts! How many duties simultaneously discharged! Homage is rendered to God through the address 'Father', a testimony of faith in his name, an act of submission with regard to his will, a call to hope in the coming of his kingdom, a request for life as expressed in 'Bread', a suppliant acknowledgment of debts, a fervent plea for defence against temptations. What is astonishing? Only God could have taught us how he wants to be prayed to. It is, indeed, he who arranged the religious rite of prayer, animates it with his spirit the moment it issues from his mouth, and confers on it the privileges to transport us to heaven by touching the heart of the Father through the words of the Son."[16]

Notes

1. Augustine, between 393 and 396, in his *De sermone Domini in monte*, book II, no. 38 (Migne, vol. XXXIV, cols, 1286–1287; Mutzenbecher, pp. 128–30), explained the Lord's Prayer in terms of both the seven gifts of the Holy Spirit and the seven Beatitudes (he counted them differently from us). Evidently, medieval authors have not failed to exploit this idea of Augustine's.
2. Here, for instance, is the opening of a commentary from MS *24870* of the *fonds français* of the Bibliothèque Nationale in Paris: "Pater noster qui est in caelis. Septem petitiones sunt in oratione dominica ut VII dona mereamur spiritus sancti . . . VII virtutes per quas veniamus ad VII beatitudines. Septum enim vitia sunt principalia . . ." (p. 43, col. 1.)

3. Thus two fifteenth-century manuscripts in the Bibliothèque Nationale in Paris: 1. *Fonds français*, no. *19 24* (folio 1 recto): "This is the Lord's Prayer divided into seven sections or prayers corresponding to the seven days of the week according to Brysines of Torenterim, most learned and eloquent theologian (a marginal note written about 1560 gives the genealogy of the Caurel family); 2. *Fonds français*, new acquisitions, No. *4 186*, manuscript formerly in the possession of Anne de Polignac.

4. Thus Mother Angélique Arnauld in an unpublished commentary copied in manuscripts *5 370* and *7 391* of the Bibliothèque de l'Arsenal in Paris.

5. For instance St Teresa of Avila, in chapters 26 to 44 of *The Way of Perfection*.

6. At a certain period, the fashion was established of commenting on the Lord's Prayer backwards, beginning with the seventh petition. Thus: before 1109 St Anselm of Canterbury; before 1117 Anselm of Laon; around 1195 Innocent III; about the twelfth century pseudo-Bernard; before 1203 Alain of Lille; before 1220 Günther the Cistercian; before 1240 Edmond of Canterbury; before 1277 Humbert of the Romans and others; and quite recently Archbishop Anthony Bloom.

7. Karl Barth, *Prayer According to the Catechism of the Reformation.* Stenographic Records of Three Seminars. Adapted by A. Roulin. Transl. by Sara F. Terrien (Philadelphia, The Westminster Press, 1952), p. 20. From *Prayer*, by Karl Barth, translated by Sara F. Terrien; Westminster Press, copyright 1952 by W. L. Jena. Used by permission.

8. Translated from *Institution de la Religion Chrestienne*, ed. J. Pannier, Book III, "On Prayer", p. 168. Peguy celebrates "the first time that the Lord's Prayer went forth on the face of the earth" in *Le Mystère de la Charité de Jeanne d'Arc* (Paris, Gallimard, 1943), pp. 199–200.

9. Translated from Raïssa Maritain, *Notes sur le "Pater"* (1962), pp. 147, 150–1.

10. Barth, *op. cit.*, pp. 34–6. See also No. 7.

11. H. Bremond, *Histoire littéraire du sentiment religieux* ..., VII, pp. 10, 13–4. H. Bremond has once more taken up these fine explanations in his *Introduction à la philosophie de la prière* (Paris, Bloud & Gay, 1929), pp. 15–6, 18–20.

12. By taking into account, in this way, the whole context of the Lord's Prayer, one can better see the seriousness of the misinterpretation that would be committed were one to require of our Heavenly Father not to expose us to, or not submit us to, temptation: such an assumption would do injury to his fatherly goodness and would contradict our attitude of filial adoration.

13. Vladimir Soloviev, *Les Fondements Spirituels de la Vie*, translated from the original Russian of 1883 (Paris, G. Beauchesne, 1932).

14. R. Maritain, *op. cit.*, pp. 153, 155, 156, 157–8.

15. Adolf von Harnack, *What is Christianity?* Translated (from the original *Das Wesen des Christentums* [Leipzig, 1900]) by Thomas Bailey Saunders (New York, Harper, 1957), pp. 64–5.

16. Tertullian, *De Oratione*, chapters 2 and 9 (Migne, vol. I, cols. 1153 & 1164–5; Brepols, vol. I, pp. 288 & 263).

PART FOUR

PRACTICAL APPLICATIONS

10

The Use of the Lord's Prayer in the Primitive Church*

Gordon J. Bahr

There is no lack of exegetical works on the Lord's Prayer. In addition to the material available in the standard commentaries a wide variety of articles and monographs try to explain what the words of the Lord's Prayer mean.

But when we ask how the Lord's Prayer was used in the Primitive Church, the secondary literature is of small service. In the literature to which I have had access, only five authors discuss the way in which the Primitive Church used the Lord's Prayer. Four of these limit their comments to one or two statements, or, at most, a short paragraph; the fifth author devotes an entire article to the subject, but reaches conclusions which are open to question.[1] The reason for the paucity of statements on this subject is easily found: the primitive Christian sources give us no clear description of the way in which the Church of that period used the Lord's Prayer. Perhaps some of the statements about the Lord's Prayer and prayer in general from the literature of the first two centuries will enable us to conjecture how the Lord's Prayer must have been used in the earliest Christian communities.

Origen in his treatise *On Prayer* twice calls the Lord's Prayer an outline or sketch: "And now we shall come to the next task, wishing to consider the prayer outlined by the Lord and with what power it has been filled." Then follows the Matthean form of the Lord's Prayer: "And first of all it is observed that Matthew and Luke are thought by many to have recorded the same prayer sketched out because it is necessary to pray thus."[2]

Origen is not the first to speak of the Lord's Prayer as an outline. Tertullian, in his treatise on prayer, says: "Jesus Christ our Lord has marked out for us disciples of the New Covenant a new outline of prayer."[3]

* Reprinted, with permission, from the *Journal of Biblical Literature*, vol. LXXXIV (1965), pp. 153–9.

The assumption that the Lord's Prayer is an outline for prayer may be lurking behind the word *outos* which is often used to introduce the text of the prayer. Origen uses it,[4] and before him the *Didache*,[5] and before that, the Gospel according to Matthew.[6] Harnack,[7] Zahn,[8] Fiebig,[9] and Lohmeyer[10] agree that this word does not mean that the Lord's Prayer is to be repeated verbatim, but that it is merely an example of *how* one should pray. I would suggest that it is an example of the ideal prayer in the sense that it is an outline of the parts which the ideal prayer should contain and of the items which the ideal prayer should include. To borrow Tertullian's words, "But with what propriety has divine wisdom set up the order of the prayer, that after heavenly things, that is, after God's Name, God's will, and God's kingdom, it should make place for petition for earthly necessities too."[11] Tertullian's observation is of utmost importance, and I shall return to it later.

Origen tells us which parts a prayer should contain: "It seems to me that, having taken up the parts of prayer, I should thus bring the matter to an end. It appears to me that there should be four parts in the outline. These I have found scattered in the Scriptures. And each should compose his prayer according to these. These are the parts: so far as one is able, at the beginning and in the exordium of the prayer one must express the *praise* of God through Christ ... And after this, each must place *thanksgiving*, both communal, for the benefits toward all, and for those which have come to the individual from God. And after thanksgiving, it seems to me that one must become a sharp accuser of one's own sins before God ... And after *confession*, it seems to me that one must add, fourthly, *petition* for the great and heavenly things.... And in addition to all this, one must bring the prayer to an end with *praise* of God through Christ in the Holy Spirit."[12] Origen's prescriptions contain provisions for heavenly things and earthly necessities, as Tertullian has said.[13] Or, as Tertullian says in another place, the Lord's Prayer "... embraces the characteristic functions of prayer, the honour of God and the petitions of man ..."[14]

These sources agree that prayer needs an outline, and that the outline should have two parts: one devoted to the praise of God and one devoted to the petitions of man. Now that we have the skeleton of prayer, how do we clothe it with flesh? Origen provides the answer. He says that, using the arrangements which he proposes, we should fill it in according to our ability.[15] That means that once we have the proper outline in mind, we are free to fill in that outline with our own words.

The text of the Lord's Prayer is to be composed in the presence of the worshipping congregation. Cyprian says of the Lord's Prayer: "Our prayer is public and common".[16]

Not all modern scholars agree with Cyprian that the Lord's Prayer was the prayer of the community.[17] But it seems to me that the plural form of the Lord's Prayer in both Matthew and Luke strongly suggests that these authors assumed that it was basically a prayer used by a group. The context in which it is set, although not original, also supports this interpretation.

Following the Lord's Prayer, the individual brought before God his own private petitions. Tertullian says: ". . . the appointed and customary prayer having been sent ahead as a foundation or accessory required for his desires, it is permitted to add other petitions . . .".[18] Thus provision was made for both public and private prayer within the context of congregational worship.

The *Didache* has preserved the following singular[19] but highly suggestive instruction following the Lord's Prayer: "Three times a day thus shall you pray."[20] I shall return to this rule in a moment.

To recapitulate: up to this point I have shown that the Lord's Prayer is an outline for prayer; that it contains two parts, one heavenly, the other earthly; that it has no fixed text; that it is a communal prayer; that private petitions may follow it; and that it is to be prayed three times a day.

The things which these Christian authors wrote about the form and use of the Lord's Prayer were also written by Jewish authors about the Eighteen Benedictions (*Amidah*).

This chief prayer of the Jewish liturgy was also originally not a prayer with a fixed text, but merely an outline for prayer, and had to be filled in by the person using it. For example, the Talmud relates the following incident which occurred sometime after the year 130:[21] "We learn in a *baraitha*: It happened to one disciple that he went down before the Ark (to lead the congregation in prayer) in the presence of Rabbi Eleazar, and he lengthened (the Eighteen Benedictions) too much. His disciples said to him, 'Our master, how much this one lengthened them!' He said to them, 'Is he lengthening more than Moses, our master, as it is written of him, '. . . forty days and forty nights . . .'?"[22] Again it happened to a disciple that he went down before the Ark in the presence of Rabbi Elazar. And he shortened too much. His disciples said to him, 'How much this one shortens them!' He said to them, 'Is he shortening more than Moses, our master, as it is written, 'O God, heal her now, I beseech you' '?'"[22] This makes it quite clear that the text of the Eighteen Benedictions was not fixed, and that not more than an outline existed which was filled in at will. A number of other texts indicate the same, among them the following story about Rabbi Akiba who was martyred about 132: "Rabbi Judah said, 'When Rabbi Akiba was praying with the community he used to shorten (the Eighteen Benedictions when saying them) before them. When he was praying privately, one would leave him on this side (of the room) and come (back) and find him on the other side because of the kneeling and prostration which he practised'."[23] We even get strong prohibitions against reciting a fixed prayer:[24] Rabbi Eliezer (ben Hyrcanus—late first century)[25] says, "He who makes his prayer (of the Eighteen Benedictions) a fixed thing, his prayer is not supplications for grace."

As late as the fourth century, we are told that one should strive for variety in his prayer, and that new material should be introduced every day.[26]

Even the outline of the Eighteen Benedictions remained unfixed for a long time. Only at the end of the first century were the eighteen parts of the prayer put in order. At this time a benediction (or rather, a malediction) was added to the existing eighteen.[27] And as late as the third century a Babylonian scholar could say that there is no order in the middle section of the Eighteen Benedictions.[28]

The Eighteen Benedictions fall into three parts: the first part, consisting of three benedictions, gives praise to God; the last part, consisting of three benedictions, gives thanks to God; and the middle section contains the petitions of the praying congregation. This tripartite arrangement probably existed long before the time when the Eighteen were arranged in order at the end of the first century.[29] The Tannaitic *midrash* on Deuteronomy attributes this threefold division to the first sages,[30] an indication that it must have been of considerable antiquity already at that time.

Thus the Eighteen Benedictions exhibit the pattern: praise, petition, thanksgiving. We have seen that Origen prescribes a five part outline of praise, thanksgiving, confession, petition, and praise. These two outlines are really identical; they consist of praise, petition, and praise, for giving thanks to God amounts to praising him.

The Lord's Prayer has the same tripartite outline. The first part offers praise to God by asking that his name be hallowed, his kingdom come, his will be done. Then come the petitions for human needs, and finally, the doxology again praises God. The need to provide a third part for the Lord's Prayer, which did not appear in the original outline, may account for the later addition of the doxology. Several scholars[31] have pointed out that the addition is merely a reflection of the first part of the prayer.

I have already indicated that the Eighteen Benedictions formed a congregational prayer, as its plural form also suggests. Under certain circumstances it was also said privately,[32] for one could not always be with a group of people at the time for prayer.

Jewish congregational prayer of this period made provision for private as well as public petitions.[33] For we learn in a *baraitha*: Rabbi Eliezer (ben Hyrcanus—late first century) says, "A man should petition for his needs and after that say the Eighteen Benedictions. As it is said, 'A prayer for one afflicted when he is faint and pours out his thought before the Lord. May the Lord hear my prayer; let my cry come unto you.'[34] Thought means only the Eighteen Benedictions. As it is said, 'And Isaac went out to meditate in the field.'[35] Rabbi Joshua (ben Hananiah—a contemporary of R. Eliezer) says, "Let him say the Eighteen Benedictions and after that let him petition for his needs. As it is said, 'I will pour out my thought before him, my trouble I will tell before him.'"[36] We have already seen that Tertullian is of the opinion that personal petitions should follow the prescribed and customary Lord's Prayer.

Finally, the Eighteen Benedictions were prayed three times each day. Rabban Gamaliel (late first century) says, "Every day a man must pray the Eighteen (Benedictions)." Rabbi Joshua (ben Hananiah—a contemporary of Rabban Gamaliel) says, "An abstract of the Eighteen." Rabbi Akiba (martyred ca. 132) says, "If his prayer is fluent in his mouth, let him pray (the full) Eighteen; but if not, an abstract of the Eighteen."[37] The times for prayer were morning, afternoon, and evening: "The morning prayer (may be said) until midday ... The afternoon prayer (may be said) until evening ... The evening prayer, there is no fixed time for it ..."[38] This recalls the highly important directive which follows the Lord's Prayer in the *Didache*: "Three times a day thus shall you pray." Here the similarity in usage between the Eighteen Benedictions and the Lord's Prayer is obvious.[39]

I have indicated a number of ways in which the Lord's Prayer and the Eighteen Benedictions are similar: both are outlines for prayers; both prayers have the same tripartite outline; the words of the two prayers are not fixed; both are congregational prayers; private petitions follow both; and both are used three times a day. These observations suggest that the primitive church used the Lord's Prayer in exactly the same way as the contemporary synagogue used the Eighteen Benedictions.

Notes

1. Carl Steuernagel, "Die ursprüngliche Zweckbestimmung des Vaterunser", in *Wissenschaftliche Zeitschrift der Karl-Marx-Universität Leipzig,* 3 (1953–4), Gesellschafts- und sprachwissenschaftliche Reihe Heft 2/3, pp. 217–20. Steuernagel conjectures that, at the request of his disciples, Jesus wanted to give them directions for saying the *havinenu* or shortened middle portion of the Eighteen Benedictions which was used on the Sabbath. But Steuernagel does not give a satisfactory explanation for the laudatory character of the opening statements of the Lord's Prayer, nor is he able to show that such a sabbatical shortening of the Eighteen Benedictions was customary prior to the first amoraic generation. (*Editors' Note*: There is no indication in the sources that the *havinenu*, an abbreviation of the *weekday* Eighteen Benedictions, was *ever* used on the Sabbath—although both the *havinenu* and the Sabbath Prayer presuppose a structure of Seven Benedictions.)
2. Origen, *Peri Euches* 18, 1.
3. Tertullian, *de Oratione* 1.
4. *Loc. cit.*
5. 8, 2.
6. 6 : 9.
7. Adolf Harnack, "Über einige Worte Jesu, die nicht in den kanonischen Evangelien stehen, nebst einem Anhang über die ursprüngliche Gestalt des Vater-Unsers", in *Sitzungsberichte der königlich preussischen Akademie der Wissenschaften* (1904), p. 205.
8. Theodor Zahn, *Das Evangelium des Matthäus*[2], p. 268.
9. Paul Fiebig, *Das Vaterunser: Ursprung, Sinn und Bedeutung des christlichen Hauptgebetes*, pp. 27 f.
10. Ernst Lohmeyer, *Das Vater-unser*, pp. 10 f.
11. *Op. cit.*, ch. 6.
12. *Op. cit.*, ch. 33.
13. *Op. cit.*, ch. 6 quoted above.
14. *Op. cit.*, ch. 1.
15. *Op. cit.*, ch. 33 quoted above.
16. Cyprian, *de Dominica Oratione*, ch. 8. Cf. Origen, *op. cit.*, ch. 33 quoted above; also *Apostolic Constitutions* ii, 36 and iii, 18.
17. Congregational prayer: Lohmeyer, *op. cit.*, p. 11; Harnack, *op. cit.*, p. 208; E. F. Scott, *The Lord's Prayer*, p. 25; Theodor Zahn, *Das Evangelium des Lukas*, p. 444. Private prayer: Gustaf Dalman, *Die Worte Jesu*, p. 364; Heinz Schürmann, *Das Gebet des Herrn*, p. 113.
18. *Op. cit.*, ch. 10.

19. *Ap. Const.* vii, 24 is probably dependent upon *Didache* 8. Cf. *Ap. Const.* ii, 36: twice daily.
20. *Didache* 8, 3.
21. B. *Berakhoth* 34a. Parallels: *Mekhilta* on Exodus 15:25; *Sifré* on Num. 12:13 (paragraph 105, ed. Friedmann, p. 28b).
22. Deut. 9:25 f., Num. 12:13. The proof texts have been chosen to represent the extremes of length and brevity.
23. *Tosephta Berakhoth* 3:5. See also *Mishnah Ta'anith* 2:2 and next note.
24. *Mishnah Berakhoth* 4:4; see also *Mishnah Abhoth* 2:13.
25. So Bacher, *Tannaiten* I², p. 103.
26. B. *Berakhoth* 29b.
27. B. *Berakhoth* 28b–29a. (*Editors' Note*: For another view of what constituted the nineteenth benediction, see above, chapter 3.)
28. B. *Berakhoth* 34a.
29. Ismar Elbogen, *Der jüdische Gottesdienst*⁴, pp. 31 f.
30. *Sifré* on Deut. 33:2. Cf. *Mishnah Rosh Hashanah* 4:5.
31. Lohmeyer, *op. cit.*, p. 172; Zahn, *Matthäus*, p. 284; Dalman, *op. cit.*, p. 363.
32. *Tosephta Berakhoth* 3:5 and 3:7; b. *Abodah Zarah* 7b. See also *Mishnah Berakhoth* 4.
33. B. *Abodah Zarah* 7b.
34. Ps. 102:1 f.
35. Gen. 24:63.
36. Ps. 142:3. Here thought (= the Eighteen Benedictions) precedes personal petitions.
37. *Mishnah Berakhoth* 4:3; cf. *Mishnah Ta'anith* 2:2.
38. *Mishnah Berakhoth* 4:1.
39. Adolf Harnack, "Die Lehre der zwölf Apostel nebst Untersuchungen zur ältesten Geschichte der Kirchenverfassung und des Kirchenrechts", pp. 27 f.; Eduard Freiherr von der Goltz, *Das Gebet in der ältesten Christenheit*, p. 190.

11

The Lord's Prayer in Pastoral Usage

Josef Bommer

The Lord's Prayer is the most frequently recited prayer in Christendom, and rightly so. It plays a major rôle in all Christian churches and is most widely applied, in liturgical life and as a proclamation, as prayer and as kerygma. The Lord's Prayer is recited because it is the prayer of the individual and the prayer of the community, primarily in the liturgy. But the Lord's Prayer is also interpreted in sermons and catechesis. It has to be expounded to children and even more to adults.

Both forms of pastoral use of the Lord's Prayer have a long and honourable *history*. Yet the Lord's Prayer, in spite of its many versions, seems to have been mainly a prayer of the individual in early times.[1] The instruction contained in the *Didache* 8,2—to recite it three times daily—is probably to be understood in this sense. This admonition recurs again and again in patristic times, as in the writings of Ambrose (*De virg.* III, 4, 19). The baptized are admonished to say the Lord's Prayer and the symbolum daily upon rising and before retiring, a prayer regulation with repercussions up to the present time. In this regard, Augustine emphasizes above all the petition for forgiveness (*Ep.* 149,16). The Lord's Prayer is for him a means leading to forgiveness of sins. In addition there is the petition for bread which similarly points towards Christian everyday life but very soon acquires a eucharistic colouration. The Lord's Prayer becomes a communion prayer.

In the liturgical context, the Lord's Prayer makes its first appearance at Baptism (*Apostolic Constitutions* VII, 45). There evolves the custom, in connexion with the catechumenate, to entrust the Lord's Prayer to candidates for Baptism shortly before their baptism. The Lord's Prayer becomes part of the arcane discipline. Since the seventh century, then, the *traditio orationis dominicae*, together with the *traditio symboli*, has been amplified into a solemn rite (*Ordo Rom.* XI).

It is understandable that the revision of the baptismal liturgy which followed on the Second Vatican Council restored the Lord's

Prayer to a preferred position. After baptism, after the anointing with chrism, after the handing over of the white robe and the donation of a burning candle, there follows, in connexion with the end of the baptismal ceremony, an exhortation to the congregation to recite the Lord's Prayer. The priest invites those present to do so in the following words: "Dear Brothers and Sisters! This child was given new life through baptism, and thus it is called and is a child of God. At Confirmation it will receive the abundance of the Holy Spirit. In the midst of the congregation it will step up to the altar, call God its Father and partake of the Table of the holy sacrifice. Us, too, has the Lord accepted as his sons and daughters; therefore we pray vicariously for this child as the Lord taught us to pray." The liturgical rubrics further state: "All recite (or sing) the Lord's Prayer together with the celebrant" (nos. 34 and 35 of the new baptismal Order).

A proper celebration of the transmission of the Lord's Prayer has been provided again today in the rite of the Baptism of Adults. This rite, however, is unlikely to be practised frequently because the custom of child baptism by far predominates. The rite is called "Celebration of incorporating adults into the Church". According to the early Christian catechumenate, this incorporation is to take place along different stages spread over a longer period of time. Three stages are mentioned: celebration of acceptance, celebration of inscription, and celebration of incorporation. The celebration of the inscription is divided into celebration of penitence (Scrutinies) and into Transmissions. There is a celebration of transmission of confession of faith and *celebration of transmission of the Lord's Prayer*. (The ancient *traditio orationis dominicae* is again revived.) The ritual instructions state: "Applicants for Baptism are also handed the Lord's Prayer which has of old been the prayer of those who have received the spirit of being children of God through baptism. Those newly baptized recite it during the first celebration of the Eucharist in which they fully participate, together with the others who have been baptized. The transmission of the Lord's Prayer takes place in the week after the third celebration of penitence."

The celebration as such is amazingly rich in its procedure. First there are recommended readings from the Old Testament (such as Hos. 11:1, 3–4, 8c–9: With cords of love will I draw you to me). Psalms, too, are recited. Psalms 23 and 103 call God "shepherd" and "father". The reading from the Epistles to the Romans

(8:14–17, 26–27) speaks of our receiving the spirit which makes us into sons of God as we call out: Abba, Father!

Then there comes the transmission proper of the Lord's Prayer which is done as follows: the Deacon says: "The candidates now step forward to receive the Lord's Prayer." Thereupon the celebrant says: "We learn how the Lord taught his Disciples to pray." Then the Gospel, the joyful message according to Matthew 6:9b–13 is read, that passage from the Sermon on the Mount where Jesus teaches his disciples to pray, and speaks before them the words of the Lord's Prayer. In a short sermon (homily) the celebrant is to explain the sense and meaning of the Lord's Prayer. There follow two prayers over the candidates for baptism, whereby the second is to be recited with outstretched arms. "The celebrant spreads his hands over the candidates and says: 'Almighty, eternal God, Thou wouldst endow Thy church with ever new members. Strengthen faith and insight in our candidates that out of rebirth from water and the Holy Spirit they may become Thy children. Through Christ, our Lord. Amen.'" (Cp. Nos. 188–192 in the new *Ordo*.) Here it is interesting to note that candidates for baptism are given the Lord's Prayer but are not yet permitted to pray. That is to take place only during the first celebration of the Eucharist with the congregation.

Here we are presented with an important pastoral insight: the Lord's Prayer is the prayer of all who are baptized, and hence it is, among Christians, a profoundly ecumenical prayer. It was high time that it was given an ecumenical form so as to make common recital of the Lord's Prayer possible among all Christians as a community, not least among marriage partners and families where Christians of different denominations live together most intimately. The Catholic and the Protestant versions of the Lord's Prayer must no longer be permitted to be symbols of separation. There is no denominational controversy regarding the interpretation of this prayer.

Further: the *eucharistic interpretation* of the petition for bread leads, since the time of Tertullian (*De or.* 6) to the connexion of the Lord's Prayer with the *celebration of the eucharistic Lord's Supper* in the Eastern and Western Church. The Lord's Prayer becomes a Prayer of Communion. It is allotted an irrevocable place in the Catholic Mass, in the Protestant Lord's Supper and in the liturgies of all eastern rites where, in every instance, the Lord's Prayer is emphatically recited by all of the people or representatively said or sung by the choir. Pope Gregory the Great gave the prayer its present place in the Catholic Mass: before the breaking of the bread. Vatican II, in renewing the liturgy, changed the prayer from that of the celebrating priest into that of the whole people.

Immediately after the Eucharistic High Prayer, the "Canon", there follows a solemn introduction which exhorts the congregation to recite or to sing the Lord's Prayer: "In obedience to the word of our Lord and Redeemer and according to his divine instruction we dare to say . . ." or: "Let us pray as the Lord taught us to pray . . ." or: "We are called children of God and such we are. Therefore we pray full of confidence: . . .". And lastly a further possibility: "We have received the Spirit which makes us into children of God. Therefore we dare to say . . .". Upon the Lord's Prayer proper there still follows an amplification: "Redeem us, Lord, almighty Father, from all evil and give peace in our days. In your pity, come to our help and save us from confusion and sin so that, full of confidence, we wait for the coming of our redeemer Jesus Christ." There follows the well-known addition from the *Didache*: "For Thine is the kingdom and the power and the glory in eternity. Amen." Thus, in each celebration of the Eucharist, the Lord's Prayer is assured a pre-eminent place. Here the Lord's Prayer is always communal prayer: that is, it is to be recited or sung in unison by the congregation. Melodies are available which originated with the Gregorian chant. Of course, the singing or recital of the Latin text is also possible and permitted: "Pater noster . . .".

The Lord's Prayer has its place, too, in the penitential liturgy. Just as in the celebration of the Eucharist it was, above all, the petition for bread which justified its liturgical usage, so here it is the well-known petition for forgiveness: "Forgive us our debt as we forgive our debtors". And further: "Lead us not into temptation but deliver us from evil". Such sentences inevitably led to the inclusion of the Lord's Prayer in the confession and also in the anointing of the sick. For both are the eminent sacraments of penitence. In the celebration of confession and penitence, the Lord's Prayer is to be said immediately before the absolution, in connexion with the prayer of confession and repentance. It follows an introduction which could be as follows: "Let us pray to God our Father in the words which Christ taught us, so that he should forgive our guilt and redeem us from evil." Upon the Lord's Prayer proper there follows the amplification: "Lord, help your servants who confess that they are sinners in your Church. Redeem them from sin through service in your Church so that they can thank you with renewed hearts" (*Ordo* No. 54). In the liturgy for the sick the Lord's Prayer follows the anointing and is introduced in a similar or in the same manner as in the celebration of the Eucharist. If it can be done, the receiving of Holy Communion, the Mass of the Sick, the viaticum, follow immediately upon the anointing of the sick (*Ordo* No. 20).

The Lord's Prayer has its place in the Canonical Hours, in the breviary or *officium*. Benedict of Nursia prescribes it in his rule (chapter 13) for the conclusion of all Canonical Hours, as follows: for Matins and Vespers the whole is to be sung by the leader, but for the remaining Hours only the beginning and end: a custom which, according to Jungmann, probably goes back to the arcane discipline. The officiating priest sang or recited only "Pater noster", and the community of monks would pray the rest in silence. Only the concluding sentence again rang out aloud and solemnly: "et ne nos inducas in tentationem!" To which all present responded: "Sed libera nos a malo. Amen." ("Our Father", . . . "And lead us not into temptation, but deliver us from evil. Amen.")

In the renewed breviary or Prayer of Hours of the priest, every time of prayer (every Hour) can again be concluded with the Lord's Prayer.

That the Lord's Prayer also is part of the Prayers at Mealtime is due to the petition for bread: "Give us this day our daily bread." And many a Catholic family has remained faithful to this practice to this day and recites the Lord's Prayer before or after the main meal.

In the catechetical frame of reference, too, the Lord's Prayer is prominent even in early times.

The catechetical interpretation of the Lord's Prayer is most closely connected with baptism and the baptismal catechumenate. Starting as a narrative catechesis where the redemptive acts of God are related (Augustine: *De catechizandis rudibus*), it develops towards more systematic instruction in which belief and the symbolum, hope and the Lord's Prayer, love and the decalogue (Augustine: *Enchiridicon*) are combined in a manner which now seems strange. Furthermore, the Lord's Prayer is interpreted in the homily, and in this connexion it appears as the Christian doctrine of prayer.

Even today, especially in the Catholic Church, the Lord's Prayer is taught to children at an early age. The Lord's Prayer is learned by heart and may, among all other prayers, be the one which many Christians even today are able to recite by heart. But the Lord's Prayer is not a children's prayer. Essential statements in it are of necessity obscure to children, especially the central statement concerning the coming of God's kingdom. That is why explanation and expounding of the Lord's Prayer are part of adult catechesis and proclamation during worship.

1. The danger of the Lord's Prayer as anybody's prayer

Even these few notes show how broad and universal the use of the Lord's Prayer is in Christian churches and, in part, in Christian life. Closely connected with this is the danger to the Lord's Prayer. This prayer became over-used, especially in the Catholic Church. Quantitative accumulation has made the Lord's Prayer anybody's prayer. Its wide usage has led to a dangerous trivialization. An "off-season" for the Lord's Prayer has been demanded so that its value can be rediscovered, and the weight of its petitions felt anew.[2]

The danger comes from two directions: first, from a *magical* understanding of religion and prayer; and, second, from embarrassment. The Lord's Prayer seems to be the simple way out of an embarrassment vis-à-vis prayer. Someone who cannot pray any more recites the Lord's Prayer or asks others to recite it. There is a rather sad Catholic tradition of using the Lord's Prayer as a stopgap; this estranged it and, without regard to the peculiar significance of its individual petitions, used the Lord's Prayer for opinions and purposes which had nothing or little to do with the substance of its statements. Thus the Lord's Prayer was used to pray for the poor souls, for good weather, for better attendance at church, for the purity of youth, for the peace of the world. This may be well meant—but constitutes a violation. We recall times when, after the sermon, the Mass or another service, numerous Lord's Prayers were appended for such and such requests, and the subsequent bawling of the children, the incomprehensible babbling of the men and a vociferous drone from the women induced one's worst fears as regards the granting of such requests. Even worse is the misuse of the Lord's Prayer as a liturgical yardstick (silent prayer "the length of a Lord's Prayer" or the famous "five times the Lord's Prayer").[3] What Catholic does not recall the famous-infamous penances: "As a penance say the Lord's Prayer and the creed five times . . .". Through endless repetition the Lord's Prayer became totally worn out and meaningless. The fivefold repetition of the Lord's Prayer for the five holy wounds called to mind a prayer-mill. The Lord's Prayer was reeled off. Where one could not think of anything else to pray, when the priest had no other idea and wanted to save himself the trouble and hazard of a personal prayer, the Lord's Prayer was made to serve. Misused indulgence practices (*toties quoties*) and liturgies which prescribed several recitals of the Lord's Prayer during the course of one divine service, pointed in the same direction.

Much has been improved here, not least on account of the post-conciliar Catholic reformation. Vestiges of these manifest mis-usages are regrettably still frequent enough. They repeatedly call for a corresponding catechesis and a more profound theological proclamation by way of expounding the Lord's Prayer. From time to time, an interpretation of the petitions of the Lord's Prayer should be incorporated in the increasingly popular cyclical sermons. Most valuable examples and suggestions are available.

But the Lord's Prayer may well be the favourite prayer of the praying Christian, and no one would be so foolish or inexperienced to demand that each recital of the Lord's Prayer should call forth the utmost intensity and an exhaustion of all the theological depths of the petitions of the Lord's Prayer. Repetition, too, is not wholly bad. It can also express a genuine law of life. There can, indeed, be prayer situations where the worshipper repeats the Lord's Prayer several times. However, that cannot be prescribed. The individual petitions lend themselves excellently to meditation. Here, above all, prayer, including the Lord's Prayer, should not be only on a rational level. Strong emotional powers play a part here. Intellectual understanding is not everything and, above all, not the only thing. We can and must not only think but feel. Habit, too, is under certain circumstances, a genuine help in life, as long as it does not become habitualness and casualness. Learning prayers and saying prayers by heart is, from this standpoint, absolutely justified. Each priest or pastor has had unforgettable encounters with the seriously ill and dying who, in the extremity of physical and spiritual weakness, whispered the Lord's Prayer. It was learned by rote, of course. But it helped all the same. When biblical texts make too great demands on us, when individually formulated prayers have become impossible because they are spiritually too exhausting, then, in many cases, there remains the Lord's Prayer, recited by heart since childhood, which has accompanied many Christians throughout life and constituted their morning and evening prayer throughout long years. Who could belittle something like that and denigratingly speak of a prayer mill? Psychologists of religion are of a different opinion here.

2. *The Lord's Prayer and its crisis due to more profound difficulties*

The above danger to the Lord's Prayer, however, is not the only one. It would be relatively easy to remove it.

Other difficulties go deeper. I am not here thinking of difficulties with prayer in general. The whole problem of prayer, of which naturally the Lord's Prayer is a part, is not under discussion here. I am thinking of *difficulties* arising out of the *content* of the Lord's Prayer. Otto Betz has summed these up as follows: "Again and again we pray, in the Lord's Prayer, for the coming of God's kingdom. And at once an uneasiness creeps in: are we really to pray for the fall of this world and the coming of the other-worldly kingdom? Are we to devalue today for the sake of tomorrow? Are we to emphasize the relativity of time for the sake of eternity? Our temporal existence is precious to us, it is precisely the limited nature of our history which endears it to us; the world is for us no vale of tears which we are yearning to leave. And we also have a secret suspicion that the Lord's Prayer calls forth a posture which is designed to keep us in a status of irresponsibility and dependence. Are we to understand ourselves as children of a mighty father who holds everything in his hand and who again and again makes plain to us how powerless we are and that everything revolves around him? We are to show concern for *his* holiness, *his* will is to be fulfilled, *his* kingdom is to start. Is it surprising that especially young people admit they no longer want to recite the Lord's Prayer, that it seems to them a late reflection of a patriarchal view of society? If God alone is the one who acts and we are nothing but his powerless creatures, puppets in his play, then we do not even want to play long. We have lived as minors long enough, we have that up to here."[4] It is not my task here to analyze all these difficulties and to put against them a comprehensive exposition of the Lord's Prayer. All the same, I want to name them briefly because, and to the extent that, they have pastoral significance.

Already the appellation of the Deity as "father" is among these difficulties. What does "father" mean to us in a fatherless time? "Speaking of God as Father strikes us today mostly as a hackneyed cliché which seldom coincides with our experience of life. In dark hours, to call God 'father' can be an infuriating imposition which sounds naive and contradicts reality."[5] "In addition to the embarrassment of talk about God there is another one. 'Father' seems semantically replete. Therefore the word no longer yields anything, and has become a word shell ... And how, finally, can one evince an emancipatory interest in a father who is (semantically) dead or not yet quite dead? In this light: is the cause of Jesus emancipative? Then one has to posit another Jesus, and one creates him: the protesting Jesus."[6] It should be clear that the loss of the father is closely connected with the loss of authority. What is fashionable babble in this and what a genuine problem need not be decided here. We can probably not dispense with the paternal appellation of God because "Abba, dear father", holds too central a place in the New Testament. It will have to be a question of cleansing the father concept, of seeing the father not as oppressor but as redeemer, and of putting filiality in place of infantility. "I am here—as your father!" It is a question of discipleship and of understanding that the appellation "father" includes a new, fellow-human relationship.

If, going beyond the appellation, we look at the petitions of the Lord's Prayer, then the first three petitions deal with God's cause before man: the sanctification of the name, the coming of the kingdom and the realization of God's will: concepts for discussion, with which today's man has difficulties. What, to him, is a God who is intent upon being honoured, hallowed and praised? What, to him, is a kingdom in the midst of a democratic era? Does that not signify dominion and suppression? What, to him, is a divine will which he can hardly grasp and which forces him into resignation and into an attitude of obedience? There arises the thorny problem of divine providence, the danger of misuse: all too often the will of God was proffered to cover up misuse of power in matters great and small, to bend men in one's own interests, to stabilize sociological conditions. Alfred Delp, the German Jesuit martyr, who during the weeks preceding his death meditated on the Lord's Prayer wrote that the most pious of prayers could easily become blasphemy if it was recited in acceptance, or even furtherance, of conditions which killed man, made him unreceptive to God, and let his spiritual and religious organs wither away of necessity.[7]

All these and many similar misunderstandings can be countered only with an always new, carefully and theologically accountable exposition of the Lord's Prayer, and more difficult hermeneutical problems must not be skirted here: what does it mean: "hallowed be Thy name?" No incense is demanded here but the worshipper asks for God himself: God is to be shown forth as the holy one. God should prove himself to be God. His kingdom should come, and this kingdom is our final redemption, the happiness and salvation for us and the whole world. No false eschatology is proclaimed here, nor a pure this-worldliness. God's dominion would set man free, in this time and during his life, so that through this time and through his life he should gain eternal life. The petition for the realization of God's will should, finally, not be construed as a humble, resigning self-surrender to God's will nor as an obedient assurance to fulfil God's will. No, the worshipper asks of God to raise up his will, and this will is not directed against man but leads him towards his goal. In this and in similar manner the Lord's Prayer should be brought close to modern man, and this requires a great and difficult translation process. The Lord's Prayer can continue to be used in pastoral work only if we are permitted to reinterpret it continually, to explain it in accordance with the prevailing new life situation. Of course, this does not mean arbitrariness. The criteria of scientifically grounded scripture interpretation are to be strictly adhered to. But pure historicism does not help. Above all, the *spirit* of the Lord's Prayer has to be explained and made clear, and such an explanation goes beyond a purely verbal understanding towards an actualization in which the modern Christian rediscovers, in the petitions of the Lord's Prayer, his life and his concerns. Not dead formulae should be handed down if the recital of the Lord's Prayer is to continue maintaining its central significance in Christian churches and in the life of worshipping Christendom.

These considerations are, then, valid for the remaining petitions in which man's cause is treated before God: the petition for bread, the petition for forgiveness and the petition for redemption. The pain is tangible here, real, always and at all times: the pain of hunger, the pain of guilt, the pain of temptation. Here, too, the usability of the Lord's Prayer for pastoral purposes depends on whether we are able to express this threefold pain in the language of modern man, to bring it close to his experience and then to place it within the wider context of redemptive history. The Lord's Prayer and the beatitudes express that we men are thoroughly hungry beings; and also those of us to whom daily bread in the literal sense presents no problem, suffer from this hunger. Life and want are one.

The petition for forgiveness of guilt and the existence of an all-inclusive community of forgiveness may, among all the statements of the Lord's Prayer, be those which are most easily understood. Today's man, too, knows of guilt, also of his guilt and he knows entanglement with guilt even if he calls these things by other names. Everyday life is being discussed here, and something is being demanded of him as a precondition, as it were, so that God can act: Forgive, and you shall be forgiven! This and the preceding petition for bread make clear: the Lord's Prayer makes men into brothers. "A we-world is being delineated" (Betz).

Something similar holds true for temptation and distress, for the power of evil. For, standing in the world always means being tempted, being exposed to dangers, being threatened in manifold ways. Such threats are part of the basic experience of man, and that at all times; even if the causes of the threat may vary, perdition threatens from all sides. And thus we pray, and it is an almost absurd petition, that God may not lead us into temptation, that God may not let us succumb to temptation, that God may deliver us finally and at last from evil, free us from wickedness. And again the whole is at stake, the whole man, the whole existence of discipleship.

If in our pastoral ministry we take the trouble not only to recite the Lord's Prayer and to have others recite it often, perhaps almost too often, but to preach it, to make it the favourite subject of our message, then and only then will this prayer even today still have its great significance; and it towers, in content and form, above most other prayers, most of all above those newfangled prayers which we ourselves compose and in which we believe we have done more justice to the experience of modern man. Such endeavour in itself is to be commended, only it should not be satisfied with irrelevancies and banalities and should be more modest in its pretensions. Prayers are not manufactured on an assembly line, one does not produce them offhand.

A far too obvious, far too habitual recitation of the Lord's Prayer should be supplemented by deepening meditations on it. Then it will become apparent how wide the horizons of Christian faith and Christian life are. Then the Lord's Prayer will inculcate magnanimity, belief in the God of the Bible, knowledge of his immutability and secrecy, and of his concerned kindness and

167

nearness. The Lord's Prayer does not presuppose an uncritical understanding of the world. It critically questions the world and absolutely knows serious challenge. But it leads us men together towards a community and places us as such before our God.

The Lord's Prayer becomes a school for prayer, but at the same time it becomes the "manifesto of the Christian in the world" (O. Betz).

Notes

1. Cf. J. A. Jungmann, in *LThK*, X, 627–9.
2. Cf. O. Betz, "Manifest des Christen in der Welt. Das Vaterunser heute", in *Bibel und Kirche*, 3 (1967), pp. 86–92.
3. Cf. W. Knörzer, "Thesen zur Praxis des Vaterunsergebets", in *Bibel und Kirche*, 3 (1967), pp. 93–4.
4. O. Betz, *op. cit.*, pp. 86 ff.
5. Rolf Baumann, "Abba, lieber Vater", in *Bibel und Kirche*, 22 (1967), pp. 73–8. This passage on p. 73.
6. Otto Wanke, "Jesu Gebet als Wegweisung der Emanzipation", in *Katechetische Blätter,* 8 (1972), pp. 456 f.
7. A. Delp, *Facing Death* (London, 1962), p. 129, cited in O. Betz, *op. cit.*

12
Teaching the Lord's Prayer

Herbert Jochum

1. *The Lord's Prayer in the History of Religious Education*

The Lord's Prayer has a long tradition in the history of Christian religious education. From a form-historical point of view, the New Testament versions of the Lord's Prayer (Mt. 6:9–13, Lk. 11:2–4) can already be regarded as catechesis, as instruction for a Judeo-Christian or Gentile-Christian community.

The *Teaching of the Twelve Apostles* or *Didaché* (8:2) is the oldest Church order known to us, and its oldest layer probably dates back to the first century. Here the Lord's Prayer in the Matthew version (with the doxology from 1 Chr. 29:11) is connected with a baptismal catechesis of broad scope: the teachings, important for one about to be baptized, relate to fasting, praying and the Lord's Supper.

That the Lord's Prayer was to develop in catechetical significance as one of the fundamental short formulae of Christian belief can be seen in the famous "catecheses" of Cyril of Jerusalem which he delivered while still a presbyter during the Passion and Easter seasons of the year 350. These catecheses have been transmitted to us in the stenographic notes of a listener, and explain the confession of faith (1–19) to one about to be baptized; after the baptism, the sacraments are explained in the four so-called "mystagogic catecheses"; in the fifth "mystagogic catechesis", the Lord's Prayer is explained within a description and brief explanation of the liturgy of the mass.

2. *The Lord's Prayer as a Short Formula of the Faith*

When the Church expanded, it was soon forced to systematize its religious education in a baptismal catechumenate. The basic elements of the systematic religious education which ensued and maintained its relative stability into the middle of the twentieth century, are grounded in the question of the transmission of ecclesiastical life and belief. Christian religious instruction was almost exclusively concerned with information about the revealed truths of Christian belief in the form of church doctrine. According to this tradition, religious education is mainly an introduction to a lucid, systematically ordered corpus of knowledge concerning belief; the transmission of basic knowledge about the revealed truths concerning God and his creation, about redemption in Christ, about the Church and its sacraments, about divine will, about the perfection of the world and of man. As the West became Christianized, a religiously homogeneous society emerged. Not only was an eminent place in the educational canon assigned to religious truths in this society, but an acquaintance and facility with Christian knowledge formed an essential part of the "equipment for mastering life situations".[1] This focusing of religious education on introducing and practising the faith was justified because those addressed were regarded as already baptized believers who did not need to be prepared for a religious decision. Instead they had to be strengthened in the beliefs which they held; therefore they had to be taught the detailed contents of their faith.

The "old" formulae at the end of this process of catechetical canonization contained a systematization of the contents of Christian doctrine, available for transmission in religious education: the Apostolic Creed, the Ten Commandments, the Seven Sacraments, the Three Divine Virtues, the Four Last Things and the Lord's Prayer.

Thus, in consonance with the cognitive and pragmatic aims of religious education, the Lord's Prayer became, on the one hand, the brief formula of Christian faith, "the centre of piety and life",[2] the prayer- and life-order of the Christian",[2] and, on the other hand, the "locus" for rehearsing the different ecclesiastical occasions on which the Lord's Prayer is recited.[3]

The split in Christianity that resulted from the Reformation, for the first time cast into doubt the religio-philosophic unity of western culture. The securing and defence of what was peculiar to the two religions became the task of theology and—because catechesis depended so onesidedly on theology—one of the most important functions of religious instruction. The catechism became the programme of religious instruction, where the Lord's Prayer kept its pre-eminent place alongside the traditional brief formulae of faith. Only now did religious education come into its own as a subject for instruction with a regular teaching plan: the focal point was the study of the confession of faith, of the sacraments, of the

Ten Commandments and the Lord's Prayer. The *Catechismus Romanus* (1566), made mandatory by the Council of Trent, is divided into the corresponding four parts. In the last part which contains, first, general explanations of prayer, the Lord's Prayer is, in an extensive commentary (of sixty-five pages), didactically revealed as a short formulation of the now Christian-Catholic doctrinal structure.[4] Deharbe's commentary on the catechism, the most significant in the nineteenth century, includes a comprehensive commentary on the Lord's Prayer, which ties all classical theological tractates to individual petitions of the Lord's Prayer.[5] the first German *Einheitskatechismus* (uniform catechism) of 1925, is, at the same time, the last evidence for the use of the Lord's Prayer as a short formula, "because it contains everything essential for time and eternity".[6] The leading commentaries by Hilker[7] and Gründer[8] once more expatiate on this connexion of the Lord's Prayer with the total path of Christian salvation.

3. *In Search of a New Function*

The Lord's Prayer lost its centuries-old character as short formula of faith in the *Katholischer Katechismus der Bistümer Deutschlands* (Catholic Catechism of the German Dioceses) of 1955[9], which is an attempt to order Catholic doctrines anew and which has been translated into many languages; also in the *Arbeitsbuch zur Glaubensunterweisung: glauben-leben-handeln* (Workbook for Religious Instruction: belief-life-action) of 1969,[10] which is the present official catechism. The Lord's Prayer here has become a subject in its own right in the ecclesiological part of the catechism. This part has the sacraments as its main theme. One *Zielfelderplan für den katholischen Religionsunterricht der Schuljahre 5–10* (Goals for Catholic Religious Instruction for Grades 5–10)[11] no longer specifically mentions the Lord's Prayer under the subjects "Singing and Prayer as Forms of Religious Expression" (grade 5) and "Prayer" (grade 7).[12]

The traditional catechetic significance of the Lord's Prayer has come to an end in our days, just as the whole of the traditional religious-educational canon has been dissolved in a process of reorientation which is not yet at an end. However, the loss of the Lord's Prayer as a short formula of faith is not necessarily the end of its religious educational significance. Some see the Lord's Prayer as the (political) "manifesto of the Christian in the world".[13] Relieved of the need for ecclesiastical self-representation, and freed from christological, ecclesiological and ethical connotations, the Lord's Prayer could demonstrate its ecumenical relevance for the relationship between Christianity and Judaism, as it already did for the two branches of Christianity.[14]

4. Legitimation of the Lord's Prayer for Religious Education Today

Possible Justified Areas

The Lord's Prayer is not a part of the new curriculae for the upper grades. The following short drafts indicate existing areas where different aspects of the Lord's Prayer might be included.

(i) The Lord's Prayer as Part of a Course on the Problem of God (theology)

This course is to range from questions of the existence of God, via proofs for the existence of God, to the possibility of experiencing God in a secularized world, to the manifold aspects of views of God and what they depend on. In this connexion, the social, depth- and developmental-psychological implications of the father image could be explored. Views of God, man and the world in the Lord's Prayer could be compared with those held today.

(ii) The Lord's Prayer as Part of a Course on Religious Language (linguistics)

This course is to indicate various attempts throughout theological history to deal with the problem of speaking about God: *via eminentiae, via negativa, analogia entis*; bearing in mind that logical positivism and linguistic analysis have pronounced a verdict of senselessness over the language of religion, the meaning of language about God, as demonstrated in the Lord's Prayer, should be examined: is the Lord's Prayer a "religious language game" of the time of Jesus? Is it a legitimate language game today after the later Wittgenstein's *Philosophical Enquiries?* Are there more recent linguistic attempts to seek an answer to the postulate that religious language can be verified? Poems and parodies based on the Lord's Prayer, written for varying purposes, could illustrate the problems of religious language. An analysis of versions of the Lord's Prayer for children could help towards following up the question in what way a change in language brings about a change in theological content. The question whether such paraphrases are legitimate, whether the Lord's Prayer is to be regarded as a lasting prayer formula

172

or as a religious, basic position capable of interpretations and change, is one which goes deeper.

(iii) *The Lord's Prayer in the History of its Effectiveness* (church history)

In a course with a more pronounced church historical or ecclesiological orientation, different historical interpretations of the Lord's Prayer could elicit self-representation attempts of the Church and could stimulate discussion of historical conditions, relationships and aims. Ecclesiological, christological and ethical interpretations of the Lord's Prayer could be examined as to their intended or unintentional pedagogical, dogmatic, churchpolitical and other functions. Mistaken dogmatizing could be avoided by accompanying questions concerning changes in views about God, man and the world as held at various historical periods of the interpretations under discussion.

(iv) *The Lord's Prayer as Part of a Course on World Religions* (comparative religion)

This course could compare the main prayers of the different world religions and thus elicit whatever is specific in any one religion. For instance, a comparison of the address of God would find a father image of God in other religions (Greece, Africa). A comparative analysis would, however, show the differing semantic structures.

(v) *The Lord's Prayer as Part of a Course on Christianity and Judaism* (ecumenism)

Taking the Lord's Prayer as a paradigm, this course could make clear the essential stages in the history of the relationship between these two religions: the separation at the beginning, and the search for dialogue today. The "Christianization" of this thoroughly Jewish prayer demonstrates Christian handling of the Jewish "heritage". The Lord's Prayer, which probably took the place of the Eighteen Benedictions very early in the community of Judeo-Christians, has extraordinary significance in this process of separation. Within the community it was a verbal expression of doctrinal self-reassurance and self-representation; to the outside world it signified an expression of community membership with all the church-sociological and church-disciplinary consequences pertaining thereto. Both these functions endow the Lord's Prayer with apologetic tendencies up to today.[15] Another question is in line with the dialogue desired today: although hitherto the Christian formula for separation, *par excellence*, could the Lord's Prayer release ecumenical energies and become a verbal nucleus of what is specific to Christians and Jews vis-à-vis the same father-God?

(vi) *The Lord's Prayer as Part of a Course on Religion in Dialogue with the Sciences* (dialogue)
This course could, for instance, deal with the relationship between Christianity and Marxism by way of dialogue, or a critique of religion; it could tabulate the differences and similarities between the respective doctrines as well as the mutual challenges to the attitude of the other in interpretations of the Lord's Prayer. For instance, the loss of the eschatological element in Christianity caused, over the centuries, by a retrospective relationship of Christians to the redemptive events of the past, could be discovered and corrected not least by means of the futurist orientation of Marxism. (Cp. the versions of the Lord's Prayer by Milan Machoveč and Dorothee Sölle.)

Other partners in dialogue regarding the Lord's Prayer could be philosophy (H. R. Schlette, *Skeptisches Vaterunser* [The Skeptical Lord's Prayer]),[16] psychology (Jung, *Answer to Job*,[17] Freud, *Moses and Monotheism*).[18,19]

5. *The Lord's Prayer—Curricula for Religious Instruction in Higher Secondary Education*
(i) *Curriculum 1*
Motivation; Eliciting Problems.

(*a*) *Point of departure*
After a kind of brainstorming, individual problems of the Lord's Prayer—for instance the father problem—could be singled out, or else the whole text could be divided up. A parody of the Lord's Prayer could be used for eliciting contrasts and challenging effects.

(*b*) *Applied basis of presentation:*
Can twentieth-century man pray the Lord's Prayer at all?

(*c*) *Goal-oriented questions:*
Is the Lord's Prayer not dependent on political, socio-cultural, historical, religio-historical conditions radically different from those obtaining today? To mention only the patriarchal, agrarian society; a knowable world; a world more immediately experienced as creation; a greater proximity to one's fellow man; and so on.

What are the conditions of our epoch? Students should arrive at an analysis of the spiritual condition of today's man, awareness of self and the world, via problems of the Lord's Prayer.

(d) Reintegration structure:

One session on the Lord's Prayer could touch on the following issues:

Our Father in heaven
> God image: eclipse of God, God-is-dead theology. Theism—atheism, end of metaphysics.
> "Fatherless society", authority crisis, theodicy, Auschwitz.
> Image of man: child—brother, infantilism, projection— illusion; brotherhood of man as ineffective anticipation: *homo homini lupus*.

hallowed be your name
> theodicy problem in face of sufferings in the world.

your will be done
> use of God in education, legitimation and exercise of political power, "dieu le veult" (Old-French crusaders' cry). "God with us" (inscription on army belt buckles of German soldiers during World War I).
> In God's name ... persecution of Jews, inquisitions, burning of witches.
> Christian fatalism?

your kingdom come
> *Regnum Dei, Civitas Dei*, Church?
> Thousand-year empire, Third *Reich*?

Give us today our daily bread
> world hunger; hunger for justice, for love ... price of raw material, import duties, nations as "have-nots", Christian egotism?

forgive us our debts (guilt) as we forgive our debtors (those who have incurred guilt with respect to us)
> personal debt (guilt)—structural debt (guilt), cp. political guilt; economico-social debt (guilt): global economic structure.

and lead us not into temptation but deliver us from evil
> escape into absurdity, into nihilism as absolute godlessness, total dominion of man.

At the end of this motivation phase, the problems brought up by association should be systematized approximately according to:

- difficulties which arise out of the problem of the existence of God in general; which question the possibility of prayer in general. Today's conceptions of the self and the world—of which one must be aware—will become apparent as these difficulties are discussed;
- difficulties arising out of the God problem (the predicate "Father");
- difficulties arising out of the semantic structure of the Lord's Prayer;
- difficulties arising out of the language structure, or out of the emptiness of the language of the Lord's Prayer, which has become unimportant through excessive use.

(ii) *Curriculum 2*

(a) Point of departure:
Students generally know only one version of the Lord's Prayer, namely that of Matthew. When it is discovered that the Luke version is the text of another editor the question arises which of the two is that of Jesus, and is it not possible that a third, namely the original version, should be reconstructed. This text criticism also raises anew the question of the "true" intent of Jesus.

(b) Applied basis of presentation:
How did Jesus of Nazareth regard the Lord's Prayer?

(c) Goal-oriented questions:
- Students get acquainted with the two synoptic versions and analyse them as to differences and similarities.
- Students view the two versions within the framework of the evangelists' theology.
- Students examine Jesus' intention for the Lord's Prayer within the context of Jesus' message.

(d) Reintegration structure:

Aramaic Reconstruction	Mt. 6:9–13	Lk. 11:2–4
Father (Abba)	Our father in heaven	Father (Abba)
Hallowed be your name.	Hallowed be your name.	Hallowed be your name.
Your kingdom comes.	Your kingdom come	Your kingdom come.
	Your will be done	
	as in heaven	
	so on earth.	

176

Our bread for tomorrow (?) give us today.	Our bread for tomorrow (?) give us today.	Our bread for tomorrow (?) give us daily.
And forgive us our debts as we herewith forgive our debtors.	And forgive us our debts as we have forgiven our debtors.	And forgive us our sins, because we forgive each one who is our debtor.
And lead us not into temptation.	And lead us not into temptation, but snatch us away from evil.	

Comparison of the two versions in the light of theological conception:

Matthew	*Luke*
Prayer catechesis for Judeo-Christians	Prayer catechesis for Gentile-Christians
within the wider framework of the Sermon on the Mount (5–7)	within the wider framework of Luke's description of his journey (9:51–19:27)
within the narrower framework of a prayer catechesis (6:5–15)	within the narrower framework of a prayer catechesis (11:1–13)
(a) misuse of the prayer through "hypocrisy"	(a) Jesus—paragon of prayer
(b) misuse of prayer through "rote recital"	(b) the Lord's Prayer as example
(c) Lord's Prayer as example for correct prayer	(c) parable of the entreating friend as answer to the question how to pray
(d) forgiveness as precondition	(d) question regarding the granting of prayer
Primitive Christian prayer catechism for baptismal instruction presupposes a prayer routine, guards against misuse	Discipleship also implies correct praying. Prayer first has to be taught.

(iii) Curriculum 3

(a) Point of departure:

As the Lord's Prayer became detached from Judaism it very soon became a kind of Christian confessional formula. As, in addition, it developed into a short formula of faith, a self definition and a definition of faith had to be incorporated into the traditional text. Therefore very early and over a long period of time, christological and ecclesiological insertions were made into the Lord's Prayer.

(b) Applied basis of understanding:

How could the prayer of the Jew, Jesus of Nazareth, and that of his Jewish disciples, become a Christian prayer, one which even

177

assumed the character of a formula of divorce vis-à-vis Judaism? In the final analysis the truly complex question of the relationship between Judaism and Christianity is here raised in general. The Lord's Prayer is only one—outstanding—example.

(*c*) *Goal-oriented questions:*
- Students should be acquainted with examples of christological, ecclesiological and ethical interpretations.
- Students should essay an attempt to connect the Lord's Prayer as a short formula of faith, with all essential theological tractates.
- Students should learn to note different tendencies in these interpretations, such as pedagogical, apologetic, church-disciplinary and political intentions.
- Students should realize that, while Christian faith may, indeed, assume an implicit christology in the Lord's Prayer, such a christology, considering Jesus' own reserve, is not an absolute necessity. The Lord's Prayer was, for Jesus, exclusively addressed to the Father: is it, then, legitimately used as a prayer addressed to the Son?

(*d*) *Reintegration structure:*

Petition in the Lord's Prayer	Short formulation of Belief (Theological Tractates)	Ecclesiological-sacramental connexion	Theological-ethical connexion
Your father in heaven	CREATION Doctrine of God FATHER		belief
Hallowed be your name	Purpose of creation— God's praise	Priesthood/marriage	love of God
Your kingdom come	Doctrine of the Church christology SON	baptism	hope
Your will be done	The Commandments	confirmation	submission to God
Give us this day our daily bread	Doctrine of Grace Sacraments HOLY SPIRIT	eucharist	frugality and trust in God
Forgive us our debt, as we forgive . . .	REDEMPTION SON	penance	love of self love of neighbour
and lead us not into temptation	evil sin devil		faithfulness
but deliver us from evil	FULFILMENT The Last Things[21]	anointing the sick ("Extreme Unction")[21]	fear of God[20]

(iv) *Curriculum 4*

(*a*) *Point of departure:*
It was inevitable that the use of the Lord's Prayer became in-flated, seeing that it was recited in different personal and ecclesiastical situations from the baptismal liturgy, by way of the eucharist, and extending even to the liturgy for the dead. This applied ubiquity and universal usefulness of the Lord's Prayer have made it everybody's formula which has lost its specific meaning and which covers religious embarrassment in general. Two procedures have at present been adopted to save the Lord's Prayer from certain death through prayer: one tries to restore to the Lord's Prayer an intent formulated for our time, or to put new in-tent into the old form; the other seeks to estrange the text through linguistically creative measures in order to command the attention which it deserves.

(*b*) *Applied basis of presentation:*
Can the Lord's Prayer be saved, and is this attempt theologically justified? Can the Lord's Prayer be freed from the odium of self-centred, escapist and ritualist piety so that it can be understood as a formula for motivating a political *engagement* for Christians towards a more humane world, or is the Lord's Prayer to go into another babylonian exile?

(*c*) *Goal-oriented questions:*
- Students are to become aware of the inflated use of the Lord's Prayer.
- They are to become acquainted with attempts to instil into the Lord's Prayer social and realistic relevance.
- They should be able critically to investigate recent reinter-pretations.
- Students are to note peculiarities in content and form of Dorothee Sölle's version of the Lord's Prayer: Thou-petitions changed to "we"; argumentative structure because of apologetic defence of the Lord's Prayer.
- Students should be able to reconstruct the question put by our leftist friends: "Why do we pray?"
- Students are to become acquainted with a marxist translation of the Lord's Prayer (Milan Machovec) and be able to compare it critically with other translations (eg, Sölle).

(d) Reintegration structure:

Question of left-wing friends	Christian Answers as Cause	Consequence
self-centredness of Christians?	brotherhood as solidarity with (a) the dead; (b) the living; (c) those who come after	Our Father
Christians' escapism?	endlessness of the task, longing for happiness and salvation	in heaven
interested only in God's cause	dominion of men over men as the most prevalent form of offending God	hallowed be Your name
renunciation of self-determination and shaping the world	fear of consumer terrorization, profit-eering	Your will be done
carefreeness as irresponsibility?	fear of man's potential, doubt and irony	Your kingdom come
dispensing with one's own responsibility?	people individually and socially indispensable for life	give us this day our daily bread
admission of one's own weakness?	wrong order of this world, duty to suggest forgiveness of debt	forgive us our debt
man's bankruptcy declaration	nationalism, belief in authority, absence of controlling authority, fatalistic posture, resignation	lead us not into temptation, deliver us from evil
	need for faith, for courage in working for the kingdom	for Thine is the kingdom and the power and the glory
	belief in God	for ever. Amen.

Milan Machovec: "The Lord's Prayer".[22]

Text	Significance
Our Father, who art in a time to come	The heavenly kingdom is not a matter of space but of time
hallowed be your resonance	even the slightest echo, the most insignificant indication of the future epoch shall be holy
your kingdom shall come, your will shall be done in this future kingdom as in our life now,	all these petitions call the future into the present

180

this bread of our tomorrow give us still today.	desire for the kingdom is as self-evident as the request for bread
Forgive us our failure as we forgive those who have incurred guilt with respect to us,	call to a lasting return
and lead us not to the day of ruin, but deliver us from the evil.	save us from the distress of the End of Time.

(v) *Curriculum 5*

(a) *Point of departure* (see also 4):

The antiquated language, the "artistically wrought vocabulary"[23] is most easily overcome through free and spontaneous prayer arising out of a man's own experience. In cases where the traditional language is being selected because of lack of spontaneity or linguistic imagination of the worshipper, various means can be employed to draw renewed attention to the text.

(b) *Applied basis of presentation:*

Should or must the Lord's Prayer be reworded to avoid worn-out clichés of the imagination? Is the "necessity for destruction"[24] of the Lord's Prayer a presupposition for new religious meaning?

(c) *Goal-oriented questions:*

- Students are to familiarize themselves with modern language experiments based on the Lord's Prayer such as parodies, blasphemies, deviation of function, poems.
- They should be able to identify their authors' varying methods and purposes like expressions of distress and disappointment, pain, cynical criticism of Church and society.
- They should develop a sensitivity for the perversions of Church and society which are attacked in these ideological and critical attempts to utilize the Lord's Prayer as a weapon against the theistic concept of an omnipotent God "who rules everything so beautifully", against the official ecclesiastical sanctioning of social conditions which often are unworthy of humanity, against the spirit of materialism, against the financial preoccupation of Western society.
- Students should develop a sensitivity to the peculiar authority which the Lord's Prayer possesses as a model, often merely formal and merely through retention of the rhythmic and syntactic structure, so that it becomes a standard of individual, corporate and church comportment.

181

– In this connexion, the limits of manipulability of such a text could be discussed; when is it being destroyed by blasphemy and when, as blasphemy against God, could it be cause for litigation.[25]

6. *The Lord's Prayer as Admission of Guilt*
Peter Coryllis: "Our Father"[26]

Our father
who art banished to heaven,
soiled is thy name.
All thy kindness
was abused.
Thy will
has been trampled.
Thy love has been scorned.
Thou art praised
in heaven;
but on earth
strangled . . .

We not only succumbed
to temptation,
but have openly and unashamedly bred it.
And evil went beyond bounds.

Canst thou work
deliverance yet?
For that will I pray.

7. *The Lord's Prayer as Criticism of Capitalism and the Church*
Hans Häring, "our mammon"[27]

our mammon
who art
in the banksafe
—thy name remain
in the partnership of
world business
—thy kingdom
come
not into
strange hands

the state debt
of millions
of innocent
debtors
—do not lead them
into temptation
but deliver them
from the evil
of desiring change
in this

—thy will
be done
in the munitions industry
as it is
in the church
—our daily bread
we have
always
because we
never forgive

—for thine
is the kingdom
and the power
and the glory
of our mansions
on the côte d'azur
forever
—amen.

"The literary form has been adopted not to endow it with new semantic contents, to develop it or use it in a novel way, but to knock the one alluded to."[28] And two quantities are alluded to every time, namely capitalism which is revealed as religion, ie, the Church, and religion which is regarded as capitalistic.

Gerd Schulte, in his "Nato unser",[29] similarly uses the form of the Lord's Prayer to expose the pseudo-religious values of western ideological idols.

8. *The Lord's Prayer against God*
Gabriela Macholdt: "Our Father"[30]

Our father, who art
Neither in heaven nor on earth,
Neither in the negro slums of Harlem
Nor with the dead in Vietnam.
Derided be thy name
For thy blessing comes from nowhere.
Thy curses roar at us
And thou sendest us wars without warning.
For thy will be done
In America, as it is in Russia.
Give us today our daily compassion
And forgive us our hunger for power,
Our avarice and our hatred of our brothers.
As we forgive thy absence.
Lead us into temptation
And deliver us from all thy evils.
Amen.

This anti-prayer shows, in spite of its semantic negation, that, in a peculiar way, the I-Thou relation remains a constant for religious

183

speech. Even while attempting literary deicide or God's exorcism from the Lord's Prayer, the fantasy changes into the one ad-dressed, the exposure into a prayer to the one who is thus supposed to be prayed to death.

Even the linguistically simply irreproducible nihilistic version in a short story by Ernest Hemingway retains the I-Thou structure of the Lord's Prayer. "Our nada who art in nada, nada be thy name thy kingdom nada thy will be nada in nada as it is in nada. Give us this nada our daily nada and nada us our nada as we nada our nadas and nada us not into nada but deliver us from nada; pues nada."[31]

9. *The Lord's Prayer as song of praise of the finally secularized man in this world*
Jacques Prévert: "Pater noster".[32]

> Our father who art in heaven
> stay there
> And we will stay on earth
> Which is at times so lovely
> With its mysteries of New York
> With its mysteries of Paris
> Which absolutely outweigh the mystery of the Trinity.
>
> With its nice children and its miserable fellows
> With all the earth's marvels
> Which are here
> Quite simply are here on earth. . . .

(vi) *Curriculum 6*

(a) *Point of departure:*
Traditional educational interpretations of the Lord's Prayer refer either exclusively to the centre of Christian teaching or, by referring to its Jewish origins, try to show what is particularly Christian in contrast to Jewish belief. In the first case one can point to the request of the disciples (Lk. 11:1) and gain or retain the im-pression that the disciples lacked a tradition of prayer and that Jesus responded to their request with an *ad hoc* extempore prayer. In the second case, Jewish parallels are delineated—the *Kaddish* and the Eighteen Benedictions—absolute literary dependency is conceded but then "considerable differences" are pointed out: "In the Eighteen Benedictions, the petitions concerning actual life

precede the petition for the coming of God's kingdom. The Lord's Prayer first of all asks for the coming of God's kingdom. The Eighteen Benedictions have in a central position the petition for the coming of the kingdom, the petition for the restoration of the house of David, the destruction of the enemies, the sovereignty of the state, the splendid rebuilding of the temple and the city of Jerusalem. These political traits are completely absent from the Lord's Prayer. The Eighteen Benedictions pray for the produce of the whole year, the Lord's Prayer dares to ask only for bread for one day.[33] The Eighteen Benedictions, too, petition for forgiveness of guilt. But in the Lord's Prayer the petition for forgiveness is tied in with the assurance that the worshipper himself forgives those who have incurred guilt with respect to him."[34] "No doubt, the Lord's Prayer is spoken out of the new posture of that disciple who could address God as 'Abba'."[35] And in the *Regensburger Neues Testament* the commentary on the Lord's Prayer culminates in this final conclusion: "In spite of the obvious contact with Jewish prayers and although almost all phrases and concepts making up the Lord's Prayer are also Jewish, it is nonetheless not a Jewish prayer."[36]

It is different from Jewish prayers on account of its brevity, the "sequence of values named in it", the absence of the "patriotic-national touch aimed against Roman sovereignty" and the "cursing of the 'heretics'", the absence of "things which are usually closest to man and which occupy his worries and his wishes. Everything that is transitory, accidental and specific is absent [from the Lord's Prayer]." The worshipper does not spread out "before God a profusion of his own small wishes".[37] Especially the Aramaic "Abba"—according to Knörzer "an unheard of appellation of God"[38]—again and again induces commentators to construct a system of beliefs fundamentally different from that of Judaism.[39]

There are certainly differences in the text between the corresponding prayers: thee differences also exist in Christian prayers with similar motifs. A question to be raised is: do these differences not postulate too hastily differences between Christian and Jewish belief, differences which, in this form, are not tenable (any more)? The comparison between the Lord's Prayer and the *Kaddish* in Knörzer's commentary shows how the perspectives of evaluation and the standards of measurement vary: "In the *Kaddish* prayer of the synagogue the coming of God's dominion concerns first of all the house of Israel.... Surely the Davidic empire is meant here which, in Judaism, was expected primarily as a political, national entity for the days of the Messiah. Whereas in the Lord's Prayer the worshipper does not dare mention a point in time for the arrival of God's kingdom, so that this great undertaking may be left to God, the Israelite asks for the commencement of God's kingdom during his lifetime."[40]

The manner in which the "Israelite" understands prayer is seen in opposition to that of the modern Christian, whereby mention of the original eschatological expectation among the first Christians has been omitted. This should be the real basis for comparison, unless one were to ask a modern Jew for his commentary on the *Kaddish*.[41]

(b) *Applied basis of presentation:*
Can Christians and Jews recite the Lord's Prayer together?
This question should be divided into three didactic units: 1) the Lord's Prayer as a Jewish prayer; 2) the Lord's Prayer as a Christian prayer; 3) the Lord's Prayer as ecumenical prayer.

(c) *Goal-oriented questions:*
— Students should get acquainted with Jewish prayers related to the Lord's Prayer (the *Kaddish*, the Eighteen Benedictions).
— They are to note differences and similarities.
— The question whether the Lord's Prayer is a Jewish prayer should be approached in differing ways: literary dependency; a Jewish prayer by virtue of its being the prayer of Jesus; recitation in the spirit of Jewish piety; short formula also of Jewish faith?
— Students should recognize that the Lord's Prayer could no longer be recited by Jews because of its ecclesiological and christological interpretation.
— Students should be confronted with the question whether the Lord's Prayer could become an ecumenical prayer in view of identical difficulties facing both religions.

(d) *Reintegration structure:*
The petitions of the Lord's Prayer with parallels from Jewish prayers

Father (our, in heaven)	Our father, our king (liturgical prayer formula)
hallowed be thy name	Exalted and hallowed be His great name in the world (*Kaddish*)
Your kingdom come	May He establish His kingdom (*Kaddish*)

(Your will be done in heaven as on earth)	Your will be done in heaven above. Grant equanimity to those who revere You (*Tosephta Berakhoth* 3:7) He spoke and it came to pass, he commanded, and it stood fast (Ps. 33:9).
Give us today our daily bread	Satiate us out of Your goodness, and bless our year ... (Eighteen Benedictions)
and forgive us our debt (as we forgive our debtors)	Forgive us, our father, for we have sinned against You (Eighteen Benedictions) Forgive thy neighbour the hurt he hath done thee; and then thy sins shall be pardoned when thou prayest (Ecclesiasticus 28:2).
and lead us not into temptation (but deliver us from evil)	Look at our affliction and champion our cause, and redeem us for the sake of Your name (Eighteen Benedictions).

Study groups could also compare the Lord's Prayer with later texts of Jewish piety[42] and with Old Testamental prayer- and credal-texts.[43]

To (2): The Lord's Prayer as Christian Prayer. Cp. Curriculum 3.

To (3):

The difficulty of prayer for Christians	The difficulty of prayer for Jews
Martin Walser, *Halbzeit*[44]	Joseph Roth, *Job*[45]
Walter Dirks: "The Lord's Prayer has become recitable by Jews and has been recited by them."[46]	Baruch Graubard: "Then I discovered a token of this 'identity' in the Lord's Prayer. That was like a Jewish prayer, like an abbreviation of the Eighteen Benedictions."[47]

Could the Lord's Prayer become the prayer for a joint Christian-Jewish theopraxis, in face of the tremendous vulnerability of God and man?[48]

— Jews and Christians face the same difficulties, eg, the difficulty of praying today.
— Jews and Christians find themselves in the same theological predicament, eg, the problem of the delay in the coming of God's dominion, problem of the loving father-god compared with Auschwitz; the possibility of belief in a liberating interference of God in our world in the face of promethean self-awareness (*homo faber*), and others.
— Jews and Christians face the same worldwide tasks: endangerment of the *humanum* and the *divinum*.

187

Prayer solidarity of Christians and Jews in the Lord's Prayer

The Thou-petitions	testify to the primacy of divine will and power (loss of *divinum*)
The We-petitions	testify to concern over the loss of the *humanum* through
bread	protection from sliding into the materialist one-dimensionality of human existence,
guilt	remembrance of guilt as grounds for constant return,
evil	caution before the attractiveness of defeatist final solutions for man and world.

The Lord's Prayer as common confession of guilt for Christians and Jews, and as common petition for God's final revelation.

Notes

1. Cp. Saul B. Robinson: *Bildungsreform als Revision des Curriculum*, Berlin, ²1969, p. 45.
2. These are the subtitles in Wolfgang Knörzer, *Vater unser. Werkhefte zur Bibelarbeit 6* (Stuttgart, Verlag Katholisches Bibelwerk, ²1969).
3. A reminder is by this connexion that during the period of the new ordering of priestly formation by the Council of Trent, reciting the Lord's Prayer was among the few conditions for ordination of the lower clergy where theological requirements were modest. Godparents were also required to know it.
4. *Catechismus ex decreto concilii Tridentini*, Lat.-German ed. (Regensburg, 1902), pp. 370–436.
5. Joseph Deharbe, *Erklärung des Katholischen Katechismus* (Paderborn, ²1861–2), IV, pp. 761–96.
6. Quoted from *Katholischer Katechismus für die Diözese Trier* (1925), p. 105.
7. Otto Hilker, *Handbuch zum Einheitskatechismus*, 3 vols. (Paderborn, 1926–7), here III, pp. 210–6.
8. Joseph Gründer, *Handbuch zum deutschen Einheitskatechismus*, 3 vols. (Paderborn, 1927–9), here III, pp. 462–77.
9. Trier, 1955, pp. 132–4. Jesus teaches us to pray. The Lord's Prayer is paraphrased for children within the framework of a short catechesis on prayer.
10. Ed. by German Bishops (Freiburg, 1969), pp. 137–9. This brief paraphrase of the Lord's Prayer within the context of a catechesis on prayer mentions the Jewish prayer tradition of the disciples for the first time.
11. Compiled by a commission of the German Katecheten-Verein e. V., Munich, in co-operation with the Bischöfliche Hauptstelle für Schule und Erziehung, Munich, 1973 f. This plan for a future curriculum for Catholic religious instruction in lower secondary schools throughout the Federal German Republic is in the experimental stage and has not been officially introduced yet.
12. In the accompanying workbook for students, *Zielfelder ru 5/6* (Deutscher

Katecheten-Verein, Munich, 1975), the index prints the ecumenical version of the Lord's Prayer (p. 111). A curiosity—in the so-called materials section—is the reproduction of the Gothic Lord's Prayer of the Wulfila bible (p. 200). If the religion teacher can recite Old German, the ten-year-old pupil may find the sound exotic and pleasurable.

13. Otto Betz in "Christsein im Lichte des VU" in *Bibel und Kirche*, 22 (1967, 3), p. 86.

14. Representatives of both churches in the German-speaking areas have agreed on one text which now has official church sanction.

15. The Aramaic address "Abba" has, to this day, been the biblical basis for postulating for Jesus a particularly close relationship to God, differing from the rest of Judaism. Further deductions from this lead to the well known clichés about God of love—God of fear, grace—law, and so on.

16. Heinz Robert Schlette, *Skeptische Religionsphilosophie. Zur Kritik der Pietät* (Freiburg, 1972), pp. 84–117.

17. Carl G. Jung, *Answer to Job*, translated by R. F. C. Hull (London, Routledge & Kegan Paul, 1954), pp. 77–92.

18. Sigmund Freud, *Moses and Monotheism* (New York, Vintage Books, 1955).

19. Other areas can only be briefly indicated here: (*a*) The Lord's Prayer in a course "Introduction to Holy Scripture" (scientific method); (*b*) The Lord's Prayer in Theology and Piety Today; (*c*) The Lord's Prayer in a course "Religion and Art".

20. *Katholischer Katechismus für die Diözese Trier*, p. 105.

21. Cp. *Catechismus Romanus*, pp. 370–436; J. Deharbe, *op. cit.*, IV, pp. 761–96.

22. Milan Machovec, *Jesus für Atheisten* (Stuttgart, 1972), pp. 104 ff.

23. Martin Walser, *Halbzeit* (Frankfurt a. M., 1960), quoted in Alfons Thome, *Moderne Problemliteratur im Religionsunterricht* (Munich, 1974), pp. 55 f.

24. H. R. Schlette, *op. cit.*, p. 96.

25. This question should be dealt with in connexion with Alfred Delp, *Facing Death* (London, 1962), p. 129: "The most pious prayer can become a blasphemy if he who offers it tolerates or helps to further conditions which are fatal to mankind, which render him unacceptable to God or weaken his spiritual, moral or religious sense."

26. Kurt Marti, *Grenzverkehr. Ein Christ im Umgang mit Kultur, Literatur und Kunst* (Neunkirchen-Vluyn, 1976), p. 158.

27. Kurt Marti, *op. cit.*, p. 160; cp. also *Kapital unser* and cp. the blasphemous litany of the master merchant Jakob Fugger in Dieter Forte, *Martin Luther und Thomas Münzer* (Berlin, 1971).

28. Alex Stock, *Umgang mit theologischen Texten* (Cologne, 1974), p. 133.

29. In Wolfgang Fietkau, *Poeten beten* (Wuppertal-Barmen, 1969).

30. Kurt Marti, *op. cit.*, p. 163.

31. Ernest Hemingway, *The Essential Hemingway* (London, Jonathan Cape, [6]1961).

32. Jacques Prévert, *Paroles* (Paris, 1949), p. 70.

33. [The petition] "is phrased in such a way that also the poor man who does not know where his next meal is coming from, can recite it without reservation." Josef Schmid, *Das Evangelium nach Matthäus, Regensburger NT* (Regensburg, [4]1959), p. 131.

34. To guard against "the presumptuous self-assurance" of "Test me, Yahweh, and try me" (Ps. 26). Cp. J. Schmid, *op. cit.*, p. 133.
35. Knörzer, *op. cit.*, pp. 54 f.
36. J. Schmid, *op. cit.*, p. 134.
37. J. Schmid, *op. cit.*, pp. 134 f.
38. W. Knörzer, *op. cit.*, p. 59. Cp. also: "Judaism did not dare to address God in this childish and familiar way"; "Therefore it must have been unheard-of to Jewish ears that Jesus should have applied the simple and intimate 'Abba' of daily speech to God", J. Schmid, *op. cit.*, p. 123. On the other hand: Johann Maier describes as "un-felicitous" the attempt to interpret the Aramaic "Abba" as a term of endearment corresponding, in its use, to "Daddy" (*Abba*) in modern Hebrew; see J. Maier, "Jesus von Nazaret und sein Verhältnis zum Judentum" in W. P. Eckert & H. H. Henrix, *Jesu Jude-Sein als Zugang zum Judentum* (Aachen, 1976), p. 103, note 44. See also chapter 8 of this volume.
39. "The early Church saw in this word 'Abba' the unmistakable uniqueness of Jesus' message", W. Knörzer, *op. cit.*, p. 79. See also note 15, above.
40. W. Knörzer, op. cit., p. 52.
41. This widespread phenomenon, obviously deeply rooted in the psychological structure of man, could, following Erich Fromm and Orwell, perhaps be called "religious double-think". This type of thinking is able to measure one behaviour according to different, often opposing standards.
42. See chapter 2 of this volume.
43. See chapter 1 of this volume.
44. See note 23 above.
45. Joseph Roth, *Job. The Story of a Simple Man* (New York, Viking Press), 1931.
46. Walter Dirks, *Unser Vater und das Vaterunser* (Munich, 1972), p. 50.
47. Baruch Graubard, see chapter 4 of this volume.
48. Cp. also A. Vögtle, chapter 7 of this volume.

13

The Fatherhood of God in Modern Interpretations

Walter Strolz

Prayer, like everything in human life, is situationally conditioned. More broadly, the man who prays, no matter in what personal state he may find himself, is related to a historical period which differs from other epochs. Martin Buber has equated this period, as far as the twentieth century is concerned, with the experience of the "eclipse of God". That is his term for an epochal attitude which fundamentally characterizes our existence and exposes it to great shocks and crises of anxiety. But this analysis has nothing to do with a debilitating pessimism. Instead Buber indicates something taking place *between* God and man, and therefore in no way the mere result of a human self-encounter. "Eclipse of the light of heaven, eclipse of God—such, indeed, is the character of the historic hour through which the world is passing. But it is not a process which can be adequately accounted for by instancing the changes that have taken place in man's spirit. An eclipse of the sun is something that occurs between the sun and our eyes, not in the eye itself."[1]

Belief in the fatherhood of God is particularly affected by this historical situation. For many people, the possibility of praying to God as father is no longer given, and the very act of praying in this sense undergoes severe tests. The act of prayer has entered the area of doubt, of futility, of something that can no longer be defended. Or the unanswering silence of Him who is addressed in prayer is so oppressive, and the evil which is continued and perpetuated everywhere is so ineradicable, that anyone affected can no longer justify his turning towards the paternal countenance of God. But this severe jolt to traditional belief in God was indicated some time ago. Probably Nietzsche, in the nineteenth century, diagnosed it most precisely. In his *Beyond Good and Evil* an aphorism directly indicates experiences we shall encounter below: "Why Atheism nowadays? 'The father' in God is thoroughly refuted; equally so 'the judge', 'the rewarder'. Also his 'free will': he does not hear—and even if he did, he would not know how to help. The worst is that he seems incapable of communicating himself clearly; is he uncertain?—This is what I have made out (by questioning, and listening at a variety of conversations) to be the cause of the decline of European theism; it appears to me that though the religious instinct is in vigorous growth—it rejects the theistic satisfaction with profound distrust."[2]

When Christians converse with Jews, they too easily forget that only a small portion of the "chosen people" profess a biblical belief in God. This can be difficult for believing Jews and Christians; nevertheless, in dialogue with Judaism it is important to respect the self-understanding of the *unbelieving* as much as that of the pious Jew.[3] Opposition to traditional belief has to be taken seriously; that is a necessary part of true dialogue. In that spirit, Jean Améry writes in the final chapter of his apologia *Beyond Guilt and Expiation*: "I was sitting next to a Jewish friend during a performance of Arnold Schoenberg's 'A Survivor from Warsaw'. When the choir, with trombone trills, began 'Shema Yisrael', my companion grew deathly pale and beads of sweat appeared on his forehead. My heart did not beat faster, but I felt more destitute than my companion who had felt moved by the Jewish prayer sung to trombone blasts. I could only be a Jew full of fear and anger, not in inspiration—I thought afterwards—when fear changes to anger in order to achieve dignity. 'Hear, o Israel' is none of my business. Only a 'Hear, o world' could I shout full of anger. The six-digit number on my forearm demands this. The feeling of catastrophe, dominating my existence, demands this."[4]

But accusation against God, too, can break forth from the rebellious depths of our humanity, when Job is suddenly present again. In his sketches from 1943, the great Jewish author Elias Canetti writes: "At the Last Judgment, one single creature will arise out of every mass grave. And God should dare judge it!"[5]

In the arena of religious experience, where belief confronts the challenges of the incomprehensible, the uncompromisable, the fatal disharmony, veracity and indignation fight with a trust in God and in spite of everything the man who prays arises from this contest again and again.

We include in our Jewish–Christian dialogue this examination of some modern interpretations of the Lord's Prayer in order to show the religious consciousness which is characteristic modern man. It is not merely a question of faith-experience in the biblical sense. By taking into account Marxist and psychological approaches to the world of the Lord's Prayer, our understanding widens to include what is generally human. That helps us to uncover the significant mystery which is present whenever and wherever man is aware of himself as creature; where opposition and inability to pray conceal his yearning. The intention here is to show the connexion between present-day religious experience and the faith tradition of Israel and Christianity.

I shall begin with Walter Dirks' attempts at exegesis of the Lord's Prayer in 1972.[6] The extent of this work indicates the author's problems in finding an approach to the paternal God. Two-thirds of the book—under the title "Belief and Ideology"—examine the question whether, given the presuppositions of our time and our world, we can still trust in God as father. Dirks takes the difficulties of experiencing God after Auschwitz quite seriously: "The most profound difficulty, familiar to all of us, is Job's plaint and complaint, the difficulty which threatened to break Reinhold Schneider." From this experience he concludes that it is now a question of trusting God in such a way "that the presumptuous intent to justify him through a strictly logical theodicy becomes meaningless". In this connexion Dirks speaks of the meaning of "negative theology", and how it reminds us of the human impossibility of defining the essence of God according to the principles of our logic. It is, he says, characteristic of the 'hubris of the theologians" not to consider this factor sufficiently. The experience of God's inscrutability should permeate theology in general so that the dogmatic claim to certainty yields to "belief in the mystery".

Where he tries to identify with the spirit of the Lord's Prayer, the question of belief is posed more directly. The first petition contains an unheard-of challenge in view of the real condition of the world: "All intellectual difficulties with so-called metaphysics and transcendence further those we have emotionally and intellectually with the incalculable, the unfeasible and the invisible, all objections against the existence of an all-powerful and all-knowing being which, moreover, apparently inflicts on man unimaginable horrors, injustice and cruelty, a possibly inconclusive march through history, never ending fights against evil with slight chances of victory, furthermore the constant temptation of indifference and of the comfortable empty life—all these personal experiences contradict not only belief in God in general but particularly the laudation contained in the first petition: God, our father, you are salvation, the powerfully healing one who brings salvation."

How is man to cope with these evils and riddles in human history and the ultimately impenetrable burden of his own existence? Does the praise of God really lead to freedom? Does the one who prays become free? When Dirks interprets the following petition of the Lord's Prayer, he leaves the realm of theological argument. He is guided by this insight: "Our surest safeguard against disposing of God in our thinking and speaking is to keep as close as possible to the source: to the figure, work and word of Jesus and to his immediate witnesses."

With justification, Dirks lays particular stress on the words "our" and "us". He gives them a socio-critical emphasis and stresses the interhuman solidarity which emerges from the fourth and fifth petitions of the Lord's Prayer and is easily not heard. Dirks arranges the sixth and seventh petitions under the heading "liberation". He does not make things too easy for himself with the sixth petition, "And lead us not into temptation". Dirks knows that the secret of evil is present here; and that man's freedom of decision is posited here. "The greatest of God's offers," he says, "our freedom, presupposes the risk that its positive and productive sense can be missed." A new translation by an exegete has been suggested for this petition: "and save us out of our temptation", but I dare to doubt that this new wording really removes what is offensive to many Christians. Dirks once more takes up the question of God permitting evil, and he interprets the seventh petition of the Lord's Prayer in this manner: "Dissolve our fear, release us for trust". It seems to me that this interpretation most concretely expresses the spirit of the Lord's Prayer out of man's faith-experience.

A philosopher of religion, Heinz Robert Schlette, in his book of 1972, *Skeptische Religionsphilosophie*,[7] characterized his "hermeneutic meditations" as a "sceptical Lord's Prayer". After the extermination of more than six million Jews, many of whom believed in God, the phrase "Father in Heaven" cannot, according to Schlette, be retained *thus*: " . . . there remains possibly the desire that He might, 'at the end', after all 'exist' as something totally other, to solve all riddles and to release from all vexation. That may even be asking too much, because the triumph of the totally other beyond this ocean of tears at the end of time is no more credible than the father who makes all things well again. The metaphor of the totally other solves the problem of evil just as little as does that of the heavenly father."

By contrast, the theologian Friedrich Wulf[8] in his interpretation (1969) of the Lord's Prayer maintains this possibility fully. However, basically he does not go beyond a pastoral homily for Christians in the traditional sense.

The NT exegete F. J. Schierse, in his *The God of Jesus—A New God?*, tries to offer an anthropological framework for addressing God as "father". He points to changes in the faith-experience of God's fatherhood, in specific relation to today's situation of man vis-à-vis his religious quest for meaning. Schierse realizes that "father" as applied to God involves more than metaphor: "Of course, it is always problematical to draw conclusions from the functions and manifestations of human fatherhood which are valid for the 'essence' of God. Analogies of this type have, in the past, often led to religiously and church-politically fateful distortions as if the patriarchal system, paternalistic conduct, spiritual tutelage and authoritarian obedience had been fixed by God himself for all eternity. We have to fear that the experiences of our time, too, have given cause for one-sided exaggerations. Nonetheless, solidarity seems to us today an irrevocable characteristic of true fatherhood. A father knows himself to be partially responsible for and, in a certain sense, partially guilty of everything his children do or suffer. Experience teaches him that it is impossible to give love without incurring guilt, or that genuine authority need not fear to admit failings and limitations. To what extent do such considerations apply also to God, the father of Jesus? Can man today take seriously talk of the fatherhood of God and at the same time void it of everything which it still denotes in a communalizing reality? At least the parable of the lost son shows that the connexion between fatherly love and guilt was not foreign to the mind of Jesus."[9]

This anthropological expansion of the denotation of the divine name "father" is certainly necessary because man is fundamentally capable of belief only to the extent that he is conditioned by history and by situations. All the same, it does not suffice for approaching the divinity of God in his fatherhood. This is already indicated in the term "loss of God's function" and through the suspect question as to what function God could still pretend to. What kind of God is it who has "functions" apportioned to him, as if the human experience of God were a psychologically or sociologically determinable mechanism? Also conventional talk of the "transfer of the name 'Father' to God" implies an all too human picture of God. The conditions for the existence of the possibility of such a "transfer" are simply and unquestioningly presupposed or, to formulate the state of affairs with regard to biblical revelation: God as creator and lord of history initially grants the possibility for man to transfer anything at all. God is the sovereign giver, and only through what is "given" in the sense of having been created through God's creative word is man a being who can transmit and produce meaningful images. A great deal of thinking still has to go into the question how, with the opening up of the ontological dimension of biblical faith, the meaning of the Lord's Prayer far surpasses mere human significance.

Belief in the fatherhood of God must not be deaf to the complaint and indignation of those who no longer see the fatherly countenance of God because the pitiless silence of God in the face of murderous violence no longer lets them believe. Honesty, truth and utter realism which do not ignore past historical experiences but cope with them: that is the demand made of the believer today. Christian theology since the end of World War II has not followed the event of Auschwitz with a consideration of fundamentals truly corresponding to the basic ties between Christianity and Judaism (Romans 11:18). Assurances which are formulated differently still seem to us to be too theo-logical and to be aimed at proof and justification of God in the sense of Job's friends. The position of Jürgen Moltmann may serve as an example: "A 'theology after Auschwitz' may appear as an impossibility or as blasphemy to those who were content with theism or with a childish belief and lost it. 'Theology after Auschwitz' as borne out in retrospective work of mourning or as recognition of guilt could not exist had there not been a 'theology in Auschwitz'. Whoever falls into insoluble problems and despair after the event must remind himself that the *Shema Yisrael* and the Lord's Prayer were recited in Auschwitz".[10]

Moltmann's comments point to the Job-like situation of religious thought which seems to be prototypical for the experience of God in our century.

Schlette takes this up where he explains the petition for daily bread. He recognizes in it the theodicy problem for which there is no solution in the human realm, in sharpest contrast to the knowledge of systematic theology. Schlette asks himself: "How can 'God' be good when he permits men not only to be hungry but lets them die of starvation and at the same time recommends the petition 'Give us this day our daily bread' which, anyway, is not heard? Such thinking about 'God' seems blasphemous or, more correctly: it makes 'God' a cynic. We had better re-jettison the old metaphysical notion of 'God'."

Has the petition for daily bread, then, become redundant for Schlette because of his negative delimitation? Not at all. Man who needs bread in order to live on earth lives in a human manner only by not living by bread alone. A man who asks for bread only for one day does not close himself off satisfied and self-assured, from that which he cannot control.

Schlette says that the petition, by leaving "open the meaning of the whole, which is more than bread alone, prevents permanent satiety from being regarded as a value and yet maintains with irrefutable clarity the fulfilment of real necessities as fundamental conditions of human life on which everything else is based—but on which something else stands and has to stand!".

This interpretation comes close to what the Jewish Christian Anni Kraus says about the fourth petition in her article of 1970. She speaks of the lasting insecurity of Christian existence and of salvation as always only beginning, always happening today, no matter how that which has previously happened is at work in it. The fourth petition, according to her author, aims to keep alive in man the yearning for the absolute without depriving human life of its creative tension.

Schlette removes the petition for forgiveness of guilt from the customary moral schema of reckoning good and evil. He considers psychoanalytical and depth-psychological insights which show us how complex a phenomenon guilt is. Here we encounter not only human weakness, unintended failure, manifold forms of dependence, and reduction of the awareness of freedom but the dark aspects of human existence. To comprehend these unambiguously from a psychological or theological standpoint is beyond man's understanding. Nonetheless man is guilty and he is also responsible, up to a certain point, for his becoming guilty. Otherwise the petition of the Lord's Prayer concerning this human situation would be meaningless. Schlette modifies the idea of guilt so that it appears part of the fundamental conditions of human society: "Guilt, then, means," he writes, ". . . the refusal which is not clearly and distinctly present in consciousness, but which is probably always intermingled with freedom, the refusal to do what,

197

speaking as a Christian, I should have done: the refusal to love (and nothing else); and forgiveness does not mean a single pathetic gesture of annulling guilt (which, incidentally, would always be in danger of haughtiness) but the constant preparedness to trust the other anew and to give him a new chance, that is: the gentle *humanitas* which anticipates and 'understands' what moves man (cp. John 2 : 25) because it knows its own evil potentials."

Schlette's interpretation of the final petitions of the Lord's Prayer is annoying if one expects a clearer answer. But one could equally counter: how could there be such an answer in the face of what happened to the chosen people in Auschwitz and Treblinka? For Schlette, as for other interpreters, there arises at this point the inevitable question: how could the God of love permit this? Could it be that the Lord's Prayer is possibly nothing but a wishful text for the abused and tormented man who has more "tests" imposed on him than he can really endure? The attempts at theological justification of God collapse like houses of cards before such suffering. Does God hear the protests of men at all? Schlette retains his sceptical key note because he sees no further. The personalistic metaphor of the "Father in Heaven" can, according to him, no longer be justified.

In conclusion, Schlette decides "to maintain scepticism in all directions, vis-à-vis all language and all fixity, to mistrust apologetic confirmations which only seek to lead us back into the theoretical difficulties of a metaphoric theology which is as tempting as it makes one despair, and to despise the reality of a desire for what is perfect, whole and absolute, a desire which no fault-finding can dispel."

The Marxist philosopher Milan Machoveč offers another interpretation of the Lord's Prayer in his *Jesus für Atheisten*[11] (1973). His basic idea is to interpret the Lord's Prayer wholly in the perspective of the future, to hear in it its eschatological meaning. "We can best visualize this unapocalyptic, non-fantasizing but very radical 'life of the future' if we understand how Jesus teaches to 'pray' ..." Machovec gives a positively historico-dynamic interpretation of the Lord's Prayer. For him, the petition for the coming of the kingdom is central and this petition contains a call to action which cannot be ignored. He writes almost as a Jewish exegete: "The man 'who waits for the kingdom' is not, by any stretch of the imagination, allowed to flee 'from this world' but must accept the most demanding assignment in this world, must carry the future into the present, must not only have but must also live the 'faith', ie, the decision to undergo a change as a result of 'God's kingdom'; therefore he must also propagate it, confess it, proclaim it, win others for it ... Jesus never demands that dogmatic formulae should be learned but demands *action* in the spirit of God's kingdom."

But for Machoveč, too, the traditional Christian "concept of God as Father" has its difficulties. Because of the father–son relationship in Jesus' message, as Christian tradition has interpreted it for centuries, man has been paternalistically spoiled, even weakened. A meaning and a justification for everything were found too easily. Twentieth-century man can no longer believe like that. Man's paternalistically and providentially coloured understanding has, in view of Auschwitz, reached a major crisis-point. This crisis "... is capable of destroying everything as man reflects upon himself, because it awakes in him a feeling of complete deracination, emptiness, uselessness, senselessness. Herein lies the disturbing aspect of those marvellous, childlike experiences of the good father, 'who knows what you need' (Matthew 6:8). That, indeed, made life easier for millions and less desperate, which, in itself, would not be bad but it supported and fortified—precisely through the principle of the presumably fatherly basis of existence and especially human existence—certain infantile characteristics of human self-reflection which are certainly very nice and to a degree necessary especially in childhood, but which, to the extent that they carry over into adulthood, render one incapable of facing hard blows of fate, also on such occasions where life is no longer the paternal home."

Still Machoveč, in spite of this doubtlessly justified criticisms, does not overlook the *lasting* significance of childhood for "adults". This insight may include the possibility that, after the dismissal of the theological legitimization of God as father, one detects in the depth of a concrete experience of the human self, a sense of security which is of non-human origin.

After this Marxist attempt to interpret the Lord's Prayer, there is also the possibility of a psychoanalytical interpretation. More exactly, the exegesis of the meaning of the sixth petition of the Lord's Prayer is involved here, in Carl Gustav Jung's *Answer to Job*.[12] That work of Jung's which has occasioned the most opposition from theological circles. His interpretation shows with what passionate concern the founder of analytical psychology has

199

struggled with the riddle of the power of evil. The petition not to be led into temptation is the stumbling-block because it confronts man with the question of the origin of evil and its uncanny power in human history. Jung says: "But although Christ has complete confidence in his father and even feels at one with him, he cannot help inserting the cautious petition—and warning—into the Lord's Prayer: 'Lead us not into temptation, but deliver us from evil'. God is asked not to entice us outright into doing evil, but rather to deliver us from it. The possibility that Yahweh, in spite of all the precautionary measures and in spite of his express intention to become the Summum Bonum, might yet revert to his former ways is not so remote that one need not keep one eye open for it. At any rate, Christ considers it appropriate to remind his father of his destructive inclinations towards mankind and to beg him to desist from them. Judged by any human standards it is after all unfair, indeed extremely immoral, to entice little children into doing things that might be dangerous for them, simply in order to test their moral stamina!"

In the same chapter Jung also relates this petition to the "God of Love" and speaks of "Christ's doubt" with a view to the character of his Heavenly Father. The psychologist then raises the question whether God could really be the essence of all good if he places his creature so squarely in temptation through evil. As questionable as this opinion is, if regarded in the spirit of the NT (James 1:13), Jung comes closer to that spirit when he views the apocalyptic dimension of evil in the individuation process as man becomes whole, and when he reminds us of the final birthpangs of historical time at the approach of the anti-Christ.

Within the framework of an extensive psychology of religion,[13] Antoine Vergote examines the psychic structure and development of religious experience. Here the Lord's Prayer is not mentioned specifically, but Vergote examines at length "Religious Longing and the Father Symbol". He excludes the question of truth by speaking of a "methodological exclusion of transcendence" which is beyond objective-scientific analysis. Although ultimately this psychologist bases himself on the Kantian dualism of being and appearance and, from a philosophical viewpoint, his non-consideration of the question of truth is eventually untenable, he makes decisive points about the fatherhood of God. They are based on interviews and surveys undertaken in Belgium. Vergote carefully analyses the results. He finds that Freud's psychoanalytical critique of the God-Father concept has led to a dated critique of the idols: ie, of those images of God which man had made for himself. Vergote proves that this surely necessary destruction of all-too-human God-Father-images which Freud had undertaken had really missed what religion meant by the Fatherhood of God. The founder of psychoanalysis had not noted the fundamental religious stance of Jesus Christ as simply embodying the Father-Son relationship. However, in the history of religion, "Jesus Christ appears as the most convinced and far-sighted guarantor for the Fatherhood of God; his understanding of this divine characteristic becomes clear in all of his conduct". The result of the psychological examination of the religious experience is that the man ready for faith goes beyond psychic determinants and motivations in his acknowledgment of the world as creation, and of his fellow man. Thus he overcomes "the wall of psychologism" which is based on tacit assumptions, the range and questionableness of which are shown up by philosophical reflection.

In a sense, Vergote abandons the position of the psychologist who ignores the question of the truth of God's transcendence when he sums up as follows: "Although God is already present in the experience of the world, he withdraws from it and leaves to man the whole mystery of his existence. He answers with silence those motivations and tendencies which aim at him, and he does not resolve the doubts concerning reality or illusion of religious experience. He offers himself as salvation to hoping and longing, but thus also opens up the abyss of his otherness. He reveals to man his fatherhood and summons him to regard himself as a son. And yet this consent to divine fatherhood may take place amid doubt and conflict. Not only does this consent often appear as focal point of all illusions; it can itself cast into doubt the most powerful and secret wishes. Therefore it is at times misunderstood as the highest negation of being human. If man wants to discover the hidden meaning of divine fatherhood, he must thus undergo a fundamental change which will transform him to the root of his being and to the foundation of his religious strivings."

J. F. Six, in his article "Dieu-Père"[14] takes up the experience of the self and of history. He poses the question of the credibility of the fatherhood in today's world. The relationships which he considers are connected with the book *Die vaterlose Gesellschaft*[15] by the psychoanalyst Alexander Mitscherlich. The protest of the sons, the calling into question of paternal authority is, according to Six, to be seen against the background of psychological and sociological changes in behaviour which go back to the critical dismantling of idols. The difficulty of turning to God as father today, he says, is to be attributed to the ideological misuse of paternal authority in education and in religious life. There is, he says, no fundamental impossibility because God, in the original biblical understanding of faith, was precisely a God who was present in history for and with man as a God of liberation and of freedom. According to Six, man in our time has a great need for the *Brotherhood of all men*. Across the bridge of this fraternal relationship, established through man's createdness, man's relationship to God as the father of all could be won back.

Most of the interpretations of the Lord's Prayer cited here evince a certain disquiet. The authors need not reproach themselves for recourse to a theology of admitting evil on the part of God. The constraints of theological systematization are shattered by the distressing reality of evil. The Bible with its unique understanding of the forces that move the individual and history in the arena of the struggle between good and evil, testifies to the limited operation of evil, from Genesis to the Apocalypse.

Whatever the individual's attitude to the interpretations of the Lord's Prayer presented here, they show with what intensity faith and history interact. Traditional religious language no longer seems capable of communicating. Like a severe earthquake, the historical catastrophes of the twentieth century have deeply shaken faithful prayer to "the Father in Heaven". Yet the "shattering" experience which makes such traditional religious expressions so radically questionable is not, finally, decisive. What is decisive is the transformation of language, its severe trial in the crucible of historical crisis into which Jews and Christians were dragged. Whatever it is that the Lord's Prayer still or again says to interpreters today points to this process. It cannot be completely apprehended within the horizon of mere ecclesiastical or theological thinking. Security, up to now naively or self-centredly misunderstood as safety is, by critical analysis, shown to be unadmitted fear of the demands of what is beyond man's control. But what remains once the countenance of the paternal God withdraws from the man who prays? The call to watchful patience remains. It frees man to hope for what man cannot accomplish himself and not to be deluded through false comfort (Is. 44:20). The personal and the epochal situation of God's abandonment is, according to the prophetic faith experience, indeed hidden but irrevocably God's time (Is. 8:17, Revelations 1:8).

Notes

1. Martin Buber, *Eclipse of God. Studies in the Relation between Religion and Philosophy*, translated Maurice S. Friedman (New York, 1952), p. 34 [Corrected by present translator].
2. *Beyond Good and Evil*, translated Helen Zimmern, *The Complete Works of Friedrich Nietzsche*, ed. Oscar Levy (New York, 1914), vol. 12, p. 72.
3. Cp. J. Maier, "Kontinuität und Diskontinuität: Jüdisches Erbe im christlichen Glauben", in *Judentum im christlichen Religionsunterricht, Schriften der Evangelischen Akademie in Hessen und Nassau*, 93 (Frankfurt a. M., 1972), pp. 7–45.
4. Jean Améry, *Jenseits von Schuld und Sühne—Bewältigungsversuche eines Überwältigten* (Munich, 1970), p. 118. Cp. also as an example of Jewish contribution George Steiner, *Language and Silence* (London & New York, 1972). With reference to the death-camps of the Nazis, the introduction says that there are realities too great for hatred or forgiveness, and that one thing only must not be permitted: forgetting, for with each forgetting, those who were tortured and burned die a second time.
4. Elias Canetti, *Die Provinz des Menschen—Aufzeichungen 1942–1972* (München, 1973), p. 67.
6. Walter Dirks, *Vater unser—unser Vater* (Munich, 1973).
7. H. R. Schlette, *Skeptische Religionsphilosophie* (Freiburg i. B.), pp. 84–117.
8. F. Wulf, *Vater unser im Himmel: Meditationen über das Gebet des Herrn* (Zürich & Würzburg, 1969).
9. F. J. Schierse, "Der Gott Jesu—Ein Neuer Gott?" in *Wort und Wahrheit*, 3 (1971), pp. 204–5.
10. Jürgen Moltmann, *The Crucified God* (London & New York, 1973).
11. M. Machovec, *Jesus für Atheisten* (Stuttgart, 1973), pp. 122–3.
12. C. G. Jung, *Answer to Job*, translated R. F. C. Hull (London, 1954), pp. 78–9.
13. *Psychologie religieuse* (Brussels, 1966).
14. *Etudes* (Feb. 1975), pp. 289–99.
15. *Ideen zur Sozialpsychologie* (Munich, 1963); cp. also P. Ricoeur, "Die Vatergestalt—vom Fantasiebild zum Symbol", in P. Ricoeur, *Hermeneutik und Psychoanalyse. Der Konflikt der Interpretationen* (München, 1974), II, pp. 315–53.

14

The Liturgies of Synagogue and Church: An Introduction to the Literature

Michael Brocke

This symposium is based on several days of common thinking about the Lord's Prayer, its roots in ancient Judaism and its context. Some important additions have been made to this English edition. The symposium shows how Jews and Christians differ fundamentally in their approaches to, and attitudes towards, their respective traditions and religions. It also reveals the different ways Jews and Christians speak about their heritage. To speak, for the first time, about topics which entail and reveal as many agreements as they do differences was particularly difficult. This applies all the more when that which is common only comes into view slowly, and is accepted gradually, and there is still a lack of clarity in regard to the meaning and importance possessed and yet to be possessed by the individual common elements: whether in an historical perspective or with a view to the present and to the ecumenical future.

Neither the common elements and the original dissimilarities of the period of Christian beginnings, nor the differences and new common elements of further historical developments until the present day, have been adequately understood by those concerned or have led to practical consequences. The problems which formed the background of the symposium may be seen as the most fundamental. They may be sensed here in print; and their resolution will require much time and work.

We were unwilling and unable to outline all relevant aspects of the manifold relationships between the divine services of Judaism and Christianity. Nor were we able to delimit the vast area of Jewish prayer and liturgical celebration. Of necessity, the emphasis is primarily placed on the relationship of the Lord's Prayer to Jewish structures and contents. However, from the very beginning, it seemed essential not to strengthen the strong Christian interest in the Lord's Prayer—intelligible and justified in its own right—to the point of a false exclusivism, or to present it as uniquely interesting.

The Lord's Prayer is a highly characteristic text for the relationship and for the independence of Christian and Jewish prayer. But, beyond that, there is a closely-woven texture of basic theological convictions common to both religions, of rites, of ceremonial procedures and texts, which, to the present day, is neither seen as a whole nor recognized in its fine detail.

The following modest selected reading list is designed to point the way in this immense and practically uncharted area for the reader who wants to inquire beyond the limits of the Lord's Prayer into the liturgy of Judaism and its influence on Christian liturgy. The following references to the literature should help the interested "lay-person" and the "professional" concerned with prayer, the literature of prayer, and the historical and present-day liturgy. No claim is made to bibliographical completeness; and we have not distributed the references evenly among the various sections. There may be an abundance of easily accessible literature in one area, making it difficult to select. In another area, there may be only a few works which, moreover, are antiquated in many respects, but which have not been replaced as yet.

We have chosen basic sources and treatments, occasionally adding our own brief comments. On the whole, we have stressed Jewish liturgy *per se* as well as its relation to, and influences upon Christian liturgy. This approach commends itself all the more because the literature about the Lord's Prayer and about Christian prayer and worship is rich and easily accessible, whereas Jewish sources and literature are ignored or wrongly considered to be inaccessible. Yet the latter, not least for their own sake, deserve to be known and to be studied by Christians.

1. *The Lord's Prayer*

The most comprehensive scholarly work which has been published about the Lord's Prayer is Jean Carmignac's *Recherches sur le 'Notre Père'* (Paris, Letouzey & Ané, 1969), 608 pp. Its importance is based not least upon its bibliography of eighty pages, the most extensive listing of the literature about the Lord's Prayer. In particular, Carmignac has examined the possible relations between the Lord's Prayer and the writings of the sectarian community of Qumran. The context of Jewish liturgy is dealt with only briefly, and Carmignac's treatment cannot be regarded as the last word on this subject. The theological conclusions of Carmignac's labour of many years in connexion with the Lord's Prayer—apart from his thoughts about its "spiritual wealth", which are included in the present volume—may be found in a popular book without scholarly apparatus: *A l'écoute du Notre Père* (Paris, Editions de Paris, 1969), 117 pp.

A useful English-language exegetical exposition of the Lord's Prayer, comparing the versions of Matthew and Luke, is Philip B. Harner's *Understanding the Lord's Prayer*, (Philadelphia, Fortress Press, 1975), 149 pp.

There is no lack of pious and meditative books about the Lord's Prayer. Their importance lies in their attempts to use the example of the Lord's Prayer to calling into question the traditional images of God and man, and, with the help of the Lord's Prayer, to offer our contemporaries a new interpretation of the traditional image of God and a new way of expressing it. Walter Strolz, in his contribution to the present volume, examines some of those attempts to meet the challenge of the questionable nature of our human and divine "father images". On the other hand, Herbert Jochum's contribution offers literary illustrations of the ability of the Lord's Prayer to withstand bitter parodies or one-sided transformations.

2. Jewish Liturgy

2.1. Prayerbooks

Anyone interested in Jewish liturgy should study it in its own sources, and not primarily through quotations appearing in secondary literature. Those sources are easily accessible. All trends within English-speaking Judaism have published editions of the Jewish prayerbook with accompanying English translations. It is, however, advisable to concentrate on the more "traditional" prayerbooks. The prayerbooks of the various Reform and Liberal movements have introduced many changes which, on occasion, make it impossible for the reader to recognize the liturgical structures as they have evolved historically. Such liturgical revisions may seem to be called for, might even be justifiable, and are certainly of interest in their own right. But they are of no help to the student unfamiliar with the field who is trying to acquire a factual knowledge of classical Jewish liturgy. Modern Orthodox prayerbooks, as currently used, are to be preferred.

We have in mind such editions as the following: Philip Birnbaum, ed., *Daily Prayer Book* (New York, Hebrew Publishing Company, 1949), 790 pp.; Philip Birnbaum, ed., *High Holyday*

Prayer Book (New York, Hebrew Publishing Company, 1951), 1042 pp.; David de Sola Pool, ed., *The Traditional Prayer Book for Sabbath and Festivals* (New York, Behrman House, 1960), 879 pp.

Most widely used in England is Simeon Singer, ed., *The Authorised Daily Prayer Book* (first published in London by Eyre & Spottiswoode in 1890, it has gone through numerous editions). An extensive commentary, in a devotional and homiletical vein, on this prayerbook is contained in Joseph H. Hertz, ed., *The Authorised Daily Prayer Book—Revised Edition* (London, 1941; New York, Bloch Publishing Company,[2] 1965), 1120 pp. The Liturgy of the High Holy Days and the Three Pilgrim Festivals is available, with an English translation, in the six volumes of *Service of the Synagogue*, edited by Herbert Adler and Arthur Davis (first published by Routledge, London, 1906, and since then republished in many editions).

A commentary on the daily prayerbook, composed in the spirit of nineteenth-century Neo-Orthodoxy by Samson Raphael Hirsch (1808–1888), can be found in *The Hirsch Siddur—The Order of Prayers for the Whole Year* (New York, Feldheim, 1969), 752 pp.

Two particularly beautiful and important liturgical works have been published recently for the High Holy Days ("The Days of Awe"), ie, the New Year and the Day of Atonement. A significant scholarly achievement is the edition, by Daniel Goldschmidt, of *Mahzor layamim hanora-im* ("Prayerbook for the Days of Awe", in Hebrew only), (New York & Jerusalem, the Leo Baeck Institute & Koren, 1970), two volumes, 62 + 328 and 54 + 797 pp. This edition of the prayerbook, containing all the liturgical accretions accumulated in the whole course of liturgical development as well as all the liturgical poetry of the Ashkenazi rite for the High Holy Days, is intended not so much for practical use in worship as for the student of the liturgy and liturgical poetry, and for the collector of bibliophilic treasures.

The use of Hebrew and English, practicability and good taste distinguish the High Holy Day prayerbook issued by Conservative Judaism in the United States: Jules Harlow, ed., *Mahzor for Rosh Hashanah and Yom Kippur—A Prayer Book for the Days of Awe* (New York, The Rabbinical Assembly, 1972), 789 pp. This is an attractive prayerbook, and is convincing in its English translations. Since it contains only a few and minor changes in the traditional text (omitting, in particular, the prayers for the restoration of the sacrificial cult), it does not convey to the non-Jewish reader any really distorted picture of the traditional Jewish liturgy. The addition of medieval texts and synagogal poetry, of meditations and modern texts which conform to the spirit of the High Holy Days is indicated to the reader. This book, true to tradition and at the same time modern and enlightened, is highly recommended; we can only hope that the promised edition of the daily prayerbook by the same editor will soon see the light of day. The weekday service, adapted for the use of mourners, has already appeared: Jules Harlow, ed., *The Bond of Life—A Book for Mourners* (New York, The Rabbinical Assembly, 1975), 205 + 94 pp.

2.2. *Accompanying Commentaries to the Liturgy*

Some of the liturgical works meant for practical use contain brief explanations which, however, do not suffice in the majority of cases. If one wants to understand the liturgical structures and the underlying theological concepts, one must consult theological and historical commentaries which accompany the text. There are such works as Israel Abrahams, *A Companion to the Authorised Daily Prayerbook* (New York, Hermon Press, [2]1966), 234 pp.; and Max Arzt, *Justice and Mercy* (New York, Holt, Rinehart & Winston, 1963), 299 pp., the latter being a helpful introduction to an understanding of the High Holy Day liturgy.

Widely used as a commentary to all the prayers: Elie Munk, *The World of Prayer* (New York, Feldheim, 1961–3), two volumes, 234 and 341 pp. Munk often has profound insights into the meaning and the exegetical possibilities of individual prayers and of the service as a whole. He also makes it possible for a novice to appreciate the structure and the flow of the service, since all the prayers are reproduced in translation in their liturgical sequence, and are commented upon. The work may be considered a classic. But it is written from a deeply pious point of view, and cannot be said to have any real scientific value.

2.3. *Collections of Prayers, Anthologies*

Many popular presentations of Jewish religion and civilization, which need not be enumerated here, also contain some of the statutory and other prayers, detached from their contexts and settings. But there are also independent collections of prayers and comprehensive anthologies which are devoted exclusively to prayer texts. Outstanding among those anthologies are the following: Nahum N. Glatzer, ed., *Language of Faith* (New York, Schocken,

1967), 336 pp. This is a typographically lavish anthology, which contains mainly Hebrew, but also some Greek, Yiddish and German prayers, all with an English Translation. The subtitle, *A Selection from the Most Expressive Jewish Prayers*, as well as the organization ("Creation", "The Presence of God", "My Times are in Thy Hand", "De Profundis", "Sabbath", "Days of Awe", "Pleace", and so on) indicate the purely literary character of this selection. Unfortunately many of the prayers are reproduced in an incomplete form. A similar work, though not quite as lavish externally, is Bernard Martin, *Prayer in Judaism* (New York, Basic Books, 1968), 256 pp. It contains some fifty translated texts with commentary.

Meyer J. Perath, *Rabbinical Devotion—Prayers of the Jewish Sages* (Assen-Netherlands, Van Gorcum, 1964), 40 pp., may be regarded as a good bilingual supplement to the collections of liturgical texts for public worship. It contains twenty-seven "private" prayers of individual Rabbinic sages, as they have been transmitted by the Talmud and the *Midrash*.

A particulary useful book, provided by its editors with expert introductions, is Joseph Heinemann and Jakob J. Petuchowski, eds., *Literature of the Synagogue* (New York, Behrman House, 1975), x + 294 pp. This is a tripartite collection of texts, with a thorough but concise commentary, which does more justice to the complexity and wealth of Jewish liturgy than comparable works. It contains not only the major prayers and other items such as the Grace after Meals (Heinemann), but thirteen homilies of the Talmudic period (Heinemann), which may serve as an introduction to the ways of the *Midrash*, and, in the third section, fourteen fine samples of the various genres of synagogal poetry from its beginning through the late Middle Ages, translated into contemporary English (Petuchowski). This introduction is also valuable from the literary point of view.

A volume scheduled for publication in 1977 is Jakob J. Petuchowski, *Theology and Poetry* (London, Routledge & Kegan Paul). On the basis of annotated translations of synagogal poetry, it seeks to introduce the reader to the deeper meaning of this liturgical literature and to its unique accentuation of Rabbinic theology.

2.4. *General Introductions and Surveys of Jewish Liturgy*

There seem to be as many general introductions and devotional aids to an understanding of the spirit of Jewish prayer and worship as there are movements and trends in modern Judaism—particularly in North America. They demonstrate the pluralistic tradition of Jewish spirituality and the Jewish quest for community—from Orthodoxy to Radical Reform and the Women's Liberation Movement. We shall limit our references to the works of mainstream Orthodoxy, Conservatism and Reform.

The reader interested in a survey of ultra-traditionalist concepts and practice is referred to Abraham Kon, *Prayer* (London, Soncino Press, 1971), 277 pp. This is a translation of a Hebrew book, *Si-ah Tephillah*, which, because of its wide distribution, may already be described as typical. It stresses, in particular, the *halakhic* (ie, legal) aspects of prayer and worship, eg, the synagogue, phylacteries, the ritual fringes (*tsitsith*), and so on. Here there is no historical "earlier and later". Only a reader who already has a basic knowledge of this field will be able to use this book with profit as a reservoir of materials and as a manual of Orthodox Jewish practice. As such, the book affords an authentic insight into the mentality and religious practice of Orthodox Ashkenazi life.

A far broader yet inexpensive presentation is Abraham Millgram, *Jewish Worship* (Philadelphia, Jewish Publication Society, 1971), 673 pp. It is arranged so broadly that one might almost describe it as a handbook of Jewish lore. But many readers are liable to be confused by the mixture of piety and scholarship which prevents the book from doing justice to either.

A work of this genre which is more highly recommended is an edited extract of the material on Jewish liturgy in the *Encyclopaedia Judaica*: Raphael Posner, Uri Kaploun, and Shalom Cohen, eds., *Jewish Liturgy—Prayer and Synagogue Service through the Ages* (Jerusalem, Keter, 1975), 278 pp. The editors borrowed extensively from the store of information in the *Encyclopaedia Judaica*. However, the authors of the original encyclopaedia articles are not to be held responsible for any factual or interpretative statement in this lavishly illustrated volume. This is a gift-book which omits the technicalities of the *Encyclopaedia Judaica* and other scholarly works.

Less concerned with form and content than with the inner structure of Jewish prayer, the dialectics of spontaneity and tradition, and the problems of prayer and worship today, is a book edited by Jakob J. Petuchowski, *Understanding Jewish Prayer* (New York, Ktav, 1972), 175 pp. The first part consists of six spirited and lucid chapters by Petuchowski about the constant elements and the dynamics which characterize Jewish prayer and its history, form and freedom, tradition and renewal, and ability and inability to pray. Together with the seven brief chapters of the second part, contributed by a number of other authors (among them Abraham Joshua Heschel, Steven S. Schwarzschild, and Ernst Akiva Simon), this book offers a fundamental and topical discussion of basic facts which should not remain unknown even to Christian readers.

A popular little volume, written by a Christian clergyman, is William W. Simpson, *Jewish Prayer and Worship—An Introduction for Christians* (London, SCM Press, 1965, and New York, Seabury Press, 1967), 128 pp.

There are few works about Jewish and Rabbinic theology which devote an adequate and significant treatment to the divine service and its meaning. Something of an exception is George Foot Moore, *Judaism in the First Centuries of the Christian Era*, vol. II (Cambridge, Harvard University Press, 1927), pp. 212–38. Max Kadushin, *Worship and Ethics* (Northwestern University Press, 1964), 329 pp., is an ambitious theological work. It is not easily comprehensible but full of important insights into the intimate interdependence of prayer and deed.

2.5. *Scientific Treatments*

Still unsurpassed is the most important work of the scientific study of Jewish liturgy: Ismar Elbogen, *Der jüdische Gottesdienst in seiner geschichtlichen Entwicklung*, reprint of the third (1931) edition (Hildesheim, Georg Olms, 1962), 635 pp. In its Hebrew translation, *Hatephillah beyisrael* (Tel-Aviv, Dvir, 1972), 496 pp., the book was improved through very necessary corrections, skilful adaptations and bibliographical supplements by Joseph Heinemann in cooperation with Israel Adler, Avraham Negev, Jakob J. Petuchowski and Hayyim Schirmann. It remains an indispensable classic which, alas, has never been translated into English.

Largely based upon Elbogen, compact and lucid, but unfortunately not altogether reliable, is Abraham Z. Idelsohn, *Jewish Liturgy and its Development* (New York, Schocken [SB 149], [2]1967), 404 pp.

Joseph Heinemann, *Prayer in the Period of the Tannaim and the Amoraim* (Jerusalem, Magnes Press, [2]1966), is the most important work, using the methodology of historical and form criticism,

212

about the development of Jewish liturgy from the period of the Second Temple until approximately the end of the Talmudic period. The book is in Hebrew, and includes a brief English summary. But a completely revised and enlarged edition of this work, in English, is scheduled for publication in 1977, under the title of *Prayer in the Talmud—Forms and Patterns*. It will appear in de Gruyter's *Studia Judaica* series (Berlin & New York). It is to be hoped that those important researches will also fructify and advance the work of Christian students of the liturgy who seek to determine the structure of the *berakhah* and its relation to the *eucharistia*. All too often they stand helpless before Jewish sources and works, if they do not ignore them altogether.

Eleven older important scientific contributions to the history of the liturgy, the cycle of Torah readings, and some *genizah* and other liturgical texts, together with a scientific prolegomenon, surveying the present "state of the discipline", have become available again in Jakob J. Petuchowski, ed., *Contributions to the Scientific Study of Jewish Liturgy* (New York, Ktav, 1970), xxviii + 502 pp.

The various relevant articles in the English-language *Encyclopaedia Judaica* (Jerusalem & New York, Keter & Macmillan, 1971), 16 volumes, are rather uneven in quality. Some articles deserve to be singled out: eg, "Liturgy" by Daniel Goldschmidt, which contains brief but reliable information about the various Jewish liturgical rites, or the article about the *"Amidah"* by Joseph Heinemann and others. (Much of this material appears in an easily comprehensible and popular form, in the volume *Jewish Liturgy—Prayer and Synagogue Service through the Ages*, referred to under 2.4., above.)

More extensive surveys for the period of Late Antiquity are furnished by Shemuel Safrai and others in section two of volume one of the new multi-volume handbook, *Compendia Rerum Iudaicarum ad Novum Testamentum: The Jewish People in the First Century* (Assen-Netherlands, Van Gorcum, 1976; published in the United States by the Fortress Press, Philadelphia) (in the chapters "Religion in Everyday Life", "The Calendar", "The Temple", and "The Synagogue"); and in the expected next two volumes of the radical revision of Emil Schürer's great work, *Geschichte des jüdischen Volkes im Zeitalter Jesu Christi*, by Geza Vermes, F. Millar & M. Black. The first volume, *The History of the Jewish People in the Age of Jesus Christ*, was published in 1973 (Clark, Edinburgh).

Of interest also to readers who are affected by recent Christian, particularly Catholic liturgical reforms and discussions about them is a further work by Jakob J. Petuchowski *Prayerbook Reform in Europe* (New York, World Union for Progressive Judaism, 1968), xxii + 407 pp. It deals with the reforms of the Jewish liturgy, beginning with the nineteenth century. The current—and often heated—discussion about present-day liturgical reforms is carried on in such American Jewish periodicals as *The C.C.A.R. Journal, Conservative Judaism, Judaism, Response, Tradition*, and others.

2.6. *Studies on Specific Problems*

Most of the scholarly works mentioned so far contain extensive and reliable references to the literature which are of help in specific problems. But, in connexion with the individual topics of our symposium, we may also mention studies which, though not belonging to the field of the scientific study of liturgy, are of related interest. There is a study by S. Dean McBride, Jr, "The Yoke of the Kingdom: An Exposition of Deuteronomy 6:4–5", in *Interpretation* 27 (July 1973), pp. 273–306, which deals with the theological significance of the "Hear, O Israel!" (*Shema Yisrael*). It combines a thorough exegesis with an ecumenically orientated consciousness of the history of the efficacy of the "Hear, O Israel!" In this way, the width of meaning and the historical power of the "Hear, O Israel!" in Judaism are made to stand out. See also Arthur Marmorstein, "The Unity of God in Rabbinic Literature", in *Studies in Jewish Theology—The Marmorstein Memorial Volume*, eds. Joseph Rabbinowitz & Myer S. Lew (Farnborough, Gregg,[2] 1970), pp. 72–105, and now also Ephraim E. Urbach, *The Sages—Their Concepts and Beliefs* (Jerusalem, Magnes Press, 1975), two volumes, *passim*. The implications of the Jewish understanding of the "Unification" and the "Sanctification of the Name" (as an act of martyrdom) are shown by the first three and the tenth chapters of the powerful study on the exegesis of "The Binding of Isaac" (*Aqedah*) by Shalom Spiegel, *The Last Trial* (New York, Schocken [SB 208], [2]1969), pp. 1–27, 131–8.

3. *Relationships between Jewish and Christian Liturgy*

This is a much neglected area; there is no authoritative or even somewhat comprehensive presentation of it which may be safely recommended. Perhaps such a presentation is not yet possible—in view of the brief and halting history of mutual ecumenical interest after centuries of Christian attempts to deny the inner dependence of Christianity upon Israel.

A rich bibliography for the topic is furnished by Kurt Hruby in his article, "Joodse Liturgie" (Jewish Liturgy), which appeared in the Dutch Catholic *Liturgisch Woordenboek*, vol. I (Roermond, Netherlands, Romen & Zonen, 1958/62), cols. 1180–2. In spite of its several errors, this bibiliography is still useful. From 1960 on, we have to rely on scattered notices in scholarly periodicals on liturgy.

Because of this, it will be of interest if we refer to some more recent studies, and thereby draw attention to some long-standing problems in the study of comparative liturgy.

The importance of the Lord's Prayer and of Jesus' other private prayers does not negate the fact that the liturgical orders of the early Christian churches to a very large extent bear a Jewish stamp—also and particularly outside the passages and contexts known to us from the New Testament. It is to be welcomed that Jesus' affinity with the Judaism of his time, and therefore also the affinity of the Lord's Prayer with its Jewish context have finally been discovered. But at the same time there should also be a discovery and an investigation of the whole range of relationships between Jewish and early Christian liturgy. A great deal of pioneering work has been done in the past. Too much of it has been ignored; many leads have not been pursued.

Of late Christian declarations have, with remarkable frequency and in a very positive tone, spoken of the relationship between the Churches and Judaism in terms of the relatedness of Jewish and Christian worship. But they have never gone into detail. Those assertions, quite naturally, contain only a few basic theologoumena. Yet, in the long run, they should effect a clearer recognition than heretofore of the importance of research on the liturgical relationships and of their significance for the future. This field of research is, in the first place, important for historical reasons.

3.1.1. Early Jewish and early Christian Inter-Testamental literatures are rich in liturgical texts, the investigation of which would shed a bright light on the various functions of those texts and their provenance, whether Jewish or Christian; and, at the same time, on the exact identification of the place of those writings.

An example of a kind of liturgical text of the late biblical and early Jewish period are the "historiographical rebukes" which, in rhetorical juxtaposition of God's kindness and Israel's ingratitude, refer paranetically and with contemporary applications to the events of the Exodus from Egypt and the desert wanderings. In a decisively altered form and function, these "rebukes" reappear in the realm of Christian liturgy; and the relation of these Christian texts to their Jewish prototypes has thus far hardly been noticed. The Good Friday "Improperia" of the Catholic, Anglican and Eastern Churches are Jewish "self-critical" texts which, within their Jewish liturgical setting, most probably aimed at the contrition and the repentance of those listening to them, and which were used in the Churches for anti-Jewish polemical purposes, after having been cleverly "Christianized". Werner Schütz, "Was habe ich dir getan, mein Volk? Die Wurzeln der Karfreitagsimproperien in der alten Kirche", in *Jahrbuch für Liturgik und Hymnodik* 13 (1968), Kassel, pp. 1–38, as well as Eric Werner, "Melito of Sardes, The First Poet of Deicide", in *Hebrew Union College Annual* 37 (1966), 191–210, and David Flusser, "Hebrew Improperia", in *Immanuel* (Jerusalem), no. 4 (1974), pp. 51–4, are important contributions to the history of the traditions of "Improperia". But they fail to point in the right direction, which is to look for, and to investigate early Jewish "Improperia". My study on the post-biblical roots of Christian "Improperia" texts by the present writer will appear in the quarterly, *Kairos* (Salzburg), 19 (1977).

3.1.2. Until now we have few certain answers to the question as to what similarities and dissimilarities belong to the period of Christian origins, and why numerous dissimilarities seem to have arisen very early. The number of contacts between the two liturgies and their significance has been a subject of debate for the last several decades. Yet even today it is still too early to raise this question, since no real progress has been made in this area since W. O. E. Oesterley (*The Jewish Background of the Christian Liturgy*, Oxford, 1925), Frank Gavin (*The Jewish Antecedents of the Christian Sacraments*, London, SPCK, 1928), C. W. Dugmore (*The Influence of the Synagogue upon the Divine Office*, Oxford, 1944), and Anton Baumstark (*Comparative Liturgy*, London, 1958).

O. S. Rankin, "The Extent of the Influence of the Synagogue Service upon Christian Worship", in *Journal of Jewish Studies* 1 (1948–9), pp. 27–32, has a brief discussion about the differences in the estimate and the evaluation of those contacts between the two classic works of Oesterley and Dugmore—the latter being desirous of minimizing the number of such contacts. In any case, there can be no doubt that many contacts which have not yet been discovered or adequately elucidated did in fact exist. On the other hand, there has been a tendency to overestimate some similarities which should rather be explained in terms of the strong trend in the early Middle Ages to revert to Old Testament ideas and ideals. (See Raymund Kottje, *Studien zum Einfluss des Alten Testaments auf Recht und Liturgie des frühen Mittelalters. Bonner historische Forschungen* 23, Bonn, [2]1970.) Nor has there only been a one-way influence. Some palpable Christian influences on Jewish liturgy in the course of history can also be discerned. This is an area which needs to be much more thoroughly investigated before we can offer a clear resumé of sound answers.

3.1.3. Our knowledge about the time of origin and the possible forms of the regular and consecutive reading of the Pentateuch, and its division into pericopes to constitute a presumed lectionary cycle of from three to three and a half years, is unsatisfactory: notwithstanding the confident assertion of some scholars that such a cycle existed at the time of Jesus. Thus far there has been no proof of the existence of this so-called "triennial cycle" before the end of the first century CE. Joseph Heinemann, "The Triennial Lectionary Cycle", in *Journal of Jewish Studies* 19 (1968), pp. 41–8, has pointed out the grave shortcomings of studies by A. Guilding, L. Crockett and others, who had attempted to prove the early existence of a fixed cycle of Petateuchal readings. The state of our actual knowledge has been well documented by Charles Perrot, in *La lecture de la Bible dans la Synagogue. Les anciennes lectures palestiniennes du Shabbat et des fêtes* (Coll. Massorah I, 1; Gerstenberg; Hildesheim, 1973), 300 pp. A brief and more popular statement of Perrot's results can be found in his article, "La lecture de la Bible dans les synagogues au premier siècle de notre ère", in *La Maison-Dieu* 126 (1976), pp. 24–41. In view of the meagre results so far obtained in this area, the need for an acquaintance with relevant studies about this topic, which have been written in Hebrew, and the desirability of a greater cooperation with scholars in the field of Judaic studies would seem to be indicated.

3.1.4. Our knowledge of early Christian poetry and hymnology will only be able to advance by means of more thorough research.

The outline drawn by Jefim (Hayyim) Schirmann, "Hebrew Liturgical Poetry and Christian Hymnology", in *Jewish Quarterly Review*, New Series, 44 (1953–4), pp. 123–61, is still valid. The works of Ephrem Syrus, Romanos "Melodus", and the homilies of Asterios Sophistes, to name only three important authors, are among those to be investigated thoroughly in relation to early synagogal poetry and Rabbinic *midrash*. See also David Flusser, "Sanktus und Gloria", in *Abraham Unser Vater—Festschrift für Otto Michel* (Leiden-Cologne, Brill, 1963, pp. 129–52); and *idem*, "Jewish Roots of the Liturgical Trishagion", in *Immanuel* (Jerusalem), no. 3 (Winter 1973–4), pp. 37–43.

To be used with caution, but still suggestive mines of information, are the studies by Eric Werner, particularly his book, *The Sacred Bridge—The Interdependence of Liturgy and Music in Synagogue and Church during the First Millennium*, London, Dennis Dobson, New York, Columbia University Press, 1959, xx + 618 pp. An abbreviated edition of this work, omitting the strictly musicological portion, is now available in paperback form, with the subtitle, *Liturgical Parallels in Synagogue and Early Church* (New York, Schocken, 1970), 364 pp. See also Eric Werner's contribution, "Musical Traditions and their Transmitters between Synagogue and Church", in *Yuval* 2 (Jerusalem, Magnes Press, 1975), pp. 163–82.

3.1.5. In contrast to the dearth of studies in the various fields we have mentioned previously, a considerable amount of research has been done on the Eucharist and eucharistic prayer. A breakthrough towards an adequate understanding of the Jewish *berakhah* and its importance for an understanding of *eucharistia* was made by J. P. Audet, in "Literary Forms and Contents of a Normal *eucharistia* in the First Century", in *Papers presented to the International Congress on "The Four Gospels in 1957"*. *Texte und Untersuchungen* 73 (Berlin, 1959), pp. 643–62. The same materials, in a French version, are contained in "Esquisse historique du genre littéraire...", *Revue Biblique* 65 (1958), pp. 371–99. For a discussion of Audet, Ligier and others, see the latest publication in this field: Thomas J. Talley, "Von der Berakah zur Eucharistia. Das eucharistische Hochgebet der alten Kirche in neuerer Forschung. Ergebnisse und Fragen", in *Liturgisches Jahrbuch* 1976, pp. 93–115. Typical as well as regrettable is the fact that Talley, in dealing with the *berakhah*, is solely dependent upon the work of Finkelstein, and appears to be unacquainted with that of Heinemann and others.

3.1.6. If, in spite of the relatively large number of studies on the eucharistic anaphora, there has not been much progress in this area, the situation is even worse in other areas, which, in comparison, have been greatly neglected. This does not mean that those areas are of any less interest. On the contrary, they are historical questions of interest in themselves, and, at the same time, the answers to them could be of potential advantage to a number of practical problems in the field of pastoral liturgy. Some of those almost neglected areas are, for example, the prayers in the *ordo commendationis animae*, the prayers for the dying and the dead, as well as some other "paradigma prayers" which are definitely of Jewish origin. This has long been known. (See Menahem Zulay, *Zur Liturgie der babylonischen Juden*, Stuttgart, 1933; and Eric Werner, *The Sacred Bridge*, p. 48.) But the subject has never been fully investigated.

Allen Cabaniss, "A Jewish Provenience of the Advent Antiphons?", in *Jewish Quarterly Review*, New Series, 66 (1975), pp. 39–56, thinks that the "great O-Antiphons" might be of Jewish origin; but he is not wholly convincing. The revival of "biblicist" interest in the Old Testament could just as easily have been responsible for their biblical allusions and coloration. Further research here should prove fruitful.

3.2. The above are but a few of the many and various aspects and problems of research. Comparative research could be of great importance not only for the sake of historical criticism, but for a better self-understanding on the part of the Christian Church by way of understanding and accepting its Jewish heritage. We can learn much from the reasons for the loss of some parts of that heritage, for the transmission of other parts in their original form, and for the functional transformation of others—sometimes to serve the Churches' need for anti-Jewish polemics, as in the case of the "Improperia", mentioned under 3.1.1., above. It should be noted that, even in their present modified Western form, these "Improperia" still betray the traces of centuries of anti-Jewish polemics. In this we have a perfect illustration of how historical and practical Christian interests can be combined in the study of comparative liturgiology.

That such comparative studies be made possible is a demand addressed to all those who are concerned. Otherwise the confident statements of so many recent ecclesiastical declarations will have been made in vain. The concern, shared by many, for the great fundamental values which Judaism and Christianity have in common will not stand the test of time, and will be of no consequence, if that concern is not based on a detailed, knowledgeable and positive reference to the pluriform elements of the hallowed patterns and texts of both unique traditions.

Contributors

BAHR, Gordon J. is Professor of Bible at Claflin College, Orangeburg, SC (USA). He was born in 1926 in Berlin, Wisconsin, and obtained his BA at Wartburg College, Waverly, Iowa, his BD at Wartburg Theological Seminary, Dubuque, Iowa, and his PhD at Hebrew Union College, Cincinnati, Ohio. His publications include "Paul and Letter Writing in the First Century" (in *Catholic Biblical Quarterly*, vol. 28, 1966), "The Subscriptions in the Pauline Letters" (in *Journal of Biblical Literature*, vol. 87, 1968), and "The Seder of Passover and the Eucharistic Words" (in *Novum Testamentum*, vol. 22, 1970).

BOMMER, Josef, born in 1923 in Zürich, Switzerland, has been Professor of Pastoral Theology at the Theological Faculty of Lucerne since 1972. Among his publications are *Vom Beten des Christen* (1966), *Beichtprobleme Heute* (1968), *Einübung ins Christliche* (1970), and *Plädoyer für die Freiheit* (1971).

BROCKE, Michael teaches Judaic Studies at the University of Regensburg, Federal Republic of Germany. He was born in 1940 in Frankenthal, Germany, and studied at the universities of Saarbrücken, Jerusalem and Vienna, obtaining his PhD degree in Vienna. He has written about the doctrines of Rabbinic Judaism and early synagogal poetry in its relation to Talmud and Midrash.

CARMIGNAC, Jean is an auxiliary vicar in Paris and a biblical scholar specializing in Qumran studies. He was born in Paris in 1915, and studied in Rome at the French Seminary, the Gregorian University and the Biblical Institute. He was ordained in 1937. From 1939 to 1943, he was Professor of Sacred Scriptures and Basic Ethics at the Major Seminary of Saint-Dié. From 1954 to 1956, he was associated with the Ecole Biblique in Jerusalem. Since 1954, he has devoted himself to the study of the manuscripts of the Dead Sea Scrolls, founding, in 1958, the *Revue de Qumrân*, which he has continued to direct ever since. In 1957, he published *Docteur de Justice et Jésus-Christ*; and, between 1961 and 1964, together with several collaborators, he published the French translation of all Qumran texts known at that time. His *Recherches sur le "Notre Père"* appeared in 1969; and he is currently working on the formation of the Synoptic Gospels.

DEISSLER, Alfons was born in 1914 in Weiterung bei Bühl, Baden, Germany. Since 1951 he has been Professor of Old Testament Exegesis and Literature at the University of Freiburg im Breisgau. Among his publications are *Psalm 119 und seine Theologie* (1955), *Das Alte Testament und die neuere katholische Exegese* (⁵1968), *Ich werde mit dir sein. Meditationen aus den fünf Büchern Mose* (1969), and *Die Grundbotschaft des Alten Testaments* (⁴1974).

GRAUBARD, Baruch was born in 1900 in Skole, Galicia, Poland. He died in 1976 in Munich. He taught Post-Biblical Judaism at the University of Marburg, Germany, from 1950 to 1958. Among his publications are *Gelesen in den Büchern Mose* (1965), and *Wort, das euer Leben ist. Aus der Glaubenserfahrung Israels* (1974).

HEINEMANN, Joseph was Associate Professor of Hebrew Literature at the Hebrew University, Jerusalem. He was born in 1915 in Munich, and received Rabbinic Ordination at the Rabbinical Academy of Mir, Poland, his MA at the University of Manchester, and his PhD at the Hebrew University, Jerusalem. He died in 1978. His publications include *Prayer in the Period of the Tannaim and the Amoraim* (Hebrew, 1964), and *Aggadah and its Development* (Hebrew, 1974). His English *Prayer in the Talmud: Forms and Patterns* is scheduled for publication in 1978. He published numerous studies in the fields of Jewish Liturgy and Rabbinic Literature.

JOCHUM, Herbert is Director of Studies and head of the department of Catholic Religious Studies at the Staatliches Studienseminar in Neunkirchen, Saar, Federal Republic of Germany, and teaches Catholic theology and relgious education at the Hochschule des Saarlandes in Saarbrücken. Born 1937 in Hüttingweiler, Saar, he studied theology, philosophy and German language and literature at the universities of Vienna and Saar-brücken. He has written about the presentation of Judaism in religious education. He is Catholic president of the Society for Christian–Jewish Cooperation in the Saar.

LAUER, Simon was born in 1929 in Mannheim, Germany. He has lived in Switzerland since 1938. He has a PhD, and is a teacher in St Gallen. In 1972 he attended the Synod as an observer on behalf of the Swiss Union of Israelite Congregations. He has published articles and book reviews in the *Journal of Jewish Studies* and the *Israelitisches Wochenblatt für die Schweiz*.

OESTERREICHER, John M. is Director of the Institute of Judaeo–Christian Studies at Seton Hall University, South Orange, NJ (USA). He was born in 1904 in Stadt Liebau (then Austria, now Czechoslovakia). He is a Monsignor and a DDr. h.c. He has edited five volumes of *The Bridge: A Yearbook of Judaeo–Christian Studies* (1955–1970) and several monographs devoted to modern Christian–Jewish dialogue. His publications include *Auschwitz, the Christian, and the Council* (1965), *The Rediscovery of Judaism* (1971), and a survey of the history and investigations of the meaning of the conciliar statement on the Church and the Jews, published as part of the three-volume *Commentary on the Documents of the Second Vatican Council.*

PETUCHOWSKI, Jakob J. is Research Professor of Jewish Theology and Liturgy at the Hebrew Union College—Jewish Institute of Religion in Cincinnati, Ohio (USA). He was born in 1925 in Berlin, and obtained his BA at the University of London and his BHL, Rabbinic Ordination, MA and PhD at the Hebrew Union College in Cincinnati, Ohio. He has been Director of Jewish Studies at the Hebrew Union College, Jerusalem, and Visiting Professor of Jewish Philosophy at Tel-Aviv University. His publications include *The Theology of Haham David Nieto* (²1970), *Ever Since Sinai* (²1968), *Prayerbook Reform in Europe* (1968), *Heirs of the Pharisees* (1970), and *Understanding Jewish Prayer* (1972). His *Theology and Poetry* is scheduled for publication in 1977. He has published many articles in the fields of Rabbinics, Jewish Theology and Liturgy.

STROLZ, Walter has been an Editor for Verlag Herder, Freiburg im Breisgau, Germany since 1959. He was born in 1927 in Schoppernau, Voralberg, Austria, and holds a PhD. His publications include *Der vergessene Ursprung* (1959), *Menschsein als Gottesfrage* (1965), *Hiobs Auflehnung gegen Gott* (1967), *Schöpfung und Selbstbesinnung* (1973), and *Gottes verborgene Gegenwart* (1976). He has edited *Jüdische Hoffnungskraft und christlicher Glaube* (1971) and other works.

VÖGTLE, Anton is Professor of New Testament Exegesis and Literature at the University of Freiburg im Breisgau. He was born in 1910 in Villingen, Hohenz., Germany. His publications include *Tugend- und Lasterkataloge im Neuen Testament* (1936), *Das öffentliche Wirken Jesu auf dem Hintergrund der Qumranbewegung* (1958), *Das Neue Testament und die neuere katholische Exegese* (1967), *Das Evangelium und die Evangelien* (1971), and *Messias und Gottessohn* (1971). He is a co-editor of Herder's *Theologischer Kommentar zum Neuen Testament* and of the journal *Bibel und Leben*.